Politics in Time

Politics in Time

HISTORY, INSTITUTIONS, AND SOCIAL ANALYSIS

Paul Pierson

PRINCETON UNIVERSITY PRESS

PRINCETON AND OXFORD

Library of Congress Cataloging-in-Publication Data
Pierson, Paul.
Politics in Time : history, institutions, and social analysis / Paul Pierson.
p. cm.
Includes bibliographical references and index.
ISBN 0-691-11714-4 (alk. paper) —ISBN 0-691-11715-2 (pbk. : alk. paper)
1. Political science. 2. Time—Sociological aspects. I. Title.
JA78.P54 2004
320'.01—dc22
2003063294

British Library Cataloging-in-Publication Data is available

This book has been composed in Electra
Printed on acid-free paper. ∞
www.pupress.princeton.edu

Printed in the United States of America

10   9   8   7   6   5   4

For Tracey

CONTENTS

List of Figures and Tables   ix

Acknowledgments   xi

Introduction: Placing Politics in Time   1

CHAPTER ONE
Positive Feedback and Path Dependence   17

CHAPTER TWO
Timing and Sequence   54

CHAPTER THREE
Long-Term Processes   79

CHAPTER FOUR
The Limits of Institutional Design   103

CHAPTER FIVE
Institutional Development   133

CONCLUSION
Temporal Context in Social Science Inquiry   167

Bibliography   179

Index   195

LIST OF FIGURES AND TABLES

FIGURES

1.1. Payoffs with increasing returns to scale.   23

3.1. A basic threshold model.   87

3.2. Time horizons in different social science accounts.   92

3.3. A threshold model with a structural cause.   94

5.1. Sources of resilience over time.   151

5.2. Conversion costs, replacement costs, and institutional change.   156

TABLES

2.1. A Standard Cycling Problem   60

3.1. The Time Horizons of Different Causal Accounts   81

3.2. Categorizing Long-Term Processes   97

3.3. Time Horizons in Major Political Science Journals, 1996–2000   98

ACKNOWLEDGMENTS

I AM NOT SHY ABOUT ASKING FOR HELP. I have always enjoyed the social part of scholarship, the opportunities for intensive interactions with others exploring the world of ideas. In completing this project, I am struck at the long, long list of people I can now gratefully acknowledge, and in compiling this list I know I am neglecting many others who have generously offered their thoughts in the process. I have been very fortunate to be able to draw on the talents of a succession of wonderful research assistants, including Fiona Barker, Alan Jacobs, Robert Mickey, John Parrish, Andy Rudalevige, Hillel Soifer, Shannon O'Neil Trowbridge, and Jeremy Weinstein. Many of these fine young scholars have now happily landed in settings where they can concentrate on their own intellectual agendas. They have enormously enhanced my own.

I benefited greatly from discussions of this project at Brown University, Columbia University, Cornell University, the European University Institute, the Centro de Investigacion y Docencia Economicas (CIDE), the University of California at Berkeley, the University of California at Irvine, the University of Illinois, the University of Toronto, the University of Virginia, and Yale University. Workshops held at Harvard's Minda de Gunzberg Center for European Studies and at the Miller Center of Public Affairs at the University of Virginia proved enormously stimulating. I am grateful to Lisa Eschenbach, Patricia Craig, and Peter Hall for helping to organize the first of these events, and to Brian Balogh and Sidney Milkis for organizing the second and inviting me to present my work there. As I have indicated at the end of this section, earlier and quite different versions of parts of the current manuscript appeared in a number of publications. I am grateful to the publishers for permission to draw on those materials here, as well as to the anonymous reviewers who offered very useful comments on those articles. I am equally appreciative of the very thoughtful readings of the current manuscript provided by reviewers for the Princeton and Cambridge University Presses.

This project received generous financial support from the German Marshall Foundation, the Simon R. Guggenheim Foundation, the Weatherhead Center for International Affairs, and the Center for European Studies, which I gratefully acknowledge. The Center for European Studies and the Department of Government at Harvard have been stimulating and convivial places to pursue this project.

Princeton University Press has done a wonderful job. Chuck Myers embraced this project from the beginning, and offered very thoughtful feedback and consistent encouragement throughout. Alice Calaprice did splendid work with the copyediting, while Kathleen Cioffi kept a watchful eye on all phases of production. Jennifer Nippins also provided valuable help in the complex process of turning my manuscript into a book. I am grateful to them all.

I have received an enormous amount of detailed and helpful feedback on this manuscript. Among the many who kindly offered me help I would like to acknowledge Gerard Alexander, Karen Alter, Frank Baumgartner, Tim Buthe, John Carey, Daniel Carpenter, Elisabeth Clemens, David Collier, Pepper Culpepper, Jeffrey Frieden, Peter Gourevitch, Anna Grzymala-Busse, Davashree Gupta, Alan Jacobs, Ron Jepperson, Michael Jones-Correa, Ira Katznelson, Margaret Levi, Christopher Mantzavinos, Eileen McDonagh, Andrew Moravcsik, Gerardo Munck, Dietrich Rueschemeyer, Jeffrey Sellers, Alec Stone Sweet, and Julian Zelizer. I appreciate their generosity in sharing their time and insights. I cannot possibly express the extent of my gratitude to a circle of scholars who have, over many years, provided a wonderful mix of prodding, encouragement, and trenchant critique that helped to make this a better book: Danny Goldhagen, Jacob Hacker, Peter Hall, Jim Mahoney, Theda Skocpol, Allison Stanger, and Kathy Thelen. I am lucky to have such friends.

My children, Sidra and Seth, were mercifully unaware that dad was writing a book at all (though Seth, in the past few months has become proficient enough with words that he can accurately describe his father's job as "sitting at the table and drinking coffee"). They have, however, been exuberant expressions of the wonders of development, and their rapid growth has been a constant reminder that writing this book has most definitely been a slow-moving process. Finally, I dedicate this book to my wife, Tracey. She is the master juggler who stands with grace at the center of our personal three-ring circus, and of my life.

Permission to use the following materials from previously published articles is gratefully acknowledged.

Parts of Chapter One appeared in "Path Dependence, Increasing Returns, and Political Science," *American Political Science Review*, Vol. 94, No. 2, June 2000, pp. 251–67.

Parts of Chapter Two appeared in "Not Just What, but *When*: Timing and Sequence in Political Processes," *Studies in American Political Development*, Vol. 14, No. 1, 2000, pp. 73–93.

Parts of Chapter Three appeared in "Big, Slow-Moving, and . . . Invisible: Macrosocial Processes in the Study of Comparative Politics," in James Mahoney and Dietrich Reuschemeyer, eds., *Comparative Historical Analysis in the Social Sciences* (Cambridge: Cambridge University Press, 2003), pp. 177–207.

Parts of Chapter Four appeared in "The Limits of Design: Explaining Institutional Origins and Change," *Governance*, Vol. 13, No. 4, 2000, pp. 475–99.

Parts of the Conclusion appeared in "From Area Studies to Contextualized Comparisons," in Grzegorz Ekiert and Stephen Hanson, eds., *Capitalism and Democracy in Central and Eastern Europe: Assessing the Legacy of Communist Rule* (Cambridge: Cambridge University Press, 2003), pp. 353–66.

PLACING POLITICS IN TIME

> For an economic historian, time has always been something
> that is fundamentally disturbing, because there is *no time* in
> neoclassical theory. The neoclassical model is a model of an
> instant of time, and it does not therefore take into account
> what time does. . . . I will be blunt: Without a deep
> understanding of time, you will be lousy political scientists,
> because time is the dimension in which ideas and
> institutions and beliefs evolve.
> —*Douglass North (1999, p. 316)*

WE CAN BEGIN WITH AN ANALOGY. Imagine that your friend invites you to the trendiest new restaurant in town, charmingly named "The Modern Social Scientist." As an added bonus, he informs you that he knows the chef well, and that you will have a chance to tour the kitchen. When you arrive, the chef explains that the kitchen is divided into two parts. On the left, she has all the ingredients (which to your puzzlement she refers to as "variables"). These ingredients, she insists, are the freshest available and carefully selected. On the right is an extraordinary profusion of measuring devices. You express astonishment at their complexity and detailed ornamentation, and the chef explains that each requires years to learn how to operate properly.

The chef proceeds to elaborate her culinary approach: good cooking, she says, amounts to having the perfect ingredients, perfectly measured. Traditional cooks have stressed how important the cooking process itself is, including the sequence, pace, and specific manner in which the ingredients are to be combined. Not so, says the proprietor of The Modern Social Scientist. As long as you have the correct ingredients and they are properly measured, she insists, how, in what order, and for how long they are combined *makes no difference.*

Few would want to patronize a restaurant with such a philosophy of cooking, but most social scientists are working in that kind of a kitchen. Disputes among competing theories center on which "variables" in the current environment generate important political outcomes. How does the distribution of public opinion affect policy outcomes? How do individual social characteristics influence propensities to vote? How do electoral rules affect the structure of party systems? Yet the significance of such "variables" is frequently distorted when they are ripped from their temporal context. Contemporary social scientists typically take a "snapshot" view of political life, but there is often a strong case to be made for shifting from snapshots to moving pictures. This means *systematically* situating particular moments (including the present) in a temporal sequence of events and processes stretching over extended periods. Placing politics in time can greatly enrich our understanding of complex social dynamics.

This book explores a range of temporal processes that are common in political life. It seeks to distinguish various processes that unfold over substantial stretches of time, to identify the circumstances under which such different processes are likely to occur, and to highlight the significance of these temporal dimensions of social life for our understanding of important political outcomes. In doing so, I seek to demonstrate the very high price that social science often pays when it ignores the profound temporal dimensions of real social processes. The ambition, in short, is to flesh out the often-invoked but rarely examined declaration that history matters.

It is no accident that so many of the giant figures in the formative period of the social sciences—from Marx, Tocqueville, and Weber to Polanyi and Schumpeter—adopted deeply historical approaches to social explanation. This stance was not simply a quaint feature of a transitional stage to modern social analysis. It was a key source of their profound insights about the nature of the social world. Attentiveness to issues of temporality highlights aspects of social life that are essentially invisible from an ahistorical vantage point. Placing politics in time can greatly enrich both the explanations we offer for social outcomes of interest, and the very outcomes that we identify as worth explaining. The systematic examination of processes unfolding over time warrants a central position in the social sciences.

Two Illustrations

Because I am eager to contribute to the efforts of social scientists working on a wide range of matters, I initially discuss many of the issues addressed in this book at a fairly high level of abstraction. It may be of some help at the outset to briefly outline two examples of recent scholarship that offer compelling examples of the insights to be gained by shifting from a "snapshot" to a moving picture of important social processes. Daniel Carpenter's *The Forging of Bureaucratic Autonomy* (Carpenter 2001) presents a striking demonstration of how attention to a long-term sequence of causes (what I will call a "causal chain" in Chapter Three) can turn our understandings of social phenomena on their heads. He criticizes the large and influential literature on relations between legislatures and bureaucrats grounded in Principal-Agent theory (McCubbins, Noll, and Weingast 1987; McCubbins and Schwartz 1984). The literature argues that congressional "principals" have substantial political resources to assure that their bureaucratic "agents" largely comply with their preferences. Yet Carpenter persuasively demonstrates how these analyses substantially underestimate the potential for bureaucratic autonomy because they adopt a cross-sectional approach to studying what should be understood as a long-term causal chain. Under the right conditions, ambitious and entrepreneurial bureaucrats were able over extended periods of time to enhance their reputations for innovativeness and competence, and develop strong networks of support among a range of social actors. These achievements created a context in which Congress, facing pressure from below and deferring to the expertise of leading bureaucrats, essentially asked for what the bureaucrats wanted. Viewed as a moment in time, one sees what looks like congressional dominance; viewed as a process unfolding over time, *the same cross-sectional evidence* provides indications of substantial bureaucratic autonomy.

Thomas Ertman's *The Birth of Leviathan* (Ertman 1996) offers a compelling explanation of different patterns of state-building in early modern Europe that emphasizes how the results of critical junctures, and cross-national differences in the sequencing of key historical processes, generated durable variations in the structures of nation-states. Ertman emphasizes the lasting repercussions of the financing methods adopted in European states that faced military competition before the rise of modern bureaucracies. Following predecessors such as Hintze and Tilly, Ertman argues that the onset of military competition had a critical effect on patterns of European state development. Crucially, however, Ertman stresses that different states experienced intense military conflict *at different times*. He maintains (p. 26) that "differences in the timing of the onset of sustained geopolitical competition go a long way towards explaining the character of state infrastructures found across the continent at the end of the 18th century."

States confronting military competition faced the life-or-death challenge of generating sufficient revenues to wage prolonged warfare. However, the available repertoires of administrative response were conditional on the point in historical development when this challenge appeared. According to Ertman, "timing mattered because the range of 'technical resources' available to statebuilders did not remain invariant across this period." In the twelfth century, literacy was a very scarce resource and sophisticated bureaucracy an unknown organizational technology. In this historical context, monarchs were forced to rely on systems of proprietary office holding and tax farming "which were much more beneficial to [these officeholders] than to their royal employers." By contrast, countries that faced intensive military competition at a later time "found themselves in a quite different world" (p. 28). Literacy was much more common, and knowledge of more modern bureaucratic organizational forms (as well as evidence of tax farming's considerable drawbacks) was widely available. The result was that state builders in these countries could work to construct "proto-modern bureaucracies based upon the separation of office from the person of the officeholder."

Why, then, did not all states adopt the superior bureaucratic structures? Because, Ertman argues, initial outcomes were strongly self-reinforcing. Once a dense network of institutions and interests developed around tax farming, especially in

a context where monarchs often had immediate needs for revenues, it became
virtually impossible to switch over to more modern forms of financing. In the
terms I will introduce shortly, the experiences of different countries were highly
path dependent. And these different paths mattered a great deal, Ertman maintains, because the bureaucratic alternative was both more effective in waging
war and more conducive to the development of parliamentary institutions.

Ertman's powerful analysis, like Carpenter's, is built on an understanding that
social processes, such as state building and the construction of bureaucratic autonomy, unfold over time. Just as Carpenter illuminates temporally extended
but crucial causal chains, Ertman employs elements of temporality explored systematically in the chapters to follow: path dependence (Chapter One), sequencing (Chapter Two), and slow-moving processes (Chapter Three). For both
authors, the turn to history is not primarily a matter of employing narrative or
compiling historical evidence; it is the grounding for theoretical claims about
how things happen in the social world.

A "Historic Turn" in the Social Sciences?

As these illustrations attest, the social sciences have had a rich tradition of historical research. Scholarly communities devoted to extending such traditions
flourish in parts of the social sciences. Indeed, some (McDonald 1996; Bates et
al. 1998) claim to witness a "historic turn" in the human sciences as a whole. Yet
in spite of this activity there has actually been surprisingly limited attentiveness
to the specifically temporal dimensions of social processes. In contemporary social science, the past serves primarily as a source of empirical material, rather
than as a spur to serious investigations of how politics happens over time.

At least within political science, the adoption of a historical orientation has
generally failed to exploit its greatest potential contribution to the more systematic understanding of social processes. One can in fact distinguish three prominent "historic turns" in the social sciences. Each of these has added significantly
to our store of knowledge, but each has serious limitations as well. The first, especially prominent in the field of American political development, might be
termed "history as the study of the past." Here analysts study particular historical
events or processes, with a focus on offering convincing causal accounts of specific outcomes of interest. Such investigations often greatly increase what we
know about particular facets of the political histories of specific countries.

What is less clear, however, is how particular studies fit into some broader research program. Little effort is made to suggest what, if anything, might "travel"
from one investigation to another. Indeed, many historically oriented analysts
are uninterested in this question, assuming the stance of most historians: that the
rich particularities of each event or process render it unique. Alternatively, these
analysts seem to assume implicitly that a discussion of, say, social movements in

the 1920s generates clear implications for our understanding of contemporary social movements. Such an assumption is highly problematic. This first historical turn is often admired. Yet it is fair to say that the great majority of social scientists, whose principal interests lie in understanding contemporary society, sees "history as the study of the past" as largely irrelevant to their own inquiries.

A second "turn" could be termed "history as the hunt for illustrative material." Here the researcher's perspective could uncharitably be summarized as follows: "I have a model of some aspect of politics. Let me search the past for a good illustration of the model." This type of exercise is especially common among those aspiring to generate very general propositions about politics. Thus, rational choice theorists—contemporary social science's most ambitious pursuers of general propositions—comb the past for examples of credible commitment mechanisms or for solutions to a particular class of collective action problems. Given a wealth of available historical material and the often highly stylized accounts generated in these exercises, the past may well offer up the desired illustrations. Here again, however, the analyses say little or nothing about the temporal dimensions of social processes. The motivation for going back in time is simply to get at examples that may not be available in the present.

This is also the case of the third turn, which could be termed "history as a site for generating more cases." History becomes a source of data, especially for phenomena that are relatively uncommon in the contemporary environment (Bartolini 1993, p. 144). There are deep controversies about this methodological move, whether it takes the form of large-n studies (e.g., using pooled time series) or small-n studies (e.g., using some variant of Mill's methods of agreement and disagreement).[1] I share some of these critics' misgivings. My main point, however, is a different one, and it applies to all three of the turns to history that I have discussed. The best case for connecting history to the social sciences is neither empirical (turn #1) nor methodological (turns #2 and 3), but theoretical. We turn to an examination of history because social life unfolds over time. Real social processes have distinctly temporal dimensions.

Yet an exploration of these temporal dimensions of social processes is precisely the weakest link in social science's historical turn. We largely lack a clear outline of why the intensive investigation of issues of temporality is critical to an understanding of social processes. The declaration that "history matters" is often invoked, but rarely unpacked.[2] Many of the key concepts needed to underpin analyses of temporal processes, such as path dependence, critical junctures,

[1] On the former see Shalev 1999. For different views on the latter see Lieberson 1985 and Mahoney 1999.

[2] There are notable exceptions, to which the current analysis is deeply indebted. Among these I would single out Collier and Collier 1991; Katznelson 1997; Mahoney 2000; Mahoney and Rueschemeyer 2003; Orren and Skowronek 1994; Skocpol 1992; Stinchcombe 1965, 1968; Thelen 1999, 2003. The excellent essays collected in Abbott 2001 cover some of the territory I take up here, albeit in very different fashion.

sequencing, events, duration, timing, and unintended consequences, have received only very fragmented and limited discussion. To assert that "history matters" is insufficient; social scientists want to know why, where, how, and for what. As the sociologist Ronald Aminzade has put it (1992, p. 458), we seek "the construction of theories of continuity and change that are attentive to order and sequence and that acknowledge the causal power of temporal connections among events." This "requires concepts that recognize the diversity of patterns of temporal connections among events."

What is at stake in this effort to refine our theoretical understandings of the different ways in which "history matters" in explaining social phenomena? Most important, examining temporal processes allows us to identify and explicate some fundamental social mechanisms. By mechanisms I mean what Jon Elster has termed "plausible, frequently observed ways in which things happen." A number of scholars have recently emphasized that where possible—and it will not always be possible—it is extremely helpful to identify frequently recurring causal mechanisms. Jon Elster has put it most strongly in arguing that "the basic concept in the social sciences should be that of a mechanism rather than of a theory. . . . [T]he social sciences are light years away from the stage at which it will be possible to formulate general-law-like regularities about human behavior. Instead, we should concentrate on specifying small and medium-sized mechanisms for human action and interaction" (Elster 1989, p. viii).[3]

The main focus of this book is on social mechanisms that have a strong temporal dimension. Although historically oriented scholars are (rightly) skeptical about the prospects for generating anything like a general theory of politics, most social scientists remain interested in developing at least limited generalizations—arguments that can "travel" in some form beyond a specific time and place.[4] The current study seeks to address this gap by outlining mechanisms that have a strong temporal dimension. Exploring the character of these mechanisms, and the features of social contexts that generate them, can thus simultaneously address the desire of analysts to move beyond a single case and the desire of historically oriented scholars to capture how history matters. The identification and clarification of such mechanisms can enhance our ability to develop arguments about temporal processes that are both convincing and have at least limited portability.

Exploring these mechanisms, I will suggest, can lead us to reassess prominent areas of social science inquiry and conventional practices in new and fertile ways. It will often suggest new hypotheses regarding important subjects and open exciting possibilities for extending existing theoretical work in new direc-

[3]For additional discussions see Scharpf 1997, chap. 1, and Stinchcombe 1991.
[4]Indeed, one of the striking features of much of the qualitative historical literature in the field of American political development, for example, is the limited capacity of studies to actually build on their predecessors, rather than simply piling up one after another. For a discussion of the possibilities for enhancing the quality of research programs in comparative historical analysis, see the essays in Part One of Mahoney and Rueschemeyer 2003.

tions. A focus on these temporally oriented mechanisms suggests new questions and reveals new outcomes of interest—questions and outcomes that are linked to, but distinct from, existing lines of inquiry. Finally, the intensive exploration of the temporal dimensions of social processes forces us to rethink our strategies of social investigation. I cannot emphasize enough that this is *not* a book about methods. Yet how you choose to look for things depends heavily on what you think you are looking for. Hence, many of the arguments explored here have substantial methodological implications (Hall 2003).

The principal audience for this book consists of those interested in the attempt to develop claims about the social world that can potentially reach across time and space. Yet even for scholars who are dubious about the prospects for generalization or uninterested in its pursuit, theoretical explorations of historical causation remain important. It is easy to underestimate the extent to which theoretical discussions underpin, if only implicitly and by way of diffusion, all empirical research. As Fritz Scharpf (1997, p. 29) puts it,

> in a world that is exceedingly complex and in which we will often be studying unique cases, we must have a good idea of what to look for if we wish to discover anything worthwhile. Since a single data point can be "explained" by any number of regression lines, post hoc explanations are too easy to invent and usually (unless invented with the trained skill of the master historian) totally useless. The implication is that our search for explanations must be disciplined by strong *prior* expectations and that we must take the disconfirmation of such expectations as a welcome pointer to the development of more valid explanations.

In general, we will be in a much better position to carry out convincing research if we think through these prior expectations—and our justifications for holding them—explicitly and carefully. Clarifying how various temporally grounded mechanisms operate and suggesting where we should expect such processes to be at work can provide stronger theoretical underpinnings for the analyses of even those seeking to explain a single case.

Achieving greater clarity about how history imparts its effects on the present will open up possibilities for more constructive intellectual dialogue. It will help historically oriented scholars be more effective in communicating the import of their research to each other as well as to often skeptical colleagues. The social sciences are highly balkanized and tribal. In this context, there is much to be said for efforts that seek to articulate the aspirations and achievements of a body of research in a language that makes sense to those outside the tribe.[5] This is not

---

[5]Even within "tribes," communication is often hindered by the lack of a common conceptual language that allows scholars to recognize common interests—as, for instance, when scholars studying different areas of the globe lack a shared vocabulary to recognize their overlapping concerns. On this see Mahoney and Rueschemeyer 2003.

just about making oneself understood or about clearing away false disagreements—although these are important benefits. At least as significant, greater clarity and precision can reveal significant points of overlap and identify opportunities for useful exchange as well as highlight genuinely contentious issues.

In this context it makes sense to briefly situate the current discussion vis-à-vis two prominent schools of thought in contemporary political science: "rational choice theory" and "historical institutionalism." Such an effort is hazardous, since these are loose camps—"theoretical imageries," as Ronald Jepperson (1996) has usefully put it—rather than coherent theories. Yet given the tendency of many scholars to orient their work in allegiance to one camp (and often in opposition to others) it may be useful to make my own position clear: a focus on the temporal dimensions of social processes largely cuts across this divide. The systematic examination of temporal processes can usefully draw on rich contributions from each tradition, while also highlighting certain limitations. It can help to distinguish points of overlap, instances of genuine disagreement, and substantial areas in which the two traditions simply speak to different (although perhaps complementary) questions. My claim is that a focus on temporal processes can point to fruitful lines of theoretical, methodological, and substantive inquiry for those working within each of these "imageries"—although these lines will and should remain distinctive in important respects.

One would think that the issues at hand would be the natural terrain for "historical institutionalism," with its long-standing insistence that social science research should be historically grounded (Skocpol and Sommers 1980; Thelen and Steinmo 1992; Katznelson 1997). Yet those associated with historical institutionalism have generally been more explicit in discussing the "institutionalist" dimensions of their frameworks than the "historical" ones. They have concentrated on examining the impact of relatively fixed institutional features of the political landscape (such as constitutional arrangements and major policy structures). The specifically historical component of historical institutionalism has, at least until recently (Hacker 2002; Thelen 2004) generally been left unclear. As already noted, if a justification for a turn to history is given at all, it has more often been methodological rather than theoretical in nature.

Thinking more explicitly about the role of time in politics will, however, justify some of the key concerns and offer support for some key propositions advanced by historical institutionalist scholarship. It will provide stronger theoretical grounds for emphasizing the "stickiness" of inherited social arrangements, for questioning functional explanations (that is, claims that social arrangements exist *because* they meet certain needs of societies or particular powerful actors), for concentrating on issues of timing and sequence, and for investigating long-term processes of social change. More broadly, this investigation will vindicate historical institutionalism's interest in macrolevel social phenomena, as well as its cautious stance regarding social science's capacity to develop broad generalizations about social processes that apply across sweeping stretches of time and space.

At the same time, I stress that rational choice analysis, broadly defined, offers essential analytical tools for investigating temporal processes. In this book I develop theoretical arguments organized around four major themes: path dependence, issues of timing and sequence, the significance and distinctiveness of "slow-moving" processes that require attentiveness to extended periods of time, and problems of institutional origins and change. On each of these points, work drawn from economic theory, focusing on problems of strategic interaction among calculating, rational individuals, has much to offer.

Yet a focus on the temporal dimensions of political processes highlights the limits of choice-theoretic approaches as well as their strengths. Most important is the way in which micromodeling exercises that are centered on strategic interaction among individuals encourage a highly restricted field of vision, both in space and time. Among the things that tend to drop out of such exercises are issues of macro structure, the role of temporal ordering or sequence, and a whole host of social processes that play out only over extended periods of time and cannot be reduced to the strategic "moves" of "actors." Thus, a restricted field of vision adversely affects both the kinds of questions rational choice theorists tend to generate and the kinds of answers they typically provide. The critique, it should be emphasized, is not the common (in my view often misguided) one about rational choice theory's assumptions about human behavior, but about its restricted range of application. The implication is thus not that rational choice theory should be rejected, but that its scope should be placed in proper perspective. Analysts should focus on establishing how insights from rational choice can be linked to other approaches, or where other approaches are simply more appropriate for addressing particular kinds of questions (Jepperson 1996).

Clearer recognition of some of rational choice's blind spots may also facilitate efforts within that tradition to address challenging problems in convincing ways. In the pages that follow I will often criticize strong *tendencies* associated with particular techniques or theoretical approaches, while accepting—indeed emphasizing—that there is nothing about these modes of inquiry that renders these tendencies logically *necessary*. Analysts will sometimes seize on this point to suggest that the critique has little import.[6] This reaction is a mistake. The question, after all, is not just what a particular technique or theory is capable of doing in principle, but how and to what extent it is actually used in practice—a distinction that is almost always glossed over in general discussions of method and theory. To paraphrase a recent observation by Ronald Jepperson, when faced with a causal account employing a long-term temporal structure, quantitative scholars (as well

---

[6]This response has been common, although far from universal, in the reactions of rational choice scholars to some of the arguments presented in this book.

as some rational-choice theorists) might well respond by exclaiming, "I can model that!" This riposte loses much of its bite, however, if the theoretical imageries and methods these analysts employ rarely lead them to consider the outcomes or hypotheses in question in the first place (Jepperson 1996).

The thrust of the arguments in *Politics in Time* is to reconsider a wide range of theoretical approaches and methodological techniques from the vantage point of issues related to temporality. In doing so, I hope to challenge some of the tribal, polarized character of much contemporary social science. A focus on the temporal dimensions of social processes provides exciting possibilities for shaping some common—or at least overlapping—intellectual terrain for scholars working out of highly diverse research traditions. In the remainder of this introduction I briefly summarize my efforts to map out that terrain.

ANALYTICAL FOUNDATIONS

The five chapters that form the core of this book explore some key temporal dimensions of social and political processes. They explicate different ways in which things happen over time in social life, drawing attention to processes that are unlikely to be visible without specifically addressing questions of temporality. In each case, I seek to demonstrate why such processes are likely to be prevalent, the circumstances under which they should be expected, and the major implications for our efforts to understand social outcomes.

Chapter One focuses on *path dependence*. Path dependence has become a faddish term, often lacking a clear meaning. Yet there are exciting new possibilities for applying the notion in a more rigorous way to the analysis of social processes. I argue that this means focusing on the dynamics of self-reinforcing or positive feedback processes in a political system. Such processes have very interesting characteristics. They can be highly influenced by relatively modest perturbations at early stages. Thus, such processes can produce more than one outcome. Once a particular path gets established, however, self-reinforcing processes make reversals very difficult. In economics, such ideas have become increasingly popular in the investigation of new technologies (Microsoft vs. Macintosh), trade, economic geography, and economic growth.

Drawing on the research of Brian Arthur and Douglas North, I show how these ideas can be extended and modified to address issues of central importance to political scientists. There are strong grounds for believing that self-reinforcing processes will be prevalent in political life—arguably more pervasive and intense than they are in the economic sphere. Once established, patterns of political mobilization, the institutional "rules of the game," and even citizens' basic ways of thinking about the political world will often generate self-reinforcing dynamics. Once actors have ventured far down a particular path, they may find it very difficult to reverse course. Political alternatives that were once quite plausible may become irretrievably lost.

Claims about path dependence typically suggest that beginnings are extremely important. So one might ask: Why begin this discussion with path dependence? The answer is that an understanding of self-reinforcing processes is extremely helpful for exploring a wide range of issues related to temporality. Exploring the sources and consequences of path dependence helps us to understand the powerful inertia or "stickiness" that characterizes many aspects of political development—for instance, the enduring consequences that often stem from the emergence of particular institutional arrangements. These arguments can also reinvigorate the analysis of power in social relations by showing how inequalities of power, perhaps modest initially, can be reinforced over time and often come to be deeply embedded in organizations and dominant modes of political action and understanding, as well as in institutional arrangements. Path-dependence arguments also provide a useful and powerful corrective against tendencies to assume functionalist explanations for important social and political outcomes—the supposition that the existence of current social arrangements is to be explained through reference to the needs they address for the currently powerful. Moreover, an appreciation of the prevalence of path dependence forces attentiveness to the causal significance of temporally remote events or processes. Path-dependent processes exemplify what Arthur Stinchcombe has termed "historical causation," in which dynamics triggered by an event or process at one point in time reproduce themselves, even in the absence of the recurrence of the original event or process. Finally, an appreciation of positive feedback also justifies attentiveness to issues of temporal ordering. In path-dependent processes, the order of events may make a fundamental difference. In all these respects, path dependence underscores the distinctly temporal dimensions of social processes, laying a foundation for the chapters that follow.

Chapter Two explores issues of *timing and sequence* in greater detail. Social scientists tracing broad patterns of political development across a number of countries often argue that the timing and sequence of particular events or processes can matter a great deal. Settings where event A precedes event B will generate different outcomes than ones where that ordering is reversed. In Ertman's account, for example, it is the relative timing of the arrival of mass literacy and the onset of intense military competition that is crucial. The concepts of timing and sequencing are, however, more often invoked than clearly thought through. Reviewing some prominent work in comparative historical analysis, I show that sequencing arguments have been both prevalent and, often, analytically muddled. There are actually a number of distinct ways to make such claims. Different types of sequencing arguments are likely to be relevant in different settings. Clarifying these differences and specifying the mechanisms that link claims about sequences to particular outcomes are the central tasks of this chapter.

I focus on two broad classes of arguments. One class of arguments about timing and sequence focuses on *conjunctures* — interaction effects between distinct causal sequences that become joined at particular points in time. For instance, it arguably mattered a good deal for the trajectory of domestic politics whether left wing or right wing parties happened to be in power at the time when a cataclysmic event, the Great Depression, hit a particular country. Just as a falling brick has distinct consequences when it arrives at the same time as an unfortunate pedestrian, the simultaneity of two processes that in other cases occur at different times produces critical consequences. Bendix's famous analysis of what happens when the twin processes of industrialization and democratization occur at the same time is a good example.

The first part of Chapter Two explores the potential and pitfalls of such conjunctural arguments for social scientists. Historically oriented scholars rightly point out that explanations for important social outcomes often rest at least in part on such conjunctures. At the same time, however, there appear to be real limits to our capacity to use conjunctural claims to search for patterns across cases. With modest exceptions, such claims would seem to be most useful for understanding, after the fact, specific outcomes of interest. They seem less likely, however, to yield an understanding of mechanisms that could be applied in multiple settings.

This is not the case for the second class of arguments about sequencing that I consider. Many—probably most—arguments about sequencing turn out on closer investigation to be grounded in claims about positive feedback. This makes them amenable to the forms of analysis developed in my discussion of path dependence. Here, timing and sequence matter because self-reinforcing processes affecting a particular aspect of political and social life can transform the consequences of later stages in a sequence.

Linking arguments about path dependence to a focus on sequencing produces powerful theoretical synergies. Path-dependent arguments about self-reinforcement explain why and when sequencing can matter. Positive feedback processes occurring at particular times essentially remove certain options from the menu of political possibilities. By doing so, they can greatly alter the consequences of events or processes occurring at a later stage. At the same time, the specific focus on sequencing generates a rich new set of hypotheses about path-dependent processes. It can draw attention to contests over "political space" in which potential competitors seek first-mover advantages, while clarifying the likely long-term impact of initial defeats on the opportunities and constraints facing initial "losers" or groups that arrive at a later point in time. It draws attention to the significance of large-scale social changes and the importance of the timing of these changes relative to each other. Furthermore, a focus on historical sequences suggests how arguments about path dependence can address claims about political change as well as political inertia. For instance, path-dependent processes may operate to institutionalize political arrangements that prove to be particularly vulnerable to some event or process emerging at a later stage in political development.

These arguments about path-dependent sequences can both draw on and enhance arguments that rational choice theorists have developed about the temporal ordering of choices in highly institutionalized settings. Working from Arrow's paradox of voting, which suggests the likelihood of endless cycling in many collective choice situations, rational choice theorists have argued persuasively that institutional arrangements governing agenda control and decision-making procedures can produce stable outcomes. These institutional arrangements are crucial because in contexts vulnerable to cycling it can be demonstrated that the sequencing among alternative choices will determine the outcome. This whole line of argument rests on institutional mechanisms that generate path dependence: steps in a sequence are irreversible because losing alternatives are dropped from the range of possible options. By showing how such "irreversibilities" can be generated in a wide range of social contexts, however, it is possible to extend this crucial insight to a far broader set of social phenomena than those covered in the literature derived from Arrow's work. Sequencing can matter not only for collective choices within legislatures, but for *any* social process where self-reinforcement means that forsaken alternatives become increasingly unreachable with the passage of time. As I demonstrate, in comparative historical analyses powerful arguments about sequencing are often applied not to the "moves" of actors on a micro scale, but to examine the impact of large-scale social changes such as democratization, industrialization, or state building.

A striking feature of many of the arguments discussed in Chapter Two is that they draw attention to lengthy, large-scale historical processes such as democratization or state building. Chapter Three turns to a more systematic discussion of big, slow-moving aspects of the social world. If the preoccupation of Chapters One and Two is questions of temporal ordering, especially the significance of beginnings, the central preoccupation here is the long durée. The chapter examines a wide range of processes that cannot be understood unless analysts remain attentive to the unfolding of both causal processes and important political outcomes over extended periods of time. Contemporary social scientists are strongly predisposed to focus on aspects of causal processes and outcomes that unfold very rapidly. Yet many things in the social world take a long time to happen—such as the spread of literacy in Ertman's analysis, or the efforts of bureaucrats to build the foundations for autonomous action in Carpenter's study. The fact that something happens slowly does not make it unimportant.

Chapter Three also explores a range of different causal processes and outcomes that may unfold over substantial stretches of time. Some causal processes and outcomes occur slowly because they are incremental—it simply takes a long time for them to add up to anything. In others, the critical factor is the presence of threshold effects. Some social processes may have little significance until they attain a critical mass, which may then trigger major change. Other social processes involve considerable time lags between the appearance of a key causal factor and the occurrence of the outcome of interest. This may be true because the outcome depends on a "causal chain" that takes some time to work itself out (*a* causes *b*, which causes *c* . . .). Alternatively, causal processes may turn on "structural" features that involve transformations that are probabilistic during any particular period, which means that several periods may be necessary before the transformation occurs. Under conditions such as these, the social outcome of interest may not actually take place until well after the appearance of key causal factors.

Analysts who fail to be attentive to these slow-moving dimensions of social life are prone to a number of serious mistakes. They may ignore potentially powerful hypotheses. They are particularly likely to miss the role of many "sociological" variables, like demography, literacy, or technology. Their explanations may focus on triggering or precipitating factors rather than more fundamental structural causes. Indeed, by truncating an analysis of processes unfolding over an extended period of time they may end up inverting causal relationships—as Carpenter suggests in his critique of Principal-Agent theory. Perhaps most fundamental of all, they may fail to even identify some important questions about politics because the relevant outcomes happen too slowly and are therefore simply off their radar screens.

Chapters Four and Five integrate and extend the arguments of the first three chapters through a focus on issues of institutional origins and change. Questions about the effects of institutions have become central to theoretical discussions throughout the social sciences. More recently, social scientists have become interested in explaining institutional arrangements rather than simply analyzing their effects. My analysis is designed to show how systematic attention to the arguments of the first three chapters can illuminate this major topic in contemporary social theory. At the same time, in arguing for a shift in focus from the problem of institutional *selection* to the problem of institutional *development*, I further extend my critique of the ahistorical proclivities of modern social science.

As social scientists have sought to explain institutional outcomes, there has been a strong tendency to employ "functional" interpretations in which institutional arrangements are explained by their consequences. In particular, what I term "actor-based functionalism" typically rests on the claim that institutions take the form they do because powerful actors engaged in rational, strategic behavior are seeking to produce the outcomes observed. Functional explanations of institutional arrangements are often plausible, but Chapter Four demonstrates how the adoption of an extended time frame reveals numerous problems for such accounts. Functional interpretations of politics are often suspect because of the sizable time lag between actors' actions and the long-term consequences of those actions. Political actors, facing the pressures of the immediate or skeptical about their capacity to engineer long-term effects, may pay limited attention to the long term. Thus the long-term effects of institutional choices, which are frequently the most profound and interesting ones, should often be seen as the *by-products* of social processes rather than embodying the goals of social actors. A second issue related to temporal gaps between actions and outcomes concerns unintended consequences. Even where actors may be greatly concerned about the future in their efforts to design institutions, they operate in settings of great complexity and high uncertainty. As a consequence, they will often make mistakes. For these and other reasons developed in my discussion, we should generally exercise considerable skepticism about assertions that institutional arrangements will reflect the skilled design choices of rational actors.[7] Instead, we should anticipate that there will often be sizable gaps between the *ex ante* goals of powerful political actors and the actual functioning of prominent institutions.

Such gaps would not matter much for functional accounts if institutions were easily adapted in response to current needs or improved understandings of institutional shortcomings. This suggests that a central issue for institutional theory is the role of adaptation, which may play out through two important social mechanisms—learning and competition—operating over time. Although these are two very significant social processes, I argue that neither is likely to prove adequate to rescue functionalist accounts in many political contexts. This is in part because these mechanisms will often be weak in practice, but it is also because these mechanisms must also overcome substantial barriers to institutional change. This is one of the most significant implications of the earlier discussion of path dependence, although there are additional reasons why institutional redesign is often difficult in politics.

Indeed, I argue in Chapter Five that understanding how institutional arrangements can become deeply embedded over time suggests the need to reframe the topic as one of institutional *development* rather than institutional *choice*. We need to think not just about moments of institutional selection and moments of institutional change, but of processes of institutional development unfolding over significant periods of time. These processes profoundly shape the circumstances under which modifications to institutions are likely to occur, and the kinds of changes that are likely. A focus on the dynamics of institutional development, I argue, can generate quite distinctive research agendas for those interested in explaining patterns of institutional outcomes in the social world.

These five chapters provide the core of my answer to why "history matters" for social scientists. Indeed, we are now in a position to reframe the question in a more helpful way. Why do social scientists need to focus on how processes unfold over significant stretches of time? First, because many social processes are path dependent, in which case key causes are temporally removed from

---

[7]Although such claims can be, and often will be, supported by careful inquiry. The point is that such connections are often assumed or asserted without justification, and that exploring the limits of such "rational design" accounts is theoretically fruitful.

their continuing effects and a central focus of analysis is on "lost" alternatives resulting from the accumulation of self-reinforcing processes. Second, because sequencing—the temporal order of events or processes—can be a crucial determinant of important social outcomes. Third, because many important social causes and outcomes are slow-moving—they take place over quite extended periods of time and are only likely to be adequately explained (or in some cases even observed in the first place) if analysts are specifically attending to that possibility. Finally, because the task of explaining institutional outcomes is better framed as an issue of institutional development rather than one of institutional selection. Institutional development, in turn, cannot be adequately treated without attending to issues incorporating an extended time frame, including the role of time horizons, unintended consequences, learning and competitive selection processes, and path dependence.

Chapter One

POSITIVE FEEDBACK AND PATH DEPENDENCE

And the first step, as you know, is always what matters most,
particularly when we are dealing with those who are young
and tender. That is the time when they are taking shape
and when any impression we choose to make leaves
a permanent mark.
—Plato, The Republic

IMAGINE A VERY LARGE URN CONTAINING TWO BALLS, one black, one red.[1] You remove one ball, and then return it to the urn along with an additional ball of the same color. You repeat this process until the urn fills up. What can we say about the eventual distribution of colored balls in the urn? Or about a series of trials in which we fill the urn and then start over again one hundred times?

- In each individual trial we have no idea what the eventual ratio of red to black balls will be; it could be 99.9 percent red, or 0.01 percent red, or anything in between. If we were to run one hundred trials, we would probably get one hundred different outcomes.
- In any particular trial, the ratio will eventually reach an equilibrium. Later draws in a series contribute only minutely to the distribution of balls in the urn. Thus the distribution settles down onto a stable outcome.
- Sequence is thus crucial. Early draws in each trial, which have a considerable random element, have a powerful effect on which of the possible equilibria will actually emerge.

Mathematicians call this a Polya urn process. Its characteristic qualities stem from the fact that an element of chance (or accident) is combined with a decision rule that links current probabilities to the outcomes of preceding (partly random) sequences.[2] Polya urn processes exhibit positive feedback. Each step

---

[1] The following discussion relies heavily on Arthur 1994, which collects his groundbreaking essays on increasing returns and path dependence, as well as on the work of Paul David (1985, 1994, 2000), who has been an equally important contributor to the emerging literature on path-dependent processes.

[2] This case depicts a specific type of positive feedback process, in which the probability of a particular "draw" precisely equals the ratio between the two alternatives in the existing population. Arthur (1994) has shown that many of the features of this case have a greater range of application, but not all of them. It is easy to model processes with only two equilibria (e.g., Hill 1997), which probably come closer to capturing the essence of many path-dependent processes in the social world.

along a particular path produces consequences that increase the relative attractiveness of that path for the next round. As such effects begin to accumulate, they generate a powerful cycle of self-reinforcing activity.

Positive feedback processes have quite intriguing characteristics, which Brian Arthur (1994) has summarized as follows:

1. *Unpredictability*. Because early events have large effects and are partly random, many outcomes may be possible. We cannot predict ahead of time which of these possible end-states will be reached.
2. *Inflexibility*. The farther into the process we are, the harder it becomes to shift from one path to another. In applications to technology, a given subsidy to a particular technique will be more likely to shift the ultimate outcome if it occurs early rather than later. Sufficient movement down a particular path may eventually "lock in" one solution.[3]
3. *Nonergodicity*. Accidental events early in a sequence do not cancel out. They cannot be treated (which is to say, ignored) as "noise," because they feed back into future choices. Small events are remembered.
4. *Potential path inefficiency*. In the long run, the outcome that becomes established may generate lower payoffs than a foregone alternative would have. The process may be path inefficient.

To this one can add a general point of particular interest to social scientists: these are processes where sequencing is critical. Earlier events matter much more than later ones, and hence different sequences may produce different outcomes. These are processes where history matters.

The Polya urn illustration captures essential elements of "path dependence" — a term that social scientists are increasingly inclined to apply to important social processes. Claims of path dependence have figured in both classic works of comparative politics, such as Lipset and Rokkan's analysis of European party systems (Lipset and Rokkan 1967), and more recent analyses on topics such as labor incorporation in Latin America (Collier and Collier 1991), the outcome of state-building processes in Europe (Ertman 1996), and the failure of the United States to develop national health insurance (Hacker 1998). As in the Polya urn illustration, social scientists generally invoke the notion of path dependence to support a few key claims: specific patterns of timing and sequence matter; starting from similar conditions a range of social outcomes is often possible; large consequences may result from relatively "small" or contingent events; particular courses of action, once introduced, can be virtually impossible to reverse; and consequently, political development is often punctuated by crit-

---

[3] This *emerging stability* represents a critical distinction between positive feedback processes and chaotic processes that may generate *no* stable equilibrium. For an interesting discussion of this quite different framework, with applications to politics, see Fearon 1996.

ical moments or junctures,that shape the basic contours of social life (Baumgartner and Jones 1993; Collier and Collier 1991; Ikenberry 1994; Krasner 1989). All of these features stand in sharp contrast to prominent modes of argument and explanation in the social sciences, which attribute "large" outcomes to "large" causes and emphasize the prevalence of unique, predictable political outcomes, the irrelevance of timing and sequence, and the capacity of rational actors to design and implement optimal solutions (given their resources and constraints) to the problems that confront them. If path-dependence arguments are indeed appropriate in substantial areas of political life, this has considerable implications.

My analysis begins with a general discussion of path dependence that seeks to clarify some important ambiguities surrounding the concept. I then outline and investigate the distinctive characteristics of social processes subject to positive feedback. I focus here on these processes both because they are of great social significance and because social scientists are beginning to develop rigorous arguments about their causes and consequences. Positive feedback dynamics capture two key elements central to most analysts' intuitive sense of path dependence. First, they clearly reveal how the costs of switching from one alternative to another will, in certain social contexts, increase markedly over time. Second, and related, they draw attention to issues of timing and sequence, distinguishing formative moments or conjunctures from the periods that reinforce divergent paths. In a process involving positive feedback, it is not just a question of what happens, but of when it happens. Issues of temporality are at the heart of the analysis.

The following section reviews the development of arguments about positive feedback in the social science discipline where they have received the greatest attention: economics. This review suggests the wide sweep of potential applications, even in a field that might be expected to be hostile to the idea. More important, these economic applications provide the most analytically developed discussions of positive feedback. Economists have not only clarified the principal implications of path dependence but have also identified many of the specific aspects of a particular social environment that generate such processes.

The discussion of economics prepares the way for an exploration of the distinctive characteristics of *politics*. Rather than simply applying extant arguments in economics to political phenomena, we need to consider the features of the political world that require modifications in the use of path-dependence claims. I will demonstrate that arguments about positive feedback are at least as relevant to an understanding of politics as they are in other areas of the social sciences. Indeed, factors such as the prominence of collective activity in politics, the central role of formal, change-resistant institutions, the possibilities for employing political authority to magnify power asymmetries, and the great ambiguity of many political processes and outcomes make this a domain of social life that is especially prone to positive feedback.

The final section offers a preliminary assessment of what these arguments can contribute to political analysis. They provide an important caution against a too easy conclusion of the inevitability, "naturalness," or functionality of observed outcomes. Given the ubiquity of claims about efficient or functional elements in politics, this alone would be an important corrective. More significant, path-dependent arguments justify efforts to stretch the temporal horizons of political analysis. They can redirect the questions social scientists ask, contributing to a richer appreciation of the centrality of historical processes in generating variation in political life. They can also point to promising hypotheses about the sources of both political stability and political change in certain common political settings. For instance, these arguments highlight the need to consider hypotheses based on temporal ordering—the possibility that the particular sequencing of events or processes may be a key part of the explanation for divergent outcomes. They also suggest that in our search for explanation we need to think about causes and effects that are often separated in time, rather than focusing exclusively on synchronic explanations (Harsanyi 1960; Stinchcombe 1968).

PATH DEPENDENCE AND POSITIVE FEEDBACK

Analysts are increasingly inclined to invoke the concept of path dependence, but clear definitions are rare. In practice, usage tends to fluctuate between a broader and narrower conception. William Sewell, for instance, suggests path dependence means "that what happened at an earlier point in time will affect the possible outcomes of a sequence of events occurring at a later point in time" (Sewell 1996, pp. 262–63). This usage may entail only the loose and not very helpful assertion that "history matters." An alternative, narrower conception of "path dependence" has been suggested by Margaret Levi:

> Path dependence has to mean, if it is to mean anything, that once a country or region has started down a track, the costs of reversal are very high. There will be other choice points, but the entrenchments of certain institutional arrangements obstruct an easy reversal of the initial choice. Perhaps the better metaphor is a tree, rather than a path. From the same trunk, there are many different branches and smaller branches. Although it is possible to turn around or to clamber from one to the other—and essential if the chosen branch dies—the branch on which a climber begins is the one she tends to follow. (Levi 1997, p. 28)

In this conception, which will be adopted here, path dependence refers to dynamic processes involving positive feedback, which generate multiple possible outcomes depending on the particular sequence in which events unfold (Arthur 1994; David 2000).

Arthur, David, and others have argued that the crucial feature of a historical process that generates path dependence is *positive feedback* (or self-
reinforcement). Given this feature, each step in a particular direction makes it
more difficult to reverse course. As Paul David (2000, p. 8) has put it, "the core
content of the concept of path dependence as a dynamic property refers to the
idea of history as an irreversible branching process." Similarly, Jacob Hacker
(2002, p. 54) argues that "path dependence refers to *developmental trajectories
that are inherently difficult to reverse*." In the presence of positive feedback, the
probability of further steps along the same path increases with each move down
that path. This is because the *relative* benefits of the current activity compared
with once-possible options increases over time. To put it a different way, the
costs of switching to some previously plausible alternative rise.[4]

Although some prefer different definitions, I choose to employ the term "path
dependence" in this relatively restricted sense, referring to social processes that
exhibit positive feedback and thus generate branching patterns of historical development. The fuzziness that has marked the use of this concept in social science suggests that the greater range offered by looser definitions has come at a
high price in analytical clarity. Path dependence has been a victim of what Sartori called concept stretching (Sartori 1970). Different types of temporally linked
sequences are generated in different ways and have different implications (Abbott 1983, 1990). These distinctive kinds of social processes, which have been
bundled together, must be disaggregated and systematically explored. Limiting
the concept of path dependence to self-reinforcing processes in no way pre-
cludes the investigation of other ways in which sequences can matter in explaining social outcomes. It does encourage clear argument about distinct claims.[5]

However such issues of concept formation are ultimately resolved, there are
three compelling reasons for focusing special attention on processes exhibiting
positive feedback. First, such processes—in which outcomes in the early stages
of a sequence feed on themselves, and once-possible outcomes become increasingly unreachable over time—characterize many important parts of the social

[4]Like others, I will sometimes describe these dynamics as generating *irreversibilities*, but this should
be read as shorthand for "rising costs of reversal over time." It may be possible to imagine, or even
experience, a reversal in which some previously foregone alternative is recaptured. The point is that
the costs of doing so may increase sharply over time—so sharply as to make such a development
highly improbable.

[5]Another strategy would be to utilize a broader conception of path dependence and then disaggre-
gate it, exploring how distinct types of path dependence are generated in different ways, with different consequences (Mahoney 2000). Because research where path dependence is invoked without
further clarification is so prevalent, however, this option seems more problematic. Ultimately such
definitional disputes remain intractable. What is critical is that researchers should be clear and consistent about what they mean when they employ the concept, and recognize the importance of distinguishing different types of processes.

world. Second, social scientists are developing theory that makes the investigation of the causes and consequences of positive feedback a particularly promising area of inquiry. Third, a focus on self-reinforcing, path-dependent dynamics turns out to be an essential building block for exploring a wide range of issues related to temporal processes. This final claim is advanced in the chapters to follow, while the first two are developed in later sections of this chapter—a task that first requires a review of recent work on path dependence in economics.

"Increasing Returns" and Path-Dependence Arguments in Economics

Traditionally, economists have focused on the search for unique equilibria. The goal is attractive, because it suggested a world of potential predictability and efficiency. Given knowledge of existing factor endowments and preferences, equilibrium analysis might point to a single optimal outcome. Moreover, because economists assumed a context of decreasing marginal returns, this analytical goal was potentially achievable. With decreasing returns, economic actions will engender negative feedback, which will lead to a predictable equilibrium. A sharp rise in oil prices prompts increased conservation, exploration, and exploitation of other sources of energy, leading to a fall in oil prices. Each step away from equilibrium is more difficult than the one before. As Arthur (1994, p. 1) summarizes, negative "feedback tends to stabilize the economy because any major changes will be offset by the very reactions they generate. . . . The equilibrium marks the 'best' outcome possible under the circumstances: the most efficient use and allocation of resources."

During the past twenty years, however, this decreasing-returns tradition has faced a mounting challenge. Economists have exhibited a growing interest in the idea of "increasing returns"—where each increment added to a particular line of activity yields larger rather than smaller benefits. On a wide range of subjects, including the spatial location of production, the development of international trade, the causes of economic growth and the emergence of new technologies, path-dependence arguments have become prevalent. The ideas developed in this research are not entirely new.[6] Yet in the past few years, prominent mainstream economists have embraced these ideas. Their work has received considerable attention in leading journals. Douglass North, who places great emphasis on such arguments in his analysis of the development of modern capitalism, was recently awarded the Nobel Prize for economics.

Arguments about technology have provided the most fertile ground for exploring the conditions conducive to increasing returns. As Brian Arthur and

---

[6]The concept of increasing returns received attention in the work of Adam Smith and (especially) Alfred Marshall. In the twentieth century, an underground of "institutionalist" scholarship, including figures such as Kaldor, Myrdall, and Veblen, continued to explore these issues.

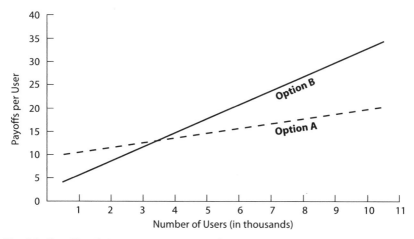

Fig. 1.1. Payoffs with increasing returns to scale.

Paul David have stressed, under conditions often present in complex, knowledge-intensive sectors, a particular technology may achieve a decisive advantage (Arthur 1994; David 1985). An early edge may trigger positive feedback effects that may lock in this technology, excluding competitors even if it is not necessarily the most efficient one in the long run. With increasing returns, actors have strong incentives to focus on a single alternative and to continue down a specific path once initial steps are taken in that direction. Path dependence arguments have been applied to the development of the "QWERTY" typewriter keyboard, the triumph of the light-water nuclear reactor in the United States, the battles between Betamax and VHS video recorders and DOS-based and Macintosh computers, early automobile designs, and competing standards for electric current.[7]

Figure 1.1, taken from Arthur's work, summarizes the process. Each technology generates higher payoffs for every user as it becomes more prevalent. In other words, these technologies are subject to increasing returns. Because technology B starts with lower payoffs, however, early users gravitate to technology A. This movement activates a process of positive feedback, improving the performance of technology A, which induces more new users to adopt it, which widens the gap between technology A and B, encouraging yet more users to gravitate to technology A. The advantages of technology A rapidly become overwhelming, even though technology B would have generated higher payoffs for all users if it had been the first to reach a critical threshold of usage (here, 3500 users). Thus

---

[7]Many of these examples have been contested by critics who deny the empirical claim that superior technologies lost out. Since these criticisms raise broader issues about the usefulness of increasing returns arguments, I will postpone discussion until the end of this section.

when a new technology is subject to increasing returns, being the fastest out of the gate (if only for reasons of historical accident) becomes critical. With increasing returns, actors have strong incentives to focus on a single alternative, and to continue moving down a specific path once initial steps are taken in that direction.

Not all technologies are prone to increasing returns. Crucially, Arthur and David addressed not only the characteristics of such processes, but the conditions that give rise to them. Understanding these conditions is essential, as we shall see, because analytically similar circumstances occur frequently in the world of politics. These arguments thus provide a foundation for developing hypotheses about when positive feedback processes are likely to operate in the social world.

Arthur (1994, p. 112) argues that four features of a technology and its social context generate increasing returns:

1. *Large set-up or fixed costs.* These create a high payoff for further investments in a given technology. With large production runs, fixed costs can be spread over more output, which will lead to lower unit costs. When setup or fixed costs are high, individuals and organizations have a strong incentive to identify and stick with a single option.

2. *Learning effects.* Knowledge gained in the operation of complex systems also leads to higher returns from continuing use. With repetition, individuals learn how to use products more effectively, and their experiences are likely to spur further innovations in the product or in related activities.

3. *Coordination effects.* These occur when the benefits an individual receives from a particular activity increase as others adopt the same option. If technologies embody positive *network externalities*, a given technology will become more attractive as more people use it. Coordination effects are especially significant when a technology has to be compatible with a linked infrastructure (e.g., software with hardware, automobiles with an infrastructure of roads, repair facilities and fueling stations). Increased use of a technology encourages investments in the linked infrastructure, which in turn makes the technology more attractive.

4. *Adaptive expectations.* If options that fail to win broad acceptance will have drawbacks later on, individuals may feel a need to "pick the right horse." Although the dynamic here is related to coordination effects, it derives from the self-fulfilling character of *expectations*. Projections about future aggregate use patterns lead individuals to adapt their actions in ways that help to make those expectations come true.

This discussion of technology is important primarily because it clarifies a set of relationships characteristic of many social interactions. New social initiatives—such as the creation of organizations or institutions—usually entail considerable start-up costs; individuals, as well as organizations, learn by doing; the benefits of our individual activities or those of an organization are often enhanced if they are coordinated or "fit" with the activities of other actors or organizations; it is frequently important to bet on the winning horse, so we adapt our actions in light of our expectations about the actions of others.

Although path-dependence arguments about technology are probably the best known, economists have applied similar analyses in a striking range of economic contexts. Both Krugman (1991) and Arthur (1994) point to the role of increasing returns in the spatial location of production. Given the importance of physical proximity in many aspects of economic life, agglomeration effects are widespread. That is, initial centers of economic activity may act like a magnet and influence the locational decisions and investments of other economic actors. Established firms attract suppliers, skilled labor, specialized financial and legal services, and an appropriate physical infrastructure. The concentration of these factors may in turn make the particular location attractive to other firms that produce similar goods. So do social networks, which facilitate the exchange of information and expertise. Increasing returns arguments help explain the prevalence of pockets of specialized economic activity, from Silicon Valley to the high-end textile manufacturers of northern Italy. Krugman (1991, p. 80) concludes: "If there is one single area of economics in which path dependence is unmistakable, it is in *economic geography*—the location of production in space. The long shadow cast by history over location is apparent at all scales, from the smallest to the largest—from the cluster of costume jewelry firms in Providence to the concentration of 60 million people in the Northeast Corridor."

These claims closely parallel recent analyses of international trade, where arguments about increasing returns have gained wide acceptance. Researchers began by focusing on economic trends that appeared anomalous from the perspective of traditional trade theory—most notably, the explosion of *intra*-industry trade after World War II (Krugman 1996). If comparative advantage results from "natural" features of different countries, one would expect most trade to occur between quite different countries, such as North-South trade of manufactured goods for raw materials. Most international trade, however, is North-North. Developed economies trade primarily with other developed countries, including extensive exchanges within particular industries. This pattern suggests a puzzle: Why have broadly similar countries developed highly specialized "niche" comparative advantages?

Increasing returns provided an answer. Knowledge-intensive sectors will be prone to positive feedback. Countries that gain a lead in a particular niche, for whatever reason, may consolidate that lead over time. The result is a high degree of specialization. Even countries with similar initial endowments develop divergent areas of economic strength. Comparative advantage is not simply given, it is often created through a sequence of events unfolding over time.[8] The relevance of increasing returns processes to the economics of trade is now widely accepted.[9]

Economists have also applied increasing-returns arguments to economic change more broadly. A prominent development in discussions of economic growth has centered on "endogenous growth" theory (Romer 1986, 1990). Economists in the 1980s became puzzled by growth rates (notably in developed countries during the post–World War II period) far greater than what measured increases in inputs of capital and labor could explain. Romer and others argue that increasing returns associated with economic applications of knowledge help account for the anomaly. Unlike capital and labor, many aspects of knowledge are nonrival— their use in one firm does not prevent their use in another. A single gain in knowledge can be applied in many settings and can lead to dramatic improvements in productivity. In short, economic growth generates positive feedback. A somewhat different analysis of growth based on increasing returns emphasizes the importance of complementarities (Milgrom and Roberts 1990; Milgrom, Qian, and Roberts 1991). Various economic activities (e.g., in information technology) may be complementary to other related activities. Improvements in a core activity can thus spill over by improving related parts of the economy. These improvements in turn may increase the attractiveness of the core activity.

Economists are now applying increasing-returns arguments to a wide range of important economic phenomena, but Douglass North's application to issues of institutional emergence and change has the most profound implications for social scientists (North 1990a). North argues that all the features that Arthur identified in investigations of increasing returns in technology can be applied to institutions. In contexts of complex social interdependence, new institutions often entail high start-up costs, and they produce considerable learning effects, coordination effects, and adaptive expectations. Established institutions will typically generate powerful inducements that reinforce their own stability and further development (David 1994). In North's words:

> All four of Arthur's self-reinforcing mechanisms apply, although with somewhat different characteristics. There are large initial setup costs when the institutions are created de novo. . . . There are significant learning effects for organizations that arise in consequence of the opportunity set provided

---

[8]It is worth noting that this research on trade has been used to derive some controversial policy implications. If first-mover advantages are significant, free trade may not be an optimal policy for a country whose trade partners are willing to subsidize emerging sectors. Under certain (restricted) conditions, a policy of "picking winners" may make economic sense (Krugman 1996; Tyson 1993). There remains considerable dispute about the significance of such opportunities for strategic intervention. Krugman, for instance, maintains that they will appear relatively infrequently, not so much because path dependence is rare, but because governments will not be able to identify winners *ex ante*.

[9]As Krugman (1996, pp. 109–110) notes, in the American Economic Association's classification system for journal articles one will now find "models of trade with increasing returns and imperfect competition" alongside the category for "conventional trade models."

by the institutional framework. . . . There will be coordination effects directly via contracts with other organizations and indirectly by induced investments through the polity in complementary activities. . . . Adaptive expectations occur because increased prevalence of contracting based on a specific institution will reduce uncertainties about the permanence of that rule. (North 1990a, p. 95)

North emphasizes that not just single institutions are subject to positive feedback. Institutional arrangements induce complementary organizational forms, which in turn may encourage the development of new complementary institutions. For social scientists interested in paths of development, the key issue is often what North calls "the interdependent web of an institutional matrix." This matrix, North emphasizes, "produces massive increasing returns" (North 1990a, p. 95). Path-dependent processes will often be evident not only at the level of individual organizations or institutions but at a more macro level that involves configurations of complementary organizations and institutions (Katznelson 1997; Hall and Soskice 2001b; Pierson and Skocpol 2002).

This argument provides the core to North's sweeping reinterpretation of economic history. The central puzzle motivating North's inquiry is the limited convergence of economic performance across countries over time. Neoclassical theory suggests that laggard countries should easily adopt the practices of high performers, which would induce fairly rapid convergence. But this does not happen. According to North, institutions, which he defines broadly to include "the rules of the game in a society or, more formally, . . . the humanly devised constraints that shape human interaction" (p. 3), explain the anomaly of continued divergence in economic performance. Once in place, institutions are hard to change, and they have a tremendous effect on the possibilities for generating sustained economic growth. Individuals and organizations adapt to existing institutions. If the institutional matrix creates incentives for piracy, North observes, then people will invest in becoming good pirates. When institutions fail to provide incentives to be economically productive, there is unlikely to be much economic growth.

For other social scientists, North's insight is crucial for two reasons. First, he highlights the parallels between characteristics of technology and certain characteristics of social interactions. In this context, it is worth noting that Arthur's arguments about technology are not really about the technology itself but about the characteristics of a technology *in interaction with* certain qualities of related social activity, such as incentives to coordinate with others or adopt behaviors based on expectations about the future. Second, North rightly emphasizes that institutional development is subject to positive feedback. Indeed, it is the role of path dependence in explaining patterns of institutional emergence, persistence, and change that may be of greatest significance for the social sciences.

The dialogue surrounding increasing returns and path dependence in economics is the impassioned discourse of an emerging paradigm. Economists talk of "new" growth theory, "new" trade theory, and so on—all based on arguments involving positive feedback. Yet despite the prevalence of such arguments and the intellectual excitement associated with them, there are excellent reasons to believe that the range of application should be at least as wide in politics as it is in economics. To understand why, it is helpful to consider the major objections to increasing-returns arguments that have recently surfaced in economics. The discussion will clarify the sources of path dependence and identify social mechanisms that might offset such processes. This clarification provides a useful analytical bridge to an investigation of path-dependent processes in politics.

In a forceful critique, Liebowitz and Margolis (1995) raise some tough questions about the economics literature on increasing returns. Two aspects of their critique are relevant here. They emphasize that only "remediable" path dependence is really of theoretical significance, and they claim that market mechanisms insure that remediable path dependence is rare. I will take up each argument in turn.[10]

Following Williamson (1993), Liebowitz and Margolis distinguish remediable and nonremediable path dependence. The latter occurs if there are no *feasible* improvements in the path, either now or in the past. Nonremediable path dependence "stipulates that intertemporal effects propagate error" (p. 207). With hindsight, we wish that some other alternative had been chosen. Yet Liebowitz and Margolis question whether nonremediable path dependence has profound implications. If we acted as best we could with the information available at the time, then the mistake was unavoidable, and we cannot reasonably describe the outcome as inefficient.

Liebowitz and Margolis argue that the only kind of path dependence with major ramifications is path dependence that is potentially remediable: "path dependence, . . . [which] supposes the feasibility, in principle, of improvements in the path . . . is the only form of path dependence that conflicts with the neoclassical model of relentlessly rational behavior leading to efficient, and therefore predictable, outcomes" (ibid). This distinction between remediable and nonremediable path dependence is crucial to their argument, because Liebowitz and Margolis believe that instances of the more theoretically troubling, remediable kind occur very infrequently.

Is their dismissal of nonremediable path dependence convincing? As Williamson notes, for policy purposes remediability is likely to be an appropriate standard. Recognizing the existence of path dependence may not help policymakers much if they do not know how to identify it *ex ante*.[11] But this objection

---

[10]Note that the Liebowitz-Margolis critique depends on *both* parts of their argument being true. The significance of path dependence for social scientists can be sustained if *either* the relevance of nonremediable path dependence or the prevalence of remediable path dependence can be sustained.

[11]As noted before, it is precisely for this reason that Krugman and others question those making broad claims about the implications of increasing returns arguments for trade policy.

loses its force if our purpose is instead to understand—perhaps *ex post*—*why* aspects of societies move in particular directions and the consequences of such movements. And, of course, it is precisely these questions about causality that are the central preoccupation of most social scientists.

The second part of the Margolis-Liebowitz analysis is the claim that remediable path dependence is rare. Their argument is straightforward. If one of two options is superior in the long run but not in the short run, then market arrangements will generally assure the adoption of the superior path. The ability of private actors to capture the returns from long-term investments prevents bad choices. Institutions of property rights, provisions for patents, and extensive capital markets insure that options with long-term promise but low short-run payoffs will nonetheless receive the support that they deserve. Economic actors, in short, calculate in the shadow of the future, and are thus unlikely to indulge in myopic, short-term maximizing behavior at their own long-term expense.

This argument has considerable merit,[12] but how much depends on the strength of these mechanisms for overcoming short-term thinking. Although Liebowitz and Margolis are more than a little complacent about the capacity of these market mechanisms to fully internalize the considerable externalities that are central to increasing-returns arguments, it is perhaps wise to leave those issues to economists. Two objections, however, are critically important. First, arguments about the farsightedness of markets seem to apply to only *some* types of path dependence in the economy. The Liebowitz-Margolis critique focuses on the decisions of firms to invest in particular technologies or products. In most of the illustrations discussed earlier (e.g., spatial agglomerations, trade specialization, endogenous growth), however, many of the benefits of increasing returns are external to individual firms and cannot be fully captured by individual investors and entrepreneurs. Thus, the mechanisms identified by Liebowitz and Margolis are unlikely to ensure that the best long-term outcome will be selected.

Perhaps more important, the Liebowitz and Margolis argument has little relevance to the development of institutions, which are also subject to increasing returns. Private actors cannot obtain patents or employ venture capital to capture the long-term economic gains from constructing key economic institutions. Indeed, the Liebowitz-Margolis argument simply assumes the presence of institutions that support their key market mechanisms. Their argument does not seem to have much relevance for North's argument about the presence in particular polities of networks or matrices of institutions and organizations. The fact that they do not even cite North's work is telling. North maintains that path-dependent processes of institutional development are crucial to the evolution of particular market economies. The farsighted financial markets central to the Liebowitz-Margolis argument are of limited help, however, in triggering such

---

[12]Arthur explicitly recognized this possibility, although as far as I know he did not systematically pursue the implications. See Arthur 1994, p. 28, fn 11.

institutional development. Rather, to a large extent, they are products of that development.

The failure of the Liebowitz-Margolis critique to address issues of institutional development in economies points to a more fundamental objection. Even if one accepts their analysis regarding the economic sphere, their arguments still have limited relevance for the analysis of other kinds of social processes. However strong market mechanisms for "farsightedness" may be, they are almost certainly far weaker in politics. At the same time, other sources of positive feedback that may be relatively unimportant in the development of technology are highly significant elsewhere. I explore both these points in the next section.

Moving from Economics to Politics

Microeconomic theory has illuminated important features of the political landscape in fields ranging from the study of party competition, to the formation of interest groups and social movements, to voting and legislative behavior. The value of economists' theoretical exports is greatly enhanced, however, if the importers take careful account of the distinctive features of the "local" environment. As Terry Moe (1990, p. 119) has put it in a related context, "the real problem is to try to identify those essential features of politics that might serve as a foundation for theory, a foundation that can take advantage of the new economics without being overwhelmed or misdirected by it." Arguments drawn from economics must be sensitive to the quite different nature of the political world.

Politics differs from economics in many ways.[13] The key is to specify which aspects are most relevant to an investigation of the sources and consequences of path dependence. Following a brief summary of the distinctive tasks of the political arena, this discussion is divided into two parts. The first considers four prominent and interconnected aspects of politics that make this realm of social life conducive to positive feedback: (1) the central role of collective action; (2) the high density of institutions; (3) the possibilities for using political authority to enhance asymmetries of power; and (4) its intrinsic complexity and opacity. After briefly explicating each, I will discuss their relevance to path dependence. *Each of these features makes positive feedback processes prevalent in politics.*

Second, I explain why the ameliorative mechanisms that Liebowitz and Margolis identify in economic systems are often ineffective in offsetting path dependence in politics. Three characteristics of politics change the picture considerably: the absence or weakness of efficiency-enhancing mechanisms of competition and learning, the shorter time horizons of political actors, and the strong status quo bias generally built into political institutions. *Each of these features makes*

---

[13]The following discussion is particularly indebted to Lindblom 1977, Moe 1984, 1990, and North 1990b.

positive feedback processes in politics particularly intense. They increase the difficulty of reversing the course down which actors have started. Path-dependent processes are now central to economic theory, and the argument here is that these dynamics will be at least as widespread and often more difficult to reverse in politics.

Sources of Positive Feedback in Politics

A fundamental feature of politics is its focus on the provision of public goods.[14] Such goods are distinguished by *jointness of supply* (where the production costs for the good are unaffected or only modestly affected by the number of those consuming it) and *nonexcludability* (where it is very costly or impossible to limit consumption to those who have paid for a good). These features, which are extremely widespread in modern life, make public goods—from national defense to environmental protection—difficult to provide through markets. Nonexcludability creates incentives for free-riding, since individuals will receive the benefits of a public good whether or not they contribute to its production. Jointness of supply means that private markets will underproduce the goods in question since private actors will tend to consider only the benefits to themselves.

The reason to emphasize these characteristics of public goods is that they help to explain a second fundamental feature of political systems: their key elements are generally *compulsory* rather than voluntary. The exercise of authority—to be blunt, coercion—combined with a complex array of complementary institutions designed to circumscribe and legitimate that authority, is necessary to generate collective provision. Legally binding rules are not just a foundation for political activity (like property rights in the economy). They are instead the very essence of politics (Lindblom 1977; Moe 1990, 2003). The focus on producing public goods, and the consequent resort to coercive authority, has a number of repercussions for the character of political life, each relevant for an assessment of tendencies toward path dependence.

THE COLLECTIVE NATURE OF POLITICS

A quick contrast with economic markets can highlight the prevalence of collective action in politics. Suppose you are working for a firm with an annoying boss and bad pay. You have a clear option: acting on your own, you can seek work elsewhere, either at one of a large number of other firms or by setting up business on your own. Your ability to move depends on the state of the labor market, but the existence of competitive options sets clear limits on how annoying your boss can afford to be and how bad the pay can get.

---

[14]In most cases, the goods in question are not "pure" public goods—a fact that would complicate the analysis but not alter the basic claims presented here. For discussions, see Mueller 1989, chap. 2, and Cornes and Sandler 1996.

Or suppose you invent a great new product. Assuming that you can get financial backing (which you should be able to do—it is a great idea, and the market generates a ready supply of venture capitalists), your prospects are good. Nothing stops you from going into business or selling the idea to someone who will. Either way, the new, superior product gets to see the light of day, and you reap considerable benefits from your innovation.

The setting of consumers, at least in the textbook case, is similarly atomistic. My decisions are essentially independent of my expectations regarding the choices of other consumers.[15] There is no need for explicit attempts to coordinate behavior; the market simply aggregates the isolated decisions of individuals.

These highly stylized examples illustrate the relative flexibility, fluidity, and atomization of economic markets. In contrast, political "markets" are generally far from flexible and fluid. In politics, the consequences of my actions are highly dependent upon the actions of others. What I get depends not just on what I do, but (mostly) on what others do. Following Olson's path-breaking work, students of politics have long recognized the "logic of collective action" (Olson 1965). Most of the "goods" produced in politics are public goods; it is difficult to limit their consumption to those who helped provide them. As a result, individuals will have a strong tendency to free-ride. Creating conditions favorable to collective action is a principal issue in political life.

The problem here is not limited to the fact that the public sector produces public goods. Given the reliance of politics on mechanisms of collective decision backed by authority, laws themselves have the character of public goods for those who benefit from them. Achieving political influence generally requires collective action. In the words of Marwell and Oliver:

> In the realm of politics and social movements, collective action gains benefits most often by affecting government policy. Collective actors bear the cost of influencing government officials, not the cost of actually providing the good. Influencing government policy almost always has very high jointness of supply . . . those paying lobbyists for tax loopholes are concerned only with the cost of lobbying, not with the cost of the lost tax revenues. The cost of cleaning up pollution may be roughly proportional to the number of polluters, but the cost of obtaining laws requiring polluters to clean up their own messes is not. An interest group or social movement campaigns for legislation of benefit to its members, but their costs are unaffected by the

---

[15]Although this represents a critical difference between economics and politics, one would need to make a number of important qualifications. The decisions of other consumers clearly do affect the price, supply, and quality of the goods available to me. Furthermore, much economic activity, both on the production and consumption side, involves significant externalities, which make the implications of consumption interdependent. As already noted, these conditions of independent consumption often do not apply to technologies involving network externalities. For a good discussion of some of these complications, see Hirsch 1977.

existence of others who would also benefit from the legislation. (Marwell and Oliver 1993, pp. 42–43)

Or, as they summarize the same point more succinctly, "laws have high joint-ness of supply" (p. 45). These circumstances generate major collective action problems.

There is another reason why political action frequently requires coordination. Many of the goals that political actors pursue have a "lumpy" or "winner-take-all" quality to them (politicians seeking reelection, coup plotters, and lobbyists either win or lose; legislation either passes or is rejected). Unlike economic markets, where there is usually room for many firms, finishing second may not count for much in politics. Indeed—the Russian Menshiviks in 1917 come to mind—it can be extremely problematic. Again, the effectiveness of my actions depends heavily on the actions of others. This is less true of some aspects of politics—such as answering an opinion poll question or voting—than others. Even in voting, however, the lumpiness of election outcomes, in the absence of a pure system of proportional representation, means that if a person does not want to "waste" her vote, her actions may well turn on what she expects others to do.

Thus, a crucial feature of most collective action in politics is the absence of a linear relationship between effort and effect. Instead, collective action frequently involves many of the qualities conducive to positive feedback (Marwell and Oliver 1993).[16] A central reason is the prevalence of adaptive expectations. Under circumstances where picking the wrong horse may have very high costs, actors must constantly adjust their behavior in the light of expectations of how they expect others to act. Whether you put energy into developing a new party, join a potential coalition, or provide resources to an interest group may depend to a considerable degree on your confidence that a large number of other people will do the same. In addition, many types of collective action involve high start-up costs. Considerable resources (material or cultural) need to be expended on organizing before the group becomes self-sustaining.

That collective action processes in politics are very often subject to positive feedback explains why social scientists have often been struck by the considerable stability of patterns of political mobilization over time. Lipset and Rokkan's work on political parties in Europe exemplifies this dynamic: key historical junctures produced major political cleavages. These political divisions became organized into political parties. Having surmounted initial start-up costs and fueled processes of adaptive expectations, these parties are reproduced through time, generating "frozen" party systems (Lipset and Rokkan 1967).

---

[16]Olson's own *Rise and Decline of Nations* (1981) is built around exactly this argument—interest groups are difficult to found but relatively easy to sustain, so we should expect them to be increasingly prevalent over time in democratic societies where severe external shocks, such as war, have been absent.

Recent work by Theda Skocpol on extensive voluntary associations in the United States provides additional strong evidence of the organizational persistence that can result from positive feedback (Skocpol 1999). Skocpol and a team of researchers identified all voluntary organizations in the United States that have ever enrolled more than 1 percent of the American population (or half that amount for single-gender groups), and tracked those organizations over time. The results, covering fifty-eight such organizations since the 1830s, reveal striking organizational continuities. Although some organizations crossed the 1 percent threshold for relatively short periods, twenty-six of the fifty-eight organizations that ever crossed the 1 percent threshold are still above it today. Of the twenty-six extensive voluntary associations in the United States today, sixteen had already reached the 1 percent mark by the 1940s, and a number of them stretch back much farther. A large number of the organizations that have fallen off Skocpol's list nonetheless stayed above it for many decades. If one examines the forty organizations on Skocpol's list founded before 1900, nineteen stayed above the 1 percent mark for at least five decades; ten of the forty are still above that threshold, a century or more after their founding.[17] In short, despite massive social, economic, and political changes over time, self-reinforcing dynamics associated with collective action processes—especially high start-up costs, coordination effects, and adaptive expectations—mean that organizations will have a strong tendency to persist once they are institutionalized.

THE INSTITUTIONAL DENSITY OF POLITICS

As much work in political science has recently stressed, efforts to coordinate actors in the pursuit of public goods often require the construction of formal institutions. Once established, these institutional constraints apply to all—those who do not approve as well as those who do—and they are backed up, ultimately, by force. The "exit" option, while central to the workings of the market, is often unavailable (or prohibitively costly) to actors who feel poorly served by existing political arrangements. Politics involves struggles over the authority to establish, enforce, and change rules governing social action in a particular territory. In short, much of politics is based on authority rather than exchange. Thus in politics, institutional constraints are ubiquitous. Both formal institutions (such as constitutional arrangements) *and public policies* place extensive, legally binding constraints on behavior.

Although unorthodox, the inclusion of public policies as well as formal institutions in this formulation is important (Pierson 1993; Pierson and Skocpol 2002; Moe 2003). While policies are generally more easily altered than the con-

---

[17]This evidence actually understates the degree of organizational persistence, since many organizations that fall below the demanding 1 percent threshold nonetheless continue to have very large memberships, and they may also have existed as quite large organizations for long periods before initially crossing that threshold.

stitutive rules of formal institutions, they are nevertheless extremely prominent constraining features of the political environment. Policies, grounded in law and backed by the coercive power of the state, signal to actors what has to be done, what cannot be done, and establish many of the rewards and penalties associated with particular activities. Most policies are also remarkably durable (Rose 1991). Especially in modern societies, extensive policy arrangements fundamentally shape the incentives and resources of political actors.

That such institutions are generally subject to positive feedback has been implicit in much recent research. Scholars have emphasized how institutions can help actors overcome various dilemmas arising from collective-choice situations—especially the need to coordinate their behavior by disciplining expectations about the behavior of others. What is absent or downplayed in these discussions, however, is a recognition that these characteristics render processes of institutional development path-dependent.

As already discussed, North's analysis highlights how institutions induce self-reinforcing processes that make reversals increasingly unattractive over time. In contexts of complex social interdependence, new institutions and policies often generate high fixed costs, learning effects, coordination effects, and adaptive expectations. Institutions and policies may encourage individuals and organizations to invest in specialized skills, deepen relationships with other individuals and organizations, and develop particular political and social identities.[18] These activities increase the attractiveness of existing institutional arrangements relative to hypothetical alternatives. In institutionally dense environments, initial actions push individual behavior onto paths that are hard to reverse. As I will explore in greater detail in Chapter Five, social actors make commitments based on existing institutions and policies. As they do so, the cost of reversing course generally rises dramatically.

Economists typically refer to self-reinforcing processes as involving a process of "increasing returns": each additional expenditure of resources generates a higher return than the one before it. As Mahoney (2001) has emphasized, this efficiency-focused (benefits per unit of expenditure) terminology makes sense for the self-reinforcing processes that interest most economists, but is not appropriate for many others. As we broaden our focus to examine other social phenomena, the more neutral language of positive feedback or self-reinforcement

---

[18]It has become common to refer to such consequences as "sunk costs." While intuitive, this terminology is unfortunate. When economists refer to sunk costs they mean costs that cannot be recovered and should be regarded as irrelevant to current choices among options. By contrast, the whole point of path dependence is that these previous choices *are* relevant to current action. In cases of increasing returns, social adaptations represent investments that yield continuing benefits. Actors may have powerful incentives to stick with a current option because they receive a continuing stream of benefits from investments already made in that option. Massive new investments would be required before some theoretically superior alternative generated the same or a higher stream of benefits.

is necessary to avoid any implicit suggestion about efficiency. This is especially important in considering two possible sources of path dependence in politics: power dynamics and patterns of social understanding.

The allocation of political authority to particular actors is a key source of positive feedback. Indeed, this represents a source of path dependence quite distinct from those discussed by Arthur and North. Where certain actors are in a position to impose rules on others, the employment of power may be self-reinforcing. Actors may utilize political authority to change the rules of the game (both formal institutions and various public policies) to enhance their power. These changes may not only shift the rules in their favor, but increase their own capacities for political action while diminishing those of their rivals. And these changes may result in adaptations that reinforce these trends, as undecided, weakly committed, or vulnerable actors join the winners or desert the losers. Many political conflicts, from the Nazi seizure of power to the gradual process through which the Labour Party supplanted the Liberals in Great Britain in the early twentieth century, reveal this sort of dynamic. Disparities in political resources among contending groups may widen dramatically over time as positive feedback sets in.

The disenfranchisement of African Americans in the post-Reconstruction American South provides a clear and poignant example of how shifts in political power can be self-reinforcing. In Alexander Keyssar's marvelous study of the history of suffrage in the United States, the end of Reconstruction precipitated a dynamic process of shifting power relations that played out over a considerable period of time (Keyssar 2000, pp. 107–16). In 1876, a contested presidential election led to the removal of federal troops from the South. In 1878, Democrats won control of both houses of Congress for the first time in twenty years. "The upshot of these events . . . ," Keyssar writes, "was to entrust the administration of voting laws in the South to state and local governments" (p. 107).

These breakthroughs, it must be stressed, did not result in immediate and total victory for Democratic "Redeemers" in the South. Instead, they ushered in a "period of limbo and contestation, of participation coexisting with efforts at exclusion" (p. 108). In many parts of the South, the Republican Party "hung on, and large, if declining, numbers of blacks continued to exercise the franchise" (p. 107):

> Periodically they were able to form alliances with poor and upcountry whites and even with some newly emerging industrial interests sympathetic to the probusines policies of the Republicans. Opposition to the conservative, planter-dominated Redeemer Democrats, therefore, did not disappear: elections were contested by Republicans, by factions within the Democratic Party, and eventually by the Farmers' alliance and the Populists. Conse-

quently, the Redeemers, who controlled most state legislatures, continued to try to shrink the black (and opposition white) electorate through gerrymandering, registration systems, complicated ballot configurations, and the secret ballot (which served as a de facto literacy test). When necessary, they also resorted to violence and fraudulent vote counts. (p. 107)

Social and political power was used over time to reinforce and consolidate political advantage. By the early 1890s, major challenges to the Redeemers began to dissipate, giving way to a durable system of planter hegemony. As late as 1964, only 10 percent of African Americans in Mississippi would be registered to vote.

A focus on path dependence can serve to refocus the attention of social scientists on the role of power (Moe 2003; Thelen 1999). In the famous community power debate of the 1960s and 1970s, Bachrach and Baratz (1962) and Lukes (1974) argued persuasively that power asymmetries are often hidden from view; where power is most unequal, it often does not need to be employed openly. Pluralist critics essentially countered that it was impossible to systematically evaluate such claims (Polsby 1963; Wolfinger 1971). Although he did not frame the issue quite this way, Gaventa (1980) demonstrated that such power asymmetries can reflect positive feedback processes operating over substantial periods of time. Processes of positive feedback can transform a situation of relatively balanced conflict into one of great inequality. Political settings where one set of actors must initially impose their preferences on another set through open conflict ("the first face of power") may change over time into settings where power relations are so uneven that anticipated reactions and agenda control ("the second face of power") and ideological manipulation ("the third face") make open political conflict unnecessary. Thus, positive feedback over time may simultaneously increase asymmetries of power and, paradoxically, render power relations less visible.

THE COMPLEXITY AND OPACITY OF POLITICS

Economic theory is built around the useful and plausible assumptions that actors know what they want, strive to get as much as they can, and are pretty good at doing so. Firms seek to maximize profits. The metric for good performance is relatively simple and transparent. Prices send strong signals that facilitate the analysis of how various features of the economic environment affect firm performance. Observable, unambiguous, and often quantifiable indicators exist for many of these features. Workers can obtain fairly good information on the wages and working conditions on offer from different firms. Consumers, too, are reasonably adept at navigating most aspects of the economic world. Links between choices and outcomes are generally clear: take a new job and your income rises; buy a car and your savings account balance shrinks. The quality of goods is usually evident in relatively short order, and repeated purchases allow consumers to sample alternatives.

Of course, one can add many complications to this simple picture of the economic realm. The market is often highly complex and confusing. Yet the presence of a unifying metric (prices), the absence of a need to coordinate many of one's economic decisions with those of other actors, the prevalence of repeated interactions, and the presence of relatively short causal chains between choices and results greatly facilitate the efforts of economic actors to establish priorities, construct sensible causal maps, and correct mistakes over time.

As I will explore in greater detail in Chapters Four and Five, politics is a far, far murkier environment (Moe 1990; North 1990b). It lacks anything like the measuring rod of price, involves the pursuit of a wide range of largely incommensurable goals, and consists of processes that make it very hard to observe or measure important aspects of political performance. And, if we believe that a system is not performing well, it is still more difficult to determine which elements in these highly complex systems are responsible and what adjustments would lead to better results. The reliance on elaborate procedures to handle collective-choice situations in politics is inescapable, but it undermines transparency—that is, it greatly increases transaction costs (Cornes and Sandler 1996; Mueller 1989). The complexity of the goals of politics, and the loose and diffuse links between actions and outcomes, renders politics inherently ambiguous. As North has argued, "political markets are far more prone [than economic markets] to inefficiency. The reason is straightforward. It is extraordinarily difficult to measure what is being exchanged in political markets and in consequence to enforce agreements" (North 1990b, p. 362).

It is important to note that North is not simply arguing that political decision making is inefficient. Rather, politics gets stuck with more difficult problems. Where transaction costs are low, market mechanisms are likely to be effective. They often break down, however, when transaction costs are very high. High transaction costs are characteristic for public goods (Cornes and Sandler 1996; Mueller 1989). Thus, it is complex and ambiguous issues and problems that gravitate toward the public sphere.

Even if mistakes or failures in politics are apparent, improvement through "trial-and-error" processes is far from automatic. Many participants in politics (voters, members of interest groups) engage in activities only sporadically. Their tools of action are often crude, such as the blunt instrument of the vote, and their actions have consequences only when aggregated. There may be long lags and complex causal chains connecting these political actions to political outcomes. The result is that mistaken understandings often do not get corrected.

The point is not that learning never occurs in politics. Rather, learning is very difficult and cannot be assumed to occur. Instead, understandings of the political world should themselves be seen as susceptible to path dependence. Drawing on work in both cognitive psychology and organizational theory, researchers argue that actors who operate in a social context of high complexity and opacity are heavily biased in the way they filter information into existing "mental maps" (North

1990b; Denzau and North 1994; Arthur 1994). Confirming information tends to be incorporated, while disconfirming information is filtered out. Social interpretations of complex environments like politics are often subject to positive feedback. The development of basic social understandings involves high start-up costs and learning effects—as Philip Converse notes, information must be stored in an effective way in order to facilitate the processing of additional information (Converse 1991). The need to employ mental maps induces positive feedback.

The path-dependent nature of views of the social world, evident at the individual level, is even more apparent at the group level. As Alexander Wendt notes, "identities and interests are not only learned in interaction, but sustained by it" (Wendt 1999, p. 331). Ideas are frequently shared with other social actors in ways that create network effects and adaptive expectations. Sociologists have emphasized that the development of norms or standards of appropriateness is a collective, self-reinforcing process. Social interactions involving activities as innocuous as a handshake "chronically reproduce" themselves (Jepperson 1991; see also Wendt 1999, pp. 184–89). Every time we shake hands, the strength of that norm is reinforced.

The same argument can be applied with considerable force to collective understandings—of how the world works, what is to be valued, what an individual's interests might be, and who that individual's friends and enemies might be—in short, to collective ideational constructs ranging from policy paradigms to full-fledged ideologies (Hall 1993; Berman 1998; Blyth 2002). Robert Wuthnow's subtle analysis of the comparative development of ideologies has elegantly shown how emerging worldviews, once they reach a critical mass, can generate a set of culture-producing institutions, organizations, and specialized actors that greatly facilitate the spread and reproduction of that ideology (Wuthnow 1989). Wuthnow demonstrates how relatively brief periods of historical openness are often followed by processes that select and then institutionalize a particular track of ideological development. His account of how "communities of discourse" often come to share, institutionalize, and reproduce a similar ideology is strikingly consistent with the framework suggested here. Berman (2003) has made a similar argument about the spread of radical Islam, in which extremists have used their control over key institutions of cultural production to foment a revolutionary transformation in citizens' worldviews—even in the absence of a revolutionary overthrow of the state itself.

North's work on "mental maps" thus converges with long-standing views of those studying political culture as well as the recent contributions of cognitive science.[19] Once established, basic outlooks on politics, ranging from ideologies

---

[19]Consider Karl Mannheim in his famous essay on generations: "It is of considerable importance for the formation of consciousness which experiences happen to make those all-important 'first impressions.' . . . Early impressions tend to coalesce into a *natural view* of the world. All later experiences then tend to receive their meaning from this original set, whether they appear as that set's verification and fulfilment or as its negation and antithesis" (Mannheim 1952).

to understandings of particular aspects of governments or orientations toward political groups or parties, are generally tenacious. They are path dependent.[20] "Social systems," as Wendt notes, "can get 'locked in' to certain patterns by the logic of shared knowledge, adding a source of social inertia or glue that would not exist in a system without culture" (Wendt 1999, p. 188).

There are, then, compelling reasons to believe that political processes will often be marked by dynamics of increasing returns. Tendencies toward positive feedback characterize four processes central to political environments: collective action, institutional development, the exercise of authority, and social interpretation. In each case, there are reasons to anticipate that steps in a particular direction can trigger a self-reinforcing dynamic. This conclusion should be underlined. By itself, it suggests why positive feedback is a critical concept for those who seek to understand the sources of political stability and change. If a recognition of the significance of self-reinforcing processes is shaking up economics, then those studying politics have at least as great a need to consider its implications.

There is also reason to believe that these effects in politics are often particularly intense. In the remainder of this section I briefly outline some reasons why, given the onset of some process of positive feedback, it is frequently more difficult to reverse course in politics than it would be in economics. These issues are pursued in greater detail in Chapters Four and Five.

Mechanisms for Reversing Course

One of the reasons economists were slow to worry about path dependence was because they believed the market provides two powerful mechanisms for exiting problematic paths: competition and learning. Competitive pressures in a market society mean that new organizations with more efficient structures will develop, eventually replacing suboptimal organizations (Alchian 1950). Learning processes within firms can also lead to correction. Firms learn from their own experiences, as well as those of other firms, and can correct mistakes over time (Williamson 1993).

It is worth emphasizing that neither of these mechanisms represents a guaranteed corrective in the path-dependent contexts explored by Arthur, North, and others. Options that gain a head start will often reinforce themselves over time, even if they have serious shortcomings. What I wish to stress, however, is

---

[20]Indeed, as marketers know well, such path-dependent cognitive effects are evident even in the less ambiguous world of consumption. This is why advertisers covet the attention of youngsters who have yet to make definitive (and resilient) choices. A telling recent example is the new marketing effort of the National Football League, which is alarmed by indications that youngsters are increasingly drawn to basketball and soccer. A former MTV executive now working on special events speaks the language of increasing returns: "It's all about getting a football . . . into a kid's hands as soon as you can. Six years old, if possible. You want to get a football in their hands before someone puts a basketball in their hands, or a hockey stick or a tennis racquet or a golf club" (Seabrook 1997, p. 47).

that these corrective mechanisms are even less effective when one shifts from firms in private markets to the world of political institutions (Moe 1984, 1990). This is clearest for mechanisms of competition. While models of competition may be helpful for understanding some important aspects of politics (such as international relations and elections), there can be little doubt that political environments are typically more "permissive" than economic ones (Krasner 1989).

As just discussed, the complexity and ambiguity of politics create serious problems for learning arguments. It may be appropriate to argue that politics sometimes involves learning processes, in which responses to public problems proceed in a trial-and-error fashion (Lindblom 1959; Heclo 1974; Hall 1993). There is little reason, however, to think that this acts as a selection mechanism with anything like the efficiency-enhancing properties of market competition in economics or Darwinian natural selection in biology. Because political reality is so complex and the tasks of evaluating public performance and determining which options would be superior are so formidable, such self-correction is often limited.

Even where learning does occur, reforms nonetheless face all the barriers to change that are characteristic of systems exhibiting positive feedback. Long movement down a particular path will have increased the costs of switching to some previously foregone alternative. Furthermore, in politics the pursuit of such change faces two additional obstacles: the short time horizons of political actors, and the strong status quo bias associated with the decision rules governing most political institutions. These factors will often make path-dependent effects particularly intense in politics.

TIME HORIZONS

A statement attributed to David Stockman, budget director during the Reagan administration, is unusual among political decision makers only for its candor. Asked by an adviser in 1981 to consider pension reforms to combat Social Security's severe long-term financing problems, Stockman dismissed the idea out of hand. He explained that he had no interest in wasting "a lot of political capital on some other guy's problem in [the year] 2010" (quoted in Greider 1982, p. 43).

Many of the implications of political decisions—especially complex policy interventions or major institutional reforms—only play out in the long run. Yet political actors, especially politicians, are often most interested in the short-term consequences of their actions; long-term effects tend to be heavily discounted. The principal reason is the logic of electoral politics. Because the decisions of voters, which determine political success, are taken in the short run, elected officials generally employ a high discount rate. They will pay attention to long-term consequences only if these become politically salient, or when they have little reason to fear short-term electoral retribution. Keynes once noted that in the long run, we are all dead; politicians have special reason to take that message to heart.

We know relatively little about the time horizons of different political actors. An interesting literature is developing on "credible commitments"—the attempt of political actors to create arrangements that facilitate cooperation (North and Weingast 1989; Shepsle 1991; North 1993). This research suggests that particular institutional designs (such as independent central banks), empowering particular kinds of political actors, may succeed in lengthening time horizons. In general, however, such mechanisms will often be of limited effectiveness in politics. As noted, the marketplace possesses some strong mechanisms for lengthening time horizons—especially the basic continuity of firms over time and the presence of capital markets. Such mechanisms in politics are generally far weaker. Monitoring political behavior over time is difficult because the interactions that go into generating performance are so complex, and even the indicators of performance are typically so limited. The relatively rapid turnover of critical positions also makes it hard to hold actors accountable. Politics, in short, lacks the characteristic property rights that facilitate the linkage of actors' decisions over time in the economic sphere. In many cases, the long term is essentially beyond the political horizon. A statesman, Bismarck said, is a politician who thinks about his grandchildren.

The different nature of time horizons in politics and in economics matters a lot. This can be seen by revisiting the Liebowitz and Margolis critique of path dependence. They properly point to key market institutions as a protection against certain kinds of remediable path dependence. If it is believed that long-term benefits will be greater using option B, then investors should gravitate toward that option even if in the short-term it will perform more poorly than option A. Thus, they argue that market mechanisms should allow the more efficient outcome (B) in figure 1.1.

In politics the outcome may well be different. Assume that the crucial decision maker is a politician up for reelection in two years. In this context, effects after the election cycle do not count for much.[21] A politician focusing on the short-term payoff would choose option A. The difference in time horizons has profound consequences. If time horizons tend to be short, then we can expect that long-term costs and benefits will have a limited effect on the chosen path. Furthermore, once on a particular path, political actors will generally have powerful incentives to stay on it. Switching costs are typically borne in the short run, and the benefits will generally only accrue in the long run, that is, to someone else.

THE STATUS QUO BIAS OF POLITICAL INSTITUTIONS

In the economic realm, an individual with a new idea for a product need only secure the finance to put it on the market. If enough consumers (choosing independently) find it sufficiently appealing, the product will be a success. Change

---

[21] These long-term effects *will* count if an actor with longer time horizons (such as an interest group) is able to make them relevant to politicians—e.g., through campaign contributions or votes. The question is whether such mechanisms are anywhere near as effective as the capital markets operative in the economic sphere. In my view, there are strong reasons to be skeptical of this, but it is clearly an issue deserving considerable attention.

can be engineered through competition against existing products. Similarly, those with property rights over a firm are generally in a strong position to remake their organizations as they choose. Lines of authority are clear, and the relevant decision makers are likely to share the same broad goal of maximizing profits.

By contrast, key features of political life, both public policies and (especially) formal institutions, are change resistant. Policies and institutions are generally *designed* to be difficult to overturn for two broad reasons. First, those who design institutions and policies may wish to bind their successors. Moe (1990) terms this the problem of "political uncertainty." Unlike economic actors, political actors must anticipate that their political rivals may soon control the reins of government. To protect themselves, these actors therefore create rules that make existing arrangements hard to reverse.

Second, in many cases political actors are also compelled to bind themselves. The key insight of the "credible commitments" literature is that actors can often do better, even in the relatively short run, if they remove certain alternatives from their future menu of options. The economy of a country will grow faster, for instance, if a monarch can credibly commit himself to refrain from expropriating an excessive amount of the hard-earned wealth of his subjects (North and Weingast 1989). This can be done if he accedes to parliamentary control over the power to tax. Like Ulysses preparing for the Sirens, political actors often bind themselves, restricting their own freedom in order to achieve some greater goal. To constrain themselves and others, designers create institutions that are sticky. Stickiness is built into the design of political institutions to reduce uncertainty and enhance stability, facilitating forms of cooperation and exchange that would otherwise be impossible.

Formal barriers to institutional reform are thus often extremely high, such as unanimity requirements in the European Union and multiple supermajorities to alter the American constitution. Of course, these obstacles may facilitate forms of cooperation and exchange that would otherwise be impossible. The relevant point here is that this institutional stickiness characteristic of political systems reinforces the already considerable obstacles to movement off an established path.[22] Combined with the weakness of competitive mechanisms and learning

---

[22]An important characteristic of political systems runs counter to this line of argument. Because politics is a powerful system for mobilizing coercive power, governments may at times be in a position to orchestrate a "jump" from one path to another. Governments, by employing sanctions, can coordinate adjustments in a way that markets might never be able to achieve. For instance, the British government was able to enact a shift to the metric system that would have been difficult or impossible to engineer through the more atomistic mechanisms of the market. And governments are clearly capable, on occasion, of mobilizing resources for more dramatic changes in course. Such possibilities, however, should not be exaggerated. The metric example represents a relatively modest instance of reversing path dependence. Switching costs were low; the problem was essentially one of coordination—inducing everyone to make the switch at the same time. For this task, the authoritative rule-setting capacities of government are of great assistance. For reasons already discussed,

processes, as well as the short time horizons characteristic of politics, the bias means that tendencies toward path dependence in political development are often particularly intense.

Politics differs from economics in many ways. Applying tools of economic analysis to politics is treacherous unless these differences are systematically considered. In the case of arguments about path dependence, attention to the character of politics suggests a striking result. The political world is unusually prone to positive feedback, and the capacities for reversing course are often weak. Both the prevalence and intensity of these processes in politics suggest that path dependence arguments offer an important tool for understanding political dynamics.

PATH DEPENDENCE AND THE STUDY OF POLITICS

To summarize briefly, in settings where self-reinforcing processes are at work political life is likely to be marked by four features:

1. *Multiple equilibria.* Under a set of initial conditions conducive to positive feedback, a range of outcomes is generally possible.
2. *Contingency.* Relatively small events, if occurring at the right moment, can have large and enduring consequences.
3. A critical role for *timing and sequencing.* In these path-dependent processes, *when* an event occurs may be crucial. Because early parts of a sequence matter much more than later parts, an event that happens "too late" may have no effect, although it might have been of great consequence if the timing had been different.
4. *Inertia.* Once such a process has been established, positive feedback will generally lead to a single equilibrium. This equilibrium will in turn be resistant to change.

There are also good reasons to think that positive feedback processes are widespread in politics, since they will be characteristic in institutional development, collective action, the exercise of authority, and the emergence of our understandings of the political world. This has fundamental theoretical implications. We need to change both the kinds of questions we ask about politics and the kinds of answers that we generate. Many of these implications will be explored in greater depth later, but a brief summary here will clarify the organizational logic of the chapters to follow.

First, path-dependent arguments point to the significance of sequencing—the temporal order in which social events or processes unfold. Most variable-

---

it is much less evident that governments will generally be willing or able to engineer shifts to a different path when switching costs are high. Cases of fundamental or revolutionary reform in well-institutionalized political systems attract our attention precisely because they are so rare.

oriented research assumes a world without positive feedback, where history washes out and sequence is irrelevant. We only need to know the values of variables at the moment of interest, not the sequence through which these factors developed. In path-dependent processes, however, positive feedback means that history is "remembered." These processes can be highly influenced by relatively modest perturbations at early stages. "Small" events early on may have a big impact, while "large" events at later stages may be less consequential. To put it another way, outcomes of early events or processes in the sequence may be amplified, while the significance of later events or processes is dampened. Thus, *when a particular event in a sequence occurs will make a big difference*. A crucial implication of path-dependence arguments is that early stages in a sequence can place particular aspects of political systems onto distinct tracks, which are then reinforced through time.

Second, a focus on path-dependent processes suggests the need to develop analyses that may incorporate substantial stretches of time. For this reason, as with their highlighting of sequencing, they justify a turn to history. At one level, of course, all social scientists agree that "history matters." The existing conditions that influence current social outcomes came into being at some point in the past. Those earlier processes are relevant to a full understanding of contemporary social events. Yet the standard assumption is that for most purposes we may safely put such issues aside. Looking back leads to the familiar problem of infinite regress. An exploration of each preceding event leads to the conclusion that some other preceding occurrence was also part of the chain of necessary events, and so on. Social scientists need to break through the seamlessness of history somewhere, and the present is as good a place to do so as any. George Homans (1967) compared the situation to that faced by mine sweepers who needed to know the magnetic charge of a ship. Such a charge resulted from an infinite range of small factors accumulated over the ship's lifetime. For practical purposes, however, a simple expedient could be used: the current charge of the ship could be measured. If the task is to understand the ship's vulnerability to mines, one can simply cut through the Gordian knot of historical regress.[23]

For many purposes, this is an appropriate approach. Social scientists often have good reason to focus on synchronic causality—to try to understand how variations in current variables affect present social outcomes. Where processes of positive feedback are significant, however, such a strategy may be problematic. Path-dependent arguments rest on what Arthur Stinchcombe has termed a conception of "historical causes" (Stinchcombe 1968, pp. 103–18; see also Harsanyi 1960; Ikenberry 1994; Jervis 2000, p. 97; Lieberson 1985)—some initial event or process generates a particular outcome, which is then reproduced through time *even though the original generating event or process does not recur*.

---

[23]For a discussion of Homans's argument, see Knapp 1983, pp. 43–45.

This is very different from the more typical search for invariant relationships among factors, in which the analyst assumes that if adding x to a setting causes y, then the removal of x should remove y as well. As Stinchcombe puts it, a "historicist explanation . . . is one in which an effect created by causes at some previous period *becomes a cause of that same effect in succeeding periods*. In such arguments, the problem of explanation breaks down into two causal components. The first is the particular circumstances that caused a tradition to be started. The second is the general process by which social patterns reproduce themselves."

In such a process the crucial objects of study become the factors that set development along a particular path—and which lie in the past—and the mechanisms of reproduction of the current path, which at first glance might seem commonplace, perhaps almost invisible or at least analytically uninteresting. This distinctive approach to explanation can be clarified through reference to the Polya urn illustration introduced at the outset. Suppose we sought to understand why the distribution of balls on the hundredth trial was 96 red/4 black. We would not be very happy with a Homans-style explanation: "because after 99 trials the distribution was 95/4, and thus there was a better than 95% probability that the next draw would also be red." What we would want to know would be the initial events that established this trajectory, and the mechanism (in this case, a process of selection governed by a particular decision-rule) that made that trajectory self-reinforcing. Thus, where historical causation is at work, explanation requires the examination of considerable stretches of time. This issue, along with others related to the investigation of long-term social processes, is taken up in depth in Chapter Three.

A third crucial implication is that path-dependent arguments provide a plausible counter to functionalist explanations of social outcomes, which too often go unchallenged. Although not always explicitly stated, functionalist arguments are prevalent in the social sciences. They are common, for instance, among those who emphasize the rational choices of individual actors that underlie political activity, and the reasonably efficient nature of collective responses to social needs (Keohane 1984; Shepsle 1986; Weingast and Marshall 1988).

Functionalist arguments take the following form: outcome X (an institution, policy, or organization, for instance) exists because it serves the function Y. In a world of purposive actors, it may indeed be the case that the effects of an institution have something to do with an explanation for its emergence and persistence. Arguments about positive feedback, however, suggest the large dangers in any assumption that an existing institution arose or continues to exist because it serves some particularly useful purpose. Thinking in functionalist terms about an existing institution, policy, or social organization may be a good way to derive causal hypotheses, but functional accounts are far from being the only plausible ones. Many alternatives to the outcome in question might have been possible, and a dynamic of positive feedback may have insitutionalized a particular option even though it originated by accident, or the factors that gave it an original advantage have long since passed away. *Rather than assuming relative efficiency as an explanation, we have to go back and look.* Thus recognizing the possibility of path dependence necessarily draws social scientists to an investigation of history, if only to evaluate the validity of functionalist assertions. As I explore in Chapters Four and Five, an investigation of path dependence can provide a basis for developing alternative hypotheses about institutional origins, stability, and change.

Consider one example. A prominent theme in recent research in comparative political economy is the idea of "varieties of capitalism." Despite increasing international economic interdependence, which seems to generate pressures toward convergence, the advanced industrial societies continue to exhibit fundamental differences in their core institutional structures (Soskice 1999; Hall 1999; Berger and Dore 1996; Hollingsworth and Boyer 1997). To date, however, this literature has done a better job of identifying and describing this diversity than it has of explaining what generates and sustains it. Hall and Soskice (2001a) have made an important step forward by emphasizing the role of institutional complementarities. The benefits of particular economic institutions and organizations are increased if they fit well in an environment populated by specific kinds of institutions and organizations.

The "varieties of capitalism" analysis persuasively illuminates distinct equilibria in different economies, but it does not address the question of how these distinct equilibria emerge. From the current analysis, one can easily see why the elaborate production systems of modern economies would be subject to positive feedback. Start-up costs, not just for new firms, but (more fundamentally) for the key organizations and institutions that link private actors, are enormous. Organizations, and the formal and informal arrangements (both public and private) that help to structure their interactions create, as North would put it, densely linked institutional matrices. Economic and social organizations and political institutions (both basic constitutional arrangements and public policy frameworks) have coevolved over extended periods of time. Coordination effects are widespread; particular courses of action are encouraged or discouraged because of anticipated actions of others in the system. Firms have developed sophisticated strategies suitable to the particular institutional matrix they confront— that is, tremendous amounts of learning by doing have occurred over time in these complex systems. In short, national economic systems are highly path dependent. They are likely to exhibit substantial resilience, even in the context of major exogenous shocks such as recent changes in the global economy.

Highlighting the possible limits of functionalist explanations reveals a final theoretical benefit of recognizing the significance of path-dependent processes: these arguments provide the basis for a revitalized effort to investigate issues of power in social life. Functionalist arguments that start from the benefits that particular actors derive from institutions and infer that their power accounted for those arrangements typically ignore important feedback processes that may generate the same observed outcome in a completely different way (Hacker and Pierson 2002). As just emphasized, an understanding of path-dependent dynamics may suggest alternative explanations for arrangements that are *too easily* attributed to power relations. At the same time, the possibility that self-reinforcing processes may magnify power imbalances over time, while simultaneously rendering those imbalances less visible, indicates that "snapshot" views will often miss important elements of power relations. In short, both these observations point to deep-rooted difficulties in the treatment of power in contemporary social science: sometimes analysts see power when it is not there, and sometimes they do not see it when it is.

Some Initial Concerns

Because the preceding discussion provides the basis for much of what follows, it may be helpful to stop and briefly address some possible objections to the line of argument developed so far.

OLD WINE IN NEW BOTTLES?

Of course, there is a long tradition of attention to history in the social sciences. Particularly for those who want answers to critical questions that grow out of the experiences of real polities, the turn to history has been common. Issues of timing, sequence, and critical junctures figure prominently in this body of work. Among many such studies, Gerschenkron's study of industrialization and state building (Gerschenkron 1962) and Lipset and Rokkan's analysis of the formation of party systems (Lipset and Rokkan 1967) are two classic examples. Indeed, it is fair to ask whether incorporating the concepts of positive feedback and path dependence into the study of politics is akin to the man who discovered that he had been speaking prose all his life. Is path dependence merely a trendy name for old ideas?

Discussions of path dependence would be worth having if they did no more than focus the attention of fad-prone social scientists on the insights and continuing relevance of this earlier body of work. Yet there is every reason to believe that the concept can do more. Awareness of the dynamics of positive feedback processes can greatly sharpen our understanding of *why* particular junctures (and which aspects of those junctures) are critical and why timing often counts for so much in politics. Most of this earlier work was vague on this crucial point. The specific characteristics of positive feedback provide a key to making sense of the complex mix of stability and change that characterize so many political processes. To repeat, Arthur's work on path dependence is groundbreaking not simply because he described the characteristics of these processes, but because he identified conditions likely to generate them. Building on North's work, we can now begin the process of adapting these arguments to the study of politics. Doing so requires careful attention to the distinctive features of the political world, such as its intrinsic ambiguity, the prevalence of highly sticky institutions, the prominence of collective action problems, and the prospects for utilizing policy authority to amplify asymmetries of power. An investigation of self-reinforcing processes can generate sharper hypotheses, based on more explicit social mechanisms, about the sources of divergent paths and social inertia.

ARE PATH-DEPENDENT ARGUMENTS JUST DESCRIPTIVE?

Without careful attention to the identification of the mechanisms at work, analyses of path dependence can easily become descriptions of what happened rather than explanations for why it happened. Thelen (1999, p. 391) nicely summarizes this concern:

> Arguments about the "freezing" or "crystallization" of particular institutional configurations . . . obscure more than they reveal unless they are explicitly linked to complementary arguments that identify the mechanisms of reproduction at work. Without these, they are at best incomplete, for they cannot explain why these patterns persisted and how they continue to dominate the political space. . . . [Sometimes] authors invoke Stinchcombe's arguments about "sunk costs" and "vested interests" that make embarking on alternative paths costly and uncertain. But such references, though a promising starting point for the analysis, cannot themselves replace the analysis; these concepts need to be applied, not just invoked. Among other things, we need to know exactly who is invested in particular institutional arrangements, exactly how that investment is sustained over time, and perhaps how those who are not invested in the institutions are kept out.[24]

The key, as Thelen suggests, is to specify the mechanisms that reinforce a particular path or trajectory. Without this, path-dependent arguments degenerate into little more than a description of stability.

At the same time, a focus on these mechanisms should help us to explain variation across settings. Although I have argued that many aspects of politics will promote strong tendencies toward self-reinforcement, not all aspects of political life are subject to positive feedback. One can think about this in terms suggested by Hannan and Freeman (1989, p. 106), who discuss the "mixing of different types of outcomes in [a] spatial or temporal distribution." Where there are long runs

---

[24]Stinchcombe (1965, p. 167) made a similar observation: "It is considerably more difficult to explain why many types of organizations retain structural peculiarities after their foundation without falling into tautologous statements about 'tradition,' 'vested interests,' or 'folkways' not being changeable by formal regulation. The problem is to specify who it is that carries 'tradition' and why they carry it, whose 'interests' become 'vested,' under what conditions, by what devices, whose 'folkways' cannot be changed by regulation, and why. This problem is at the very center of sociological theory." Stinchcombe 1965, p. 167.

of one outcome, one can describe these distributions as "coarse grained," while the opposite pattern would be fine-grained. Path-dependent processes will typically generate coarse-grained patterns of outcomes rather than fine-grained ones.

Consider a concrete example. As Mayhew notes (2002, p. 129 f.), despite a realignment literature that suggests one or another political party should gain the upper hand as a "natural" governing majority, the party with the advantage in party identification rates has shown almost no advantage in presidential elections since 1900. In other words, the outcomes of presidential elections are "fine grained" rather than "coarse grained."[25] A plausible explanation is that presidential candidates, at least in the American context, retain considerable flexibility in adopting new strategies and appeals to increase their electability. A party losing one presidential election is at little systematic disadvantage in the next. In other words, presidential elections do not appear to be highly path-dependent. Part of the reason for this outcome, however, is that losing parties are relatively free to jettison unpopular policy positions and adopt more popular ones—including ones introduced by the incumbent party. Thus, presidential elections may be fine grained in part because *policy regimes* tend to be coarse grained—that is, marked by very substantial stretches of stability (Huber and Stephens 2001; Hall and Soskice 2001a). Parties maintain their electoral competitiveness by adapting to the policy successes put in place by their competitors.

We should expect considerable variation in the extent to which strong path dependence is evident in various elements of the social world, depending on the presence or absence of the kinds of factors mentioned here, as well as the presence or absence of countervailing features of the social landscape. It is here that recent theoretical developments in work on path dependence have the greatest promise, for they offer precisely this—a set of propositions about the types of circumstances that promote positive feedback. Specifying mechanisms helps us to develop hypotheses about where we might expect (or not expect) to encounter similar dynamics—in other words, it helps us to develop portable claims.

CONTINGENCY AND DETERMINISM

Again, Thelen (1999, p. 385) has raised a reasonable concern that path-dependent models can be "too contingent and too deterministic"—that is, too open at the front end or critical juncture and too closed at the back end (once the critical juncture has passed). Critics have argued that path-dependent arguments seem to suggest a very high level of contingency at critical junctures, while the "mechanisms of reproduction" that follow generate an overly static

---

[25]Interestingly, this pattern is not always evident cross-nationally. Patterns in some countries are "coarse-grained," revealing extended periods of single-party dominance (Pempel 1990). Based on the current analysis, one could usefully focus on what factors in these different polities generate positive feedback from an electoral victory, and make it difficult for a losing party to adapt in a competitive fashion.

view of the social world (Katznelson 2003; Schwartz, n.d.). To take the starkest illustration, Arthur's Polya urn processes are totally random at the outset—the smallest perturbation can make all the difference—and yet they all settle on a particular equilibrium and then essentially stop. Positive feedback processes seem to generate only brief moments of "punctuation" in a largely frozen social landscape.

A critical feature of path-dependent processes is the relative "openness" or "permissiveness" of early stages in a sequence compared with the relatively "closed" or "coercive" nature of later stages (Mahoney 2001; Abbott 1997). Viewed *ex ante*, such processes can produce more than one possible outcome. Once a particular path gets established, however, self-reinforcing processes are prone to consolidation or institutionalization. "Critical junctures" generate persistent paths of political development.[26]

It is necessary to stress these features of path-dependent processes while avoiding a tendency to overinterpret their implications. These features of comparatively "open" processes at the outset, followed by a more constrained choice-set once reinforcement sets in, are precisely the features that make this type of process distinctive and underpin the claim that temporal sequence is crucial (Mahoney 2001). At the same time, however, such arguments rarely, if ever, suggest that "anything goes" at the initial branching point. Rather, the claim is that there may be more than one alternative (often, as in the discussions of path-dependent technologies that have been common in economics, the analysis will specify two), and that *relatively* small factors may push the outcome one way or the other. Along the same lines, claims that processes are path-dependent do not require that the factors leading to one path rather than the other be truly random, or beyond the reach of theory. Although sometimes these junctures are treated as highly contingent or random, generally analysts seek to generate convincing explanations for why one path rather than another was chosen.

The explanations, however, will often emphasize events or processes that seem "small" when compared with the large effects (major, lasting divergences across cases) that they produce once positive feedback processes have had a chance to amplify the initial repercussions. In analyzing these nonlinear processes we cannot assume that "large" effects are the results of "large" causes (Abbott 1988). To put it another way, if one imagines a counterfactual in which an alternative outcome emerges, the size of the change needed to generate the different outcome will be smaller—perhaps much smaller—at the onset of a self-reinforcing process than it will be at a later date. Hacker's analysis of the

---

[26]Although analyses invoking the language of "critical junctures" sometimes focus on large-scale, dramatic events, those qualities are neither necessary nor sufficient to generate path-dependent dynamics. In fact, the point in path-dependent analyses is that "causes" may often seem relatively small compared with their effects. What makes a particular juncture "critical" is that it triggers a process of positive feedback.

development of health-care policy in the United States offers an excellent example (Hacker 2002). Hacker does not argue that the failure of the United States to adopt national health insurance during the New Deal period was highly contingent—there were good reasons why this was the likely outcome. What he does argue is that this initial development generated powerful positive feedback, institutionalizing a set of private arrangements that made it *much* more difficult to make a transition to national health insurance at a later point in time. As a result of these self-reinforcing processes, the scale of the counterfactual needed to imagine an alternative path, Hacker suggests, is much greater in the year 2000 than it was in 1935.

If the suggestion that path-dependent arguments imply hypercontingency at the outset strikes me as a red herring, so does the suggestion that they point to a world of stasis. Nothing in path-dependent analyses implies that a particular alternative is permanently "locked in" following the move onto a self-reinforcing path. Identifying self-reinforcing processes does help us to understand why organizational and institutional practices are often extremely persistent—and this is crucial, because these continuities are a striking feature of the social world. Asserting that the social landscape can be permanently frozen is hardly credible, however, and that is not the claim. Change continues, but it is bounded change—until something erodes or swamps the mechanisms of reproduction that generate continuity. Douglass North summarizes the key point well: "At every step along the way there [are choices]—political and economic—that provide . . . real alternatives. Path dependence is a way to narrow conceptually the choice set and link decision making through time. It is not a story of inevitability in which the past neatly predicts the future" (North 1990a, pp. 98–99). The claims in path-dependent arguments are that previously viable options may be foreclosed in the aftermath of a sustained period of positive feedback, and cumulative commitments on the existing path will often make change difficult and will condition the form in which new branchings will occur.

Indeed, as I explore in greater detail in Chapters Two and Five, some of the most interesting developments in the work on path dependence focus specifically on these issues of "downstream" development in path-dependent processes. As recently emphasized by both Mahoney and Thelen, identifying the particular feedback loops (or "mechanisms of reproduction") at work will often provide key insights into the kinds of events or processes that might generate major subsequent change points (Thelen 1999, 2003; Mahoney 2001). Such junctures are usually attributed, often *ex post*, to "exogenous shocks." We should expect, however, that these change points often occur when new conditions disrupt or overwhelm the specific mechanisms that previously reproduced the existing path. Thus, a clear understanding of the mechanisms of reproduction provides an instrument for the investigation of change.

Similarly, analyses of historical sequences may focus precisely on the dynamic downstream consequences of particular patterns of instutionalization following a critical juncture. As I suggest in the next chapter, analysts sometimes wish to know about the elimination of particular alternatives at a key moment not because the outcome at that stage is permanently locked in, but because the removal of certain options through path-dependent processes creates different outcomes at a later choice-point in a historical sequence. Thus path-dependent arguments often involve a more complex position on issues of stability and change than the simple "contingency followed by lock-in" formulation suggests. When sequences involve self-reinforcing dynamics, we can expect periods of relative (but not total) openness, followed by periods of relative (but not total or permanent) stability.

A common thread runs through my discussion of each of these concerns about path-dependent arguments: the explication of specific mechanisms that generate path dependence is the key to making this a fruitful line of theorizing about the sources of social stability and change. And this in turn is the main justification for taking the time to work through key issues about these mechanisms in economic analysis, and the implications of shifting from the economic realm to the political. In the chapters that follow I will provide many illustrations of these mechanisms at work in important political processes.

Chapter Two

TIMING AND SEQUENCE

When things happen within a sequence affects
how they happen.
—*Charles Tilly (1984, p. 14)*

ARGUMENTS IN THE SOCIAL SCIENCES SOMETIMES take the following form: "the temporal ordering of events or processes has a significant impact on outcomes." These are instances in which we wish to know not just what the "value" of some variable is, but the time at which that value occurred. We want to know not just *what*, but *when*.

In practice, prominent scholars have long stressed that temporal ordering may be a critical element of explanation. There are in fact quite distinct (although sometimes hazily specified) claims about the role of sequencing at work in different analyses. I offer some suggestions about how to distinguish these arguments and suggest that they can give us considerable leverage for identifying and explaining social phenomena. An appreciation of the significance of sequences bolsters my general claim that the systematic exploration of processes unfolding over time should be central to the social sciences.

Several scholarly communities have recently tried to grapple more systematically with this issue. A number of historically oriented analysts, especially in the field of American political development, have stressed the importance of seeing distinct processes as potentially linked in highly consequential ways, depending in part on the relative timing of their development. In the first section of this chapter I explore some of the promise, as well as the difficult theoretical problems, entailed by these claims about timing and "conjunctures." I then consider recent discussions of sequences emerging from rational choice analysis. This research has made compelling theoretical arguments about the role of sequences in structuring collective choice situations. It has provided convincing evidence of these effects, but has focused most of its energies on a limited range of highly formal settings, such as legislatures.

In many ways, the accomplishments of these two literatures are perfect complements. Rational choice analysts have strong and precise theoretical arguments about why, where, and how the temporal ordering of choices can be so consequential. The price of these gains, however, has been tight constraints on the theoretical and substantive scope of these investigations. Scholarship on political development has lacked rational choice's admirable precision, but it offers much greater attentiveness to truly historical processes and a salutary focus on large-scale social and political dynamics. In this chapter, I will argue that there are genuine prospects for combining many of these strengths, and that the arguments presented in Chapter One provide a basis for doing so.

It turns out that most prominent substantive claims about the role of timing and sequence have been grounded, often implicitly, at least in part on claims about self-reinforcing or path-dependent processes. When such processes are at work, causal analysis is intrinsically historical—the order of events or processes is likely to have a crucial impact on outcomes. At the same time, explicitly addressing issues of historical sequencing clarifies how the arguments about positive feedback discussed in the last chapter can be linked to analyses that are more concerned with political change "downstream" from some branching point or critical juncture. Thus, the identification of self-reinforcing dynamics turns out to be an excellent entry-point for examining a wide range of issues related to timing, sequence, and historical process. Analyses attentive to sequence can bring important aspects of the social world into greater focus, highlighting a key contribution of historically sensitive inquiry.

Timing and Conjunctures

One prominent starting point for studies of temporal ordering has been the analysis of timing, or conjunctures—in particular, the linking of discrete elements or dimensions of politics in the passage of time. If two events or particular processes occur at the same historical moment, the results may be very different from when they are temporally separated (in some cases, regardless of the order in which they otherwise arrive). In this instance, what is being highlighted is the significance of interaction effects, and the dependence of those interaction effects upon the synchronized timing of the events or processes at hand.

To say that timing matters implies the timing of something *relative to something else.* "Time" serves as the dimension that links together quite separate social processes in highly consequential ways. Here two distinct temporal sequences converge with substantial consequences. Aminzade (1992, pp. 466–67) summarizes this type of argument:

> Sociological attempts to explain particular outcomes or patterns of development typically involve the study of multiple rather than single trajectories. Most historical sociologists reject the notion of a single master process, acknowledging multiple processes that overlap and intersect one another. Explaining a particular outcome or pattern of development thus involves a particular logic of explanation: situating events or outcomes in terms of their location in intersecting trajectories with independent temporalities. This logic is evident in numerous key works of historical sociology. . . . [T]he

focus is not on the presence or absence of certain variables or on the trajectory of a single process. It is on the temporal intersection of distinctive trajectories of different, but connected, long-term processes.

This orientation has been central to Karen Orren and Stephen Skowronek's research agenda on temporal processes (1994, forthcoming). They emphasize that different social realms interact with one another, that the different historical roots of these realms and differences in the timing of their development can profoundly shape the character of these interactions, and that these interactions are marked by tensions, dissonances, and thus an inherent dynamism. In Orren and Skowronek's view, the investigation of "collisions" and "abrasions" among distinct realms—which they term "intercurrence"—is central to the study of political development. In this view, researchers need "to locate the historical construction of politics in the intercurrence, or simultaneous operation, of older and newer governing instruments, in controls asserted through multiple orderings of authority whose coordination with one another cannot be assumed and whose outward reach and impingements upon one another are inherently problematic" (forthcoming, chap. 3, p. 52). As Orren and Skowronek detail (forthcoming), a number of recent studies in American political development have explored how particular elements of political order established at earlier moments in time, such as a reigning political coalition (Skowronek 1993), a set of legal principles (Orren 1991), or a peculiar form of local administration such as the juvenile court system (Polsky 1989), interact uneasily with other institutional and organizational arrangements established at later points in time.

This is an exciting line of inquiry. Directing attention to conjunctures or intersections of this kind is inviting, since it obviously connects the work of social science more closely to the way the world really works. Work on conjunctures and relative timing reveals a sensitivity to issues of temporal process and temporal ordering, while focusing on the thorny but central problem of explaining social change. At least as important, Orren and Skowronek's emphasis on the interactions between distinct political realms over extended periods of time invites attention to large-scale social processes. This macro-focus has held considerable appeal for the comparative historical sociologists who have played a central role in "the historic turn" among social scientists (Mahoney and Rueschemeyer 2003).[1]

But it also raises vexing problems. As Aristide Zolberg puts it in his discussion of working-class formation (1986, p. 406), "Although it is a truism among historians that World War I constituted one of the great watersheds of western history,

---

[1]Although Theda Skocpol's *States and Social Revolutions* is generally viewed as an exercise in historical sociology as a comparative method, it contains a similar appeal (1979, p. 320): "Social-scientific analyses of revolution almost *never*, as far as I can tell, give sufficient analytic weight to the conjunctural, unfolding interactions of originally separately determined processes. Yet both the causes and the development of revolutions probably have to be understood in this way, which of course means that analyses and explanations must be historically grounded."

social scientists are inclined to minimize such overwhelming 'error factors' that wreak havoc with theory construction." How can we think systematically about causal processes involving the interaction of ongoing dynamics of working-class formation and a completely separate process involving the onset of global war?

An example provided by Raymond Aron (1961, pp. 16–17) can help us explore this issue in greater depth, pointing to both the possibilities and pitfalls of such a line of inquiry.[2] A man takes the same walk every day. On one occasion, a heavy tile becomes dislodged from a building along his route. Depending upon the particular timing of these two streams of activity (strolling man, falling tile), the observed outcome will be radically different. If the two streams produce a "conjuncture," the result is calamitous.

Scharpf (1997, p. 49) suggests that analysts should regard such conjunctures as essentially irrelevant for theory development, while acknowledging that they place limits on the capacity of social scientists to predict: "Given the pervasiveness of 'Cournot effects' (i.e., the accidental intersection of unrelated chains of causation) in social and political interactions . . . even theoretically well-founded predictions may turn out to be wrong." But if Cournot effects are indeed so pervasive, many of those interested in comparative historical analysis will not find this conclusion very satisfying.

It is not clear, however, that there are any easy ways forward. If the sequences that produce the conjuncture are generally unrelated and connected only through a coincidence of timing, then it will still be impossible to anticipate such outcomes. Moreover, it may be impossible to take anything from the study of such an outcome that will help us to understand some other social setting. Peter Knapp (1983, p. 46) has summarized the issue:

> Retrospective analysis can start from the conjuncture which brings the causal sequences together. With the falling tile, the conjuncture is trivially simple. But in any case, if the causal chains are subject to lawful regularities, the outcome is still only predictable after the event, on the basis of background knowledge. It is perfectly possible to build a model of the collision. The collision is determined; it will follow from the model. Aron would say that it is determined *post hoc,* yet unpredictable, since prior to the event there is no system which includes the two sequences and it is fruitless to try to construct one. It may be perfectly useful to construct an historical model after the event, especially if the conjuncture has world-historical consequences. But we do not suppose that such a model will predict any further events of interest.

Jack Goldstone (1998, p. 833) has nicely described this as a turn to "Dr. Seuss-style" explanations: "It just happened that this happened first, then this, then that, and is not likely to happen that way again."

---

[2]The next few paragraphs draw heavily on the discussion of this issue in Knapp 1983. See also Mahoney 2000.

If our goal is to create an *"ex post* model" of a particular outcome of interest, then these "Cournot effects" may not create such a terrible problem (although the methodological challenges involved in the persuasive development of such *ex post* models of single cases are more severe than is often realized). But generally this is not all that social scientists want. At a minimum, we want to be able to take something from that specific social setting that illuminates other social processes. We want to address questions such as: "Under what circumstances are occurrences like X more or less likely?" We want more than Seussian accounts.

Yet it is a major challenge to substantiate claims about such interactions among realms even in an analysis of a single time and place. And it is even more difficult to establish more general propositions that one could take from such an analysis, beyond the sound advice to pay attention to the potential interplay among distinct social realms. We know that different social realms may "collide and abrade." That is different, however, from having ideas about when and how different social arrangements within a polity are likely to collide and abrade.[3]

Accounts of this sort can be extraordinarily vivid and may generate compelling *ex post* interpretations of particular conjunctures. These are genuinely valuable attributes. We are still, however, in the realm of Dr. Seuss. If we are dealing with conjunctures where generally disconnected realms accidentally converge, there would seem to be no prospect for developing portable claims. Even limited generalizations about conjunctures are unlikely to be possible unless the analyst can demonstrate why particular developments in one realm are *systematically* linked to those in another. Even if we do have ideas about such linkages, we still would be in search of some propositions about how different temporal orderings of these linkages (e.g., A precedes B, A follows B, A and B take place simultaneously) can be expected to influence outcomes of interest. One can find propositions of this sort in the rational choice literature on sequences, which I turn to next.

HISTORICAL SEQUENCES IN RATIONAL CHOICE ANALYSIS

Scholars employing rational choice approaches have been quite visible in the recent turn to history, and have distinctive things to say about sequencing. These efforts warrant review, because insights from rational choice theory can be useful in constructing hypotheses about the importance of temporal order in political processes. I will argue, however, that the prerequisites for successful game-theoretic analysis are highly restrictive, and thus the kinds of processes that can be examined will be of limited scope. For many investigations of historical processes, game theory can at best provide a "module" of argumentation that

---

[3]To their credit, Orren and Skowronek's forthcoming book makes a serious effort to show how this might be possible.

would then need to be connected to other modules, based on distinct bodies of social knowledge and employing other techniques of social investigation.

In key respects, the strengths and weaknesses of this rational choice research agenda have been the mirror image of those just identified in the literature on conjunctures. Rational choice theorists have generated clear and convincing claims about how and why sequencing can matter, and they have done so in a manner that lends itself to the development of clear propositions. These gains have come, however, at the cost of placing sharp limits on the kinds of sequences they examine.

In their recent volume, *Analytic Narratives*, Robert Bates and his coauthors seek to utilize game theory to develop compelling explanations of single, significant political outcomes (Bates et al. 1998). They stress that their investigations constitute a contribution to the "historic turn" in the social sciences. In extensive form, they note, "*Games explicitly take sequence into account and highlight its significance for outcomes.* They capture the influence of history, the importance of uncertainty, and the capacity of people to manipulate and strategize, as well as the limits of their ability to do so" (p. 18, emphasis added).

Indeed, game theory has paid great attention to sequence. In many types of noncooperative games, the order of moves is critical. "Battle of the sexes" games, in which both actors prefer two possible cooperative outcomes to the other alternatives but differ over which one, provide a good example. These are positive sum games with a distributional component—a common scenario in politics. In such instances, first movers will often be able to impose their preferred cooperative outcome. Games of chicken also confer substantial first mover advantages. Indeed, first movers will be advantaged in any game possessing more than one Nash equilibrium (Scharpf 1997).

The role of sequencing has been studied most extensively, and most fruitfully, in work derived from Arrow's analysis of the "paradox of voting" (Arrow 1963). This work lays out some important formal properties of sequences in social choice settings that provide a strong foundation for developing claims about temporal ordering. As is well known, Arrow's analysis of the paradox of voting demonstrates the absence of a definitive majority preference in many collective choice situations. Table 2.1 provides a standard summary, involving three choosers with equal say and divergent preference orderings among three alternatives. Such a situation does not yield a clear, determinant result. Instead, the *order* in which proposals are considered will dictate the final outcome—no minimally fair decision rules can ensure "the independence of the final choice from the path to it" (Arrow 1963, p. 120). Furthermore, if any "choice" is subject to reconsideration, the setting is inherently unstable. Given any "winning" proposal, one of the three individuals will have the incentive and capacity to propose an alternative that will be preferred by one of the two other participants. This is the problem of cycling, which has animated so much rational choice work on collective decision making and institutional effects.

TABLE 2.1
A Standard Cycling Problem

Legislator	Preference Ranking		
	1st	2nd	3rd
A	X	Y	Z
B	Z	X	Y
C	Y	Z	X

Source: Aldrich 1995, p. 38.

Note: Round-robin tournament, voting independently and sincerely. X beats Y (A,B), Y beats Z (A,C), Z beats X (B,C): Outcome: ?

This analysis has been applied and elaborated most intensively to highly institutionalized settings such as legislatures. Rational choice theorists have argued persuasively that institutional arrangements governing agenda control and decision-making procedures can play a crucial role in producing stable outcomes—structure-induced equilibria—in collective choice situations (Shepsle and Weingast 1987; Shepsle 1986; Ferejohn, Fiorina, and McCelvey 1987). They do so because these rules can create a particular sequence through which alternative proposals are considered. At the same time, the structure of those rules confers substantial power on agenda setters. Because the sequence in which alternative proposals are considered determines the eventual outcome, tremendous power rests with those actors who select the sequence.

This research on collective decision processes has strengths and weaknesses that are evident in rational choice arguments about sequencing more generally. The strengths are a clear, rigorous analysis of why ordering often matters a great deal, as well as a set of theoretical implications—about how such sequences can be structured, with what effects, in important political settings—that have lent themselves to strenuous evaluation. Yet the focus on the "moves" of "actors" is a limiting one as well, and it is evident in the broader game-theoretic literature that forms the backbone for most of the historical turn in rational choice analysis.

Indeed, it is critical to highlight the considerable limitations of a game-theoretic framework for investigating temporal sequences.[4] Four problems in particular deserve emphasis:

1. Game theory itself can say nothing about payoffs and preferences. As Scharpf notes, "Game theory as such can provide no help in identifying

[4]The following draws heavily on the thoughtful commentary of Fritz Scharpf (1997), who strongly and persuasively advocates the employment of game theory for many social science purposes. For another useful critique, see Munck 2001.

outcomes and their valuation by the 'players'; the empirical and theoretical work necessary to describe them must have been done by the researcher before it makes sense to draw up game matrices."[5] Addressing
these issues, of course, is a central concern of most comparative historical analyses.

2. Game theory needs to focus on relatively cohesive, well-integrated "composite actors." Because game theory centers on *strategic interaction*, it
   has great trouble incorporating what Scharpf calls "quasi groups" that
   cannot be treated as acting strategically but whose "utility functions are
   interdependent in such a way that certain acts by some will increase or
   decrease the likelihood that others will act in the same way." Such quasi
   groups—which would typically include voters, farmers, demonstrators,
   workers, etc.—are evidently of substantial importance for the investigation of many of the temporal sequences discussed in this book.

3. Games need to be kept very simple: few actors, few options. As Scharpf
   puts it, "Even under the best of circumstances, the cognitive complexity of identifying Nash equilibria will rapidly increase to completely
   unmanageable dimensions as the number of independent players involved and the number of their permissible strategies increase beyond a
   very few."

4. Sequences cannot be interrupted. Sequence, in these models, refers to
   an ordered alternation of "moves" by "composite actors," with preferences and payoffs fixed in advance. Needless to say, this constitutes a
   highly circumscribed depiction of historical processes. To maintain a
   sufficiently controlled sequence, time must be "squeezed," either by examining a relatively brief temporal span or by radically simplifying the
   range and extent of change in background conditions during the time
   period covered by the study.[6]

There is no denying game theory's many significant contributions to social
science, but for the investigation of historical processes these are serious limitations. As I will explore in the next section of this chapter, in most cases arguments

[5]Scharpf 1997, p. 73. Indeed, in a different publication (Bates, de Figueiredo, and Weingast 1998,
p. 628), Bates and his coauthors make the same basic point: "Game theorists often fail to acknowledge that their approach requires a complete political anthropology. . . . Game-theoretic accounts
require detailed and fine-grained knowledge of the precise features of the political and social environment within which individuals make choices and devise political strategies."
[6]But note that analytic narratives can be employed (e.g., in the chapters by Bates, Levi, and Weingast)
to specify the implications of a particular event (or other change in background conditions) for strategic interaction (Bates et al. 1998). The event marks the end of the first game and initiates a new game
with changed payoff structures. This comparative statics framework may provide a useful technique
for incorporating events into explanations, although it does not directly address issues of sequences.

about temporal sequences cannot be reduced to a sequence of "moves."[7] Reducing sequences to the order in which rational actors make moves misses what those interested in historical dynamics identify as most significant about the temporal order of events or processes—which is precisely that sequence is *given* by the way in which important social interactions unfold in time, rather than being something that someone *selects*. Indeed, where sequences really are chosen (e.g., by agenda setters in a legislature), the causal story is not about temporal order at all—it is about the institutional structure and the resources and preferences of the key strategic actors. Sequence reveals *how* powerful actors get what they want, but the sequence is itself simply a logical consequence, dictated by these other factors.

It is not surprising, in fact, that the quite successful literature developed from Arrow's work has focused so heavily on legislatures and their internal rules—a setting where it often makes considerable sense to think of actors making moves. As Scharpf himself summarizes (1997, p. 105), game theory offers the greatest analytical leverage

> in highly structured and frequently recurring interactions among a limited number of actors with a high capacity for strategic action, in situations in which a great deal is at stake, and in interest constellations with a relatively high level of conflict in which binding agreements are not generally possible. It is not surprising, therefore, that noncooperative game theory has gained its most important empirical strongholds in studies of international relations . . . of interactions in the legislative process . . . and of interactions among oligopolistic firms . . . whereas in many other areas of social science its application is viewed with much greater skepticism.[8]

When one reviews the kinds of arguments considered in this book, which often address processes covering long periods of time, involve quasi groups, and incorporate the role of events, it is difficult to see how most of them could be restated in game-theoretic terms without being distorted or drastically watered down. Even when these arguments emphasize interactions among competing groups, the point is often that some groups are able to consolidate their position

---

[7]Arguably, game theory can make a significant contribution to one form of sequencing analysis that has been prominent in comparative politics—namely, sequences involved in transitions to democracy (Przeworski 1991). The "transitology" literature focuses on relatively short time frames and, often, on strategic interaction among composite actors. To the extent that this captures the principal dynamics of the transition process, game-theoretical approaches to sequences in democratic transitions are likely to have much to offer. Precisely this, however, is hotly contested (Collier 1999; Kitschelt 2003). I will discuss in the next chapter reasons for thinking that the restricted time frames typically employed in such analyses are often highly misleading.

[8]He goes on to argue that even if game theory cannot generate predictions in other contexts, it may be useful for explanation because knowing if a particular outcome constitutes a Nash equilibrium should influence our expectations regarding its stability, even if it is not the only possible outcome.

before others even arrive on the scene. Arguments about sequence may stress, for instance, how the early emergence of certain kinds of players forecloses the possible emergence of other kinds of players (e.g., alternative organizational forms). Game theorists generally take the existence of the players as given and focus on their strategic interaction.[9]

For the issues of temporal sequencing of interest here, Scharpf is more realistic in suggesting (1997, pp. 31–34) that game theory may be most helpful in constructing particular "modules" that would need to be pieced together with other frameworks to provide a convincing account. Bates et al. might appear to have something similar in mind when they describe "analytic narratives and macro-structural analyses" as "complementary approaches to explanation." They seem to have greater ambitions, however, when they argue that analytic narratives "focus on the *mechanisms* that translate . . . macro-historical forces into specific political outcomes. By isolating and unpacking such mechanisms, analytic narratives contribute to structural accounts." The point to stress, however, is that game theory can explore only *some* mechanisms, and even those only under quite restrictive conditions.

Far more attention needs to be paid to distinguishing what game theory can do from what it cannot do, and to the question of how best to link the possible contributions of game theory together with other theoretical tool kits to address issues for which game theory alone is ill-equipped.[10] Indeed, as I argue in the next section, there are considerable possibilities for extending the important insights of rational choice work on sequences to a broader range of phenomena. In fact, it is possible to combine its strengths with some of the promise suggested by Orren and Skowronek's focus on more macro phenomena and genuinely historical processes.

SEQUENCING IN PATH-DEPENDENT ARGUMENTS

How might such an extension of these game-theoretic arguments work? The answer can be seen by returning to the basic logic of Arrow's analysis and the implications about institutional structure that rational choice theorists have derived from it. Claims about "structure-induced equilibria" rest on a specific version of the kind of path-dependent mechanisms considered in Chapter One.

[9]I am grateful to Kathleen Thelen for emphasizing the importance of this distinction.
[10]Compare Scharpf's balanced discussion to that offered in Morrow 1994. After an extended and impressive introduction to game theory for political scientists, Morrow finally concludes with a section on "the weaknesses of game theory." By this, however, he only means to highlight "cutting edge" issues (such as bounded rationality) where animated debates among game theorists are underway. He sees no need to discuss the prospect that on some matters that social scientists might wish to pursue, game theory can offer limited help or would have to be linked to other modules of argument in ways that require careful thought.

Given a particular set of institutional rules, steps in a sequence of choices become *irreversible*. The rules dictate that alternatives rejected in early rounds are
dropped from the range of possible later options (as, for example, in committee
voting rules that require a sequence of binary choices, with losers eliminated).
Absent this characteristic of irreversibility there would be cycling, rather than a
stable outcome. Sequence matters because there are irreversibilities.

It is possible, however, to expand this crucial finding to a far broader range of
social phenomena than those typically covered in the rational choice literature.
Work on path dependence shows how such irreversibilities can be generated in
a wide variety of social contexts. Thus, we can extend beyond the focus on the
"moves" of "actors" in legislatures to a broader discussion of the temporal order
in which historical alternatives present themselves, and the ways in which this
forecloses certain possibilities while enhancing the prospects of others. In comparative historical analyses, arguments about irreversibilities are often applied to
large-scale social changes such as democratization (Collier and Collier 1991;
Collier 1999), industrialization (Gerschenkron 1962; Kurth 1979), state building (Ertman 1997; Shefter 1977), or welfare state development (Pierson 1994;
Huber and Stephens 2001). Sequencing matters not only for collective choices
within legislatures, or for moves among strategic actors, but potentially for *any*
social or political process where self-reinforcement means that forsaken alternatives become increasingly unreachable with the passage of time. We can think
systematically not only about sequences of "choices" among "proposals," or
"moves" by "actors," but of sequences of social events or processes.

As I argued in Chapter One, the key mechanism at work in these path-
dependent sequences is some form of self-reinforcement or positive feedback
loop. Initial steps in a particular direction may encourage further movement
along the same path. Over time, "roads not chosen" may become increasingly
distant, increasingly unreachable alternatives. Relatively modest perturbations
at early stages may have a large influence on these processes. In many cases, the
significance of early events or processes in the sequence may be amplified,
while that of later events or processes is dampened. Thus, *when* a particular
event or process occurs in a sequence will make a big difference.

Many, perhaps even most, arguments about sequencing in the social sciences
appear to be grounded at least in part (although often only vaguely or implicitly)
on claims about path dependence and self-reinforcement. In these arguments,
early developments get deeply embedded in a particular environment, altering
the resources, incentive structures, and hence behaviors of social actors, and
thereby changing the social significance or pattern of unfolding of events or
processes occurring later in the sequence. To explore these issues, the remainder
of this section reviews three types of arguments involving positive feedback which
treat sequencing in very different ways. The first simply explores a self-reinforcing
process without placing much weight on temporal ordering. The second, which
is most common, argues that the temporal sequence of distinct processes deter-

mines outcomes because the event or process that occurs earliest will trigger positive feedback. Finally, some arguments embed an analysis of self-reinforcing processes within a broader analysis about sequences that is focused largely on downstream effects. Each of these lines of argument may be appropriate in particular circumstances; together they highlight the range of claims about sequences that can be built around a framework attentive to positive feedback.

Identifying Positive Feedback Loops

In some cases an investigator may wish to focus on a single developmental trajectory in order to show how a particular set of relationships becomes increasingly embedded over time. Terry Karl's *The Paradox of Plenty* (1997) offers a good example. Karl's study offers a compelling analysis of how "petro-states" become locked into deeply problematic developmental paths. As developing countries discover large deposits of oil, they are placed on a particular self-reinforcing trajectory. Oil resources shape the structure of organized interests and, crucially, the state itself. Karl's key observation is that with the arrival of oil resources these states are simultaneously flush with revenues but organizationally immature. The resulting state-building process leads to a particular type of political regime distinguished by deeply entrenched patterns of rent seeking. Karl shows that this pattern of institutionalized rent seeking is remarkably consistent and durable across a wide range of otherwise dissimilar countries (Venezuela, Iran, Nigeria, Algeria, and to a lesser extent Indonesia), suggesting the strength of these feedback processes.

In Karl's analysis, however, *temporal order* appears to have only a limited impact on broad outcomes:

> At least three critical junctures shape patterns of decisionmaking . . . prior to the 1973 price hike: the entry of international oil companies into weak states; the imposition of income taxes on companies as a prime source of the state's fiscal revenues; and regime changes that either reinforce or counteract reliance on oil rents. These critical junctures are path-dependent—that is, they are initially set off by the entry of the oil companies. They either occur in a distinct sequence, as they did in Venezuela, or overlap. . . . But *regardless of their timing or sequencing,* they accompany one another. The institutional legacy of these events *shapes a common decision calculus* for policymakers in petro-states. (1997, p. 197, emphasis added)

By tracing a dynamic, self-reinforcing process over time Karl is making a temporal argument, but it is not one where timing and sequence appear to be very relevant. It doesn't really matter all that much when or how these countries discovered vast oil resources; a great deal follows logically from the discovery itself.[11]

---

[11] It should be noted that Karl does complicate the analysis in a fruitful way by situating this path-dependent argument within a broader historical framework. Investigating the case of Norway, she is

Sequence-Based Arguments about Self-Reinforcement

Many works of historical sociology or political science incorporate claims about timing and sequence in a more sustained way. These analyses typically focus on processes of positive feedback that consolidate particular arrangements established at a critical juncture. Crucially, an important part of that explanation turns on issues of sequencing. In these accounts, the temporal order of key events or processes helps to determine which path of development will emerge.

A good example is Martin Shefter's classic explanation of cross-national variation in the use of party patronage (Shefter 1977). Shefter begins with the observation that there is tremendous range in the extent to which political parties base their appeals to mass electorates around patronage. This variation, he argues, cannot be explained by invoking synchronic variables (e.g., the size of immigrant populations within the electorate); rather, historical explanation is required. What is crucial, Shefter maintains, is the outcome during the initial period of democratization, when parties first had to make mass appeals. In turn, whether parties organized their strategies around patronage depended on two conditions. First, and most obviously, the party had to be in a position to offer patronage (this excluded the socialist parties of Europe and nationalist parties in much of the Third World). Second, there could not *already* be a strong, organized coalition within the party pressing for bureaucratic autonomy. Such a coalition (which, in Shefter's account, could be of "absolutist" or "progressive" origins) foreclosed the patronage option and forced the party to employ other, more collective, political appeals.

What happened at this particular juncture was "critical" because the initial form of mobilization generated positive feedback. As Shefter puts it (1977, pp. 414–15) "The way in which a party initially acquires a popular base is a character-forming or 'critical' experience . . . influenc[ing] the character of the organization the party builds, what it subsequently must do to hold on to its social base, and consequently the bargaining strength within the party of practitioners of patronage politics and of their opponents." Once entrenched, the dominant basis of political mobilization became extremely difficult to dislodge. The crucial issue therefore was one of sequencing: whether a movement advocating bureaucratic autonomy precedes or follows the onset of mass democratization. This in turn reflects different processes of state building in different countries.

---

able to argue plausibly that sequencing does in fact matter: that it is critical whether oil is discovered before or after a country experiences sustained state building. If oil is discovered first, then state building itself will be petroleum driven, producing the political pathologies that are Karl's primary concern. Where state building occurs first, however, political leaders may be in a position to successfully manage the petro boom, avoiding the destructive self-reinforcing dynamic experienced by most petro states. This raises an important issue for the investigation of sequences, however. Any comparative investigation of, say, Libya and Norway would be likely to take variation in state capacities seriously; it is not clear that attention to temporal ordering gives one extra analytical leverage.

Shefter's argument focuses both on explaining outcomes at a critical juncture and on showing that those outcomes produced self-reinforcing, path-dependent effects. His explanation for outcomes stresses the relative timing of two processes, state building and democratization. If efforts to build bureaucratic autonomy occurred after democratization, they were "too late."

Thomas Ertman's *The Birth of Leviathan* (Ertman 1996), discussed in the introduction, provides a second example. If European states faced military competition before the spread of mass literacy, they developed durable state structures quite different from those where the order of these two processes was reversed. As in Shefter's analysis, Ertman argues that initial outcomes were consequential because they were self-reinforcing. States facing early competition resorted to tax farming, which triggered the development of a dense network of institutions and interests. It became virtually impossible to switch over to more modern forms of financing, especially since monarchs generally had immediate needs for revenues. The later arrival of mass literacy thus had much more limited effects on state building than it did in settings where the temporal ordering of these two processes was reversed.

These are just two outstanding examples of this common and powerful line of argument about sequences. In these accounts, path-dependent processes are marked by critical junctures and long-enduring trajectories. The long-term outcomes of interest depend on the relative timing of important processes (Ertman: military competition vs. expansion of literacy; Shefter: democratization vs. state building), because positive feedback from one may decisively affect the consequences of the other when it occurs later. A variable's impact cannot be predicted without an appreciation for *when* it appears within a sequence unfolding over time.

Downstream Dynamics: Embedding Arguments about Positive Feedback

The arguments just discussed typically emphasize processes of institutionalization resulting from positive feedback, meaning that some process or event occurring later has less impact than it otherwise might have. These approaches are kin to game-theoretic claims about "first-mover" advantages. Whatever comes first has the greatest impact on patterns of institutionalization. Later initiatives— for mobilization, state building, and so forth—are constrained to operate within the contours established at this critical juncture.

As suggested in Chapter One, a common criticism of claims like this is that they suggest a world of stasis punctuated by only occasional bursts of change (Thelen 1999, 2003). In fact, such a depiction of social processes will often be broadly accurate, especially if one is interested in very macro phenomena such as regime formation or patterns of state building. Yet arguments about sequencing need not be based on claims about perpetual self-reinforcement, in which a path, once selected, persists indefinitely. It certainly seems plausible that issues of sequencing may be significant without implying that a particular path is necessarily "locked in." Previous events in a sequence influence outcomes and trajectories, but not necessarily by inducing continuous movement in the same direction. Indeed, the route might matter precisely because it sets the stage for a particular kind of reaction in some other direction.

The danger is that this amounts to a loose assertion that "history matters." Can we think more systematically about alternative ways in which the temporal ordering of events or processes could be consequential? James Mahoney (2001) has noted that arguments based on what he calls "event sequencing" are common in comparative historical work. The basic idea, as Mahoney puts it, is that an event or outcome at a particular juncture "may trigger a chain of causally-linked events that, once itself in motion, occurs independently of the institutions that initially trigger it. This sequence of events, while ultimately linked to a critical juncture period, may culminate in an outcome that is far removed from the original critical juncture." As Mahoney notes, an argument about "event sequencing is most effective when the events set into motion have fairly obvious linkages to one another, what Abbott calls an 'inherent logic.'"[12] Here *a* produces *b*, which produces *c*, and so on.

How do we identify such "logics," however? Reference to "event sequences" begins to sound like chaos theory, or Paul David's (1985, p. 332) unfortunate (and uncharacteristic) informal description of path dependence as a type of change where "one damn thing follows another." In Goldstone's terms, it sounds "Seussian." Mahoney, however, is grouping together two types of processes that need to be distinguished. On the one hand, we have "event chains," or tightly linked causal connections unfolding over time. These are arguments that take the form "if you get event *a*, you are highly likely to get *b*, and from *b* we would expect *c* to follow." Now, since it may take a considerable period of time for the entire chain to unfold, these are arguments that do indeed suggest the need to examine processes over time. Hence, arguments about such chains of events forms an important part of the discussion of long-term social processes, which I turn to in Chapter Three. But, like Karl's discussion of petro-states, these are not really arguments about *sequence*—that is, they do not rest on claims about the consequences of distinct temporal orderings. Thus I would distinguish arguments about event *chains* from those about event *sequences*. Event sequences are cases where different temporal orderings of the same events or processes will produce different outcomes.

When we do concentrate on event *sequences*, it turns out that we are often talking once again about processes involving positive feedback—albeit ones

---

[12]Compare Collier and Collier 1991, p. 37: "There often occurs a significant interval between the critical juncture and the period of continuity that is explained by these mechanisms of reproduction. To the extent that the critical juncture is a polarizing event that produces intense political reactions and counterreactions, the crystallization of the legacy does not necessarily occur immediately, but rather may consist of a sequence of intervening steps that respond to these reactions and counterreactions."

with more dynamic downstream characteristics. Again, we can turn to Arrow's analysis to see why this is so. For Arrow, the sequencing of proposals often matters not because the proposal that wins the first round will automatically endure. Instead, the early "winner" may be especially *vulnerable* to some specific challenger appearing at a later stage in the sequence. That challenger, however, would have been less effective if it had appeared earlier, paired against a different alternative. In a case such as this, an agenda setter may choose a sequence of votes on alternatives structured to produce an early winner that will be unable to defeat a favored proposal or amendment later on.

The equivalent argument in analyzing historical processes would be one where an early juncture generates a self-reinforcing trajectory, but one that is in turn vulnerable to particular "downstream" challenges. The sequence in which alternatives present themselves may thus be crucial to the eventual outcome, but that outcome may be far different from the initial result or trajectory that emerges at a critical juncture. Gregory Luebbert's (1991) comparative analysis of interwar Europe provides a clear example of this kind of event sequence argument. His investigation centers on the political space available for coalition formation at different stages in a historical process. In those societies that had been illiberal before World War I, the eventual alternatives proved to be social democracy or fascism. According to Luebbert, in this context "the alignment of the family peasantry was decisive." The choice of that alignment, in turn,

> was determined by whether or not socialist movements had become engaged in class conflicts within the countryside. Whenever socialists sought to organize the agrarian proletariat in politics and in the labor market, the family peasantry was pushed into the arms of fascists. Whether or not socialists sought to organize agrarian workers was in turn determined by *whether those workers were politically available or had been previously organized by another movement.* Where they had not been previously organized the logic of democratic competition, the short-term imperative of maximizing popular support, drove socialists into the void." (1991, pp. 10–11, emphasis added)

In Luebbert's argument, the political coalitions that emerged before World War I in these countries were not "locked in." On the contrary, they would give way in the wake of postwar turbulence, either to fascism or social democracy. Yet previous patterns of incorporation were vitally important, because in many cases a crucial strategic option for social democrats ("organize agrarian workers") had been removed from the range of viable alternatives. Ironically, in Luebbert's account, social democrats were *better off* when earlier stages in the sequence prevented them from employing this strategy. Here the downstream dynamic triggered by a path-dependent process of coalition formation led to social democracy, rather than fascism.

Similarly, Collier and Collier point to how previously stable arrangements can give way, but in a fashion that nevertheless signals the importance of earlier stages in a sequence. In some of their Latin American cases, elites were able to avoid labor incorporation at an initial critical juncture. Instead, they consolidated a particular kind of political regime, which Collier and Collier label "state incorporation." Because it proved to be impossible to depoliticize workers permanently, however, "state incorporation in some important respects created a greater opportunity for future polarization. This occurred for several reasons, among them that many of the legal controls of unions broke down with the competitive bidding for workers' votes under a subsequent democratic regime, and that state incorporation left unresolved the partisan affiliation of workers and unions, leaving them available for mobilization by other actors in later periods" (1991, p. 9). Here again the initial pattern of institutionalization that follows a critical juncture is not frozen in place. But when politicization of labor occurs downstream it does so under circumstances, and with results, quite different from those in force in the cases that experienced early incorporation.

Indeed, the Colliers' sweeping analysis of regime dynamics in Latin America provides a striking examination of different types of sequences and underscores many of the points I wish to emphasize here. *Shaping the Political Arena* is often cited as a powerful argument about how particular social relations and institutions established at a key historical juncture are reproduced over time. Yet the Colliers' argument about path dependence is more nuanced and dynamic. Stable institutionalization proved to be a challenge: "In all eight countries [in our study] the incorporation experience produced a strong political reaction, and in most countries this reaction culminated in the breakdown of the national political regime under which the incorporation policies had been implemented" (Collier and Collier 1991, p. 8) In fact, the Colliers identify several different sequences emerging out of a common "critical juncture" of labor's incorporation into national politics: "The legacies of some critical junctures are stable, institutionalized regimes, whereas others produce a political dynamic that prevents or mitigates against stable patterns" (p. 34). In some cases, specific relationships are institutionalized through positive feedback. Initial consolidation takes place on a basis that is sustainable over time. In other cases, there is an initial consolidation, but on terms that eventually prove to be unsustainable. In still another group of cases, what is crucial is the failure of consolidation in this initial period, and the resulting persistent instability. Thus, it is perfectly feasible for analysts of path-dependent processes to focus on "downstream" developments well past a critical juncture. In some cases, the principal concern is the eventual disruption of a self-reinforcing process; in others, the analysis usefully highlights the long-term implications of a specific pattern of consolidation having failed to occur in particular cases.[13]

---

[13]In this last instance, we see once again the particularly favorable circumstances for sequence analysis that are available to comparativists. Comparative historical analysis, as practiced by scholars like Huber and Stephens (2001), Luebbert, and the Colliers, presents good opportunities to examine alternative sequences that actually occur rather than relying exclusively on counterfactuals (Mahoney and Rueschemeyer 2003).

Arguments about positive feedback and sequencing represent a key building block for claims about why and how history matters. In all of these studies of path-dependent sequencing, particular historical sequences are crucial because initial processes generate particular, long-lasting, and highly consequential organizational forms and institutional arrangements, which alter the implications of later events or processes. In all these cases, it is not just a matter of what happens, but of *when* it happens. Some events or processes occur "too early", others "too late." We cannot explain many important political outcomes without addressing questions of temporal ordering.

Some Distinctive Features of Sequencing Arguments

A key claim of this book is that different analytic strategies may illuminate distinct aspects of social reality. Attentiveness to temporal process can help us recognize and explore parts of the social landscape that are likely to escape notice from alternative vantage points. For this reason it is worth highlighting two broad themes that feature prominently in these analyses of path-dependent sequences of development. The first focuses on *political space*; the second invokes evolving *social capacities*. These arguments are not incompatible; indeed, many analysts combine them. But they represent distinct ways in which timing and sequence can matter. Equally important, they demonstrate some of the fundamental aspects of social life that temporally sensitive analyses can help us to see more clearly.

The "Filling-Up" of "Political Space"

Many arguments about path-dependent sequences focus on competing social actors who seek to occupy some limited "political space." The crucial link to sequencing stems from the *relational* nature of these competitions. Success in struggles over political space depends not simply on the resources at one's disposal. Rather, what generally counts is the scale of those resources relative to those of other contenders. If early competitive advantages may be self-reinforcing, then *relative timing* may have enormous implications. In contexts conducive to path dependence, groups able to consolidate early advantages may achieve enduring superiority. Actors arriving later may find that resources in the environment (e.g., potential supporters) are already committed to other patterns of mobilization. Indeed, the consequences of "lateness" may be much more severe. Jared Diamond's vivid discussion of the initial clashes between Europeans and Native Americans provides a blunt but telling illustration of the relational nature of political competition. His emphasis on the head start in development that Europeans received from their favorable geo-ecological inheritance points to the brutal and enduring consequences of being "too late" (Diamond 1997). Such arguments are common for those studying interstate competition. Perry Anderson (1974), for instance, makes a similar argument about the development of Eastern European absolutism in the shadow of powerful absolutist states in Western Europe.

This type of path-dependent sequencing argument, common in comparative politics, thus takes the following form. Some actor achieves a position of influence first, and is able to use that position to consolidate its hold on a particular "political space." Challengers at later dates will often be severely disadvantaged, even though similar actors (parties, interest organizations, social movements) may fare quite well in otherwise similar contexts where they happen to arrive first. Temporal sequences are thus crucial to explaining enduring political outcomes. Classic examples from the field of West European politics would include Lipset and Rokkan's (1967) argument about enduring cleavage structures and frozen party systems, and Colin Crouch's (1986) analysis of how public authority is allocated between organized interests and civil servants in different countries.

While noting that "the metaphor of 'political space' comes up . . . time and again" in works of comparative historical analysis, Thelen (1999, 2000) has emphasized the need for caution. Claims about "vested interests" or the "filling up" of political space are often simply asserted; they need to be demonstrated. And it is certainly true that arriving first is far from a guarantee of success. Thelen in fact points to several examples of early arrivers who were ultimately unsuccessful, and she argues that "understanding when early arrival matters will hinge crucially on an analysis of the 'fit' between the organizational forms that develop and the political and economic context in which they emerge—in particular, the extent to which the latter promotes or interferes with . . . positive feedback" (Thelen 2000, p. 103).

This is absolutely right. Examining whether or not features of a particular context promote (or impede) self-reinforcing processes can increase the precision of claims like "organization A was successful because it 'fit' well in that particular context." As I suggested in the last chapter, existing research on positive feedback in social processes offers important suggestions about where to look. We would want to ask, for instance, whether start-up costs for potential alternative organizations were relatively high or low, whether organizations achieving early success would be able to exercise significant political authority, and, if so, how effectively this authority could be used to expand the group's resources or impede the progress of potential competitors, and whether other actors would face significant pressures to adapt their own behavior in light of the early success of a particular group, policy, or institution. Along these and other relevant dimensions there is likely to be considerable variation, opening the prospect of establishing sharper, testable claims about the particular contexts that may give early arrivers enduring advantages.

Even if a particular environment is conducive to positive feedback, it obviously does not follow that *any* group will be able to exploit those opportunities.

This is another way of saying, as suggested in Chapter One, that events at the beginning of a path-dependent process are not totally contingent—there may be only a few (perhaps only two) plausible alternatives. To employ the language of evolutionary theory, arriving first will not matter unless one can prosper in the ecological niches available.

Yet there remains a strong case for thinking that the sequence in which groups enter and fill political space will often matter a great deal. Since I confess that my own cultural repertoire of analogies leans heavily toward sports, I offer one here. The commercial success of a professional team sport generally hinges on a broad perception that all participating teams have a reasonable chance to win, if not this year then perhaps a few years down the road. Yet maintaining the plausibility of this "meek shall inherit" scenario requires conscious, energetic efforts to offset the tendencies for strong teams to get stronger (as they attract more revenues, better players, and better coaches). In many professional sports, rules are specifically designed to enforce a certain amount of *negative* feedback. Losing teams are given first crack at the best new talent, revenue sharing is introduced to help poor franchises, and caps are set on what individual franchises can spend on players. And of course, short of catastrophic failure losing franchises are essentially guaranteed a continued seat at the table. Even these strong countervailing efforts are often insufficient to generate anything close to parity, even over the long term.

In politics, of course, nothing like these compensatory, countervailing rules generally exist. On the contrary, as has already been discussed, there are good theoretical reasons for believing that "getting there first" often confers very substantial advantages. Start-up costs are often very high in collective action processes, and thus constitute a major barrier to entry. By contrast, it is often much easier to sustain or expand an organization once this minimum threshold has been crossed. If affiliating with organizations that fail to attract widespread support has significant drawbacks—almost always the case in politics—then individuals will make adjustments as collective action processes unfold. There will often be a tendency to affiliate with, or at least accommodate, existing groups once they reach a certain size, even among actors who would prefer some hypothetical alternative.[14] Perhaps most important, actors who achieve a critical mass of political resources may be able to manipulate the rules of the game (formal institutions) and reallocate resources (public policies) in ways that increase their organizational advantages over potential competitors. In the political world, powerful actors typically make the rules and generally have no incentives to pursue "parity"; it is a far cry from the world of team sports (Moe 2003).

---

[14]For an excellent analysis of how the adaptive expectations of voters, politicians, and interest groups generate this winnowing process for party organizations confronting different electoral rules, see Cox 1997.

Thus, arguments about political space allow us to think about dynamic relationships between early winners and "losers" in politics, and about the possibilities and constraints that may face those who lose out in early rounds. Rational choice analysts, working from Arrow's analysis of the problem of cycling, have treated this issue largely as a matter of what Riker called "heresthetics" (Riker 1986). "Losers" need to be creative in developing new issue dimensions that allow them to fragment the winner's coalition and break out of their marginal status (Shepsle 2003). While this is a relevant subject, thinking about the possible feedback effects from early losses allows one to generate considerably more developed accounts of the predicaments losers face in particular settings. Recent empirical analyses drawing on this kind of framework have shown why heresthetic moves may be ineffective. Moreover, they have identified a range of additional factors that influence the circumstances where losers may face opportunities (although often quite constrained ones) down the road (Hacker 2002; Thelen 2004).

The ideas that actors compete to occupy limited political space, and that once groups occupy this space they are often difficult to dislodge, rest on a solid theoretical base. The empirical evidence of tremendous organizational persistence across many political contexts (e.g., in party systems and structures of interest representation) is consistent with the view that organizational success frequently generates positive feedback. What has often been lacking, and what an understanding of the mechanisms of path dependence can provide, is an explicit account of the processes likely to render early advantages lasting ones. The comparative politics literature contains many arguments about competition over limited political space. If one "unpacked" these claims in order to identify the mechanisms at work, one would generally find that they relied on the kinds of processes mentioned here. They point, therefore, to the tremendous importance of the relative timing of events or processes that can influence *when* potential contenders for political space appear.

The Development of Social Capacities

A second major theme in these path-dependent sequencing arguments is the centrality of developing social capacities to many historical processes. The stock of available resources in social life—material, technological, organizational, and ideational—changes dramatically over time.[15] As I will explore in more de-

---

[15]The point here is, I think, close to what Skowronek (1993, pp. 30–31) intends with the concept of "secular time" employed in *The Politics Presidents Make*. The place of a particular presidency in a cyclical emergence and erosion of a dominant regime must also acknowledge that "[t]he resources available to presidents in getting things done have changed dramatically over the course of American history. . . . [This] parallels the development of a political universe which is in every way more fully organized and more densely inhabited. It is not just that the presidency has gradually become

tail in Chapter Three, these changes often take place very slowly. As a result, they will frequently be ignored in synchronic analyses. They may concern "sociological" variables and therefore escape the attention of even historically oriented social scientists—especially if these analysts have gotten in the habit of turning to economics for useful hypotheses. Furthermore, attention to such processes has become suspect, since in the past they were often linked to concepts of political modernization and associated with simple notions of progress, convergence, and determinism. Yet a central fact of social development is that resources that may be scarce or unavailable at one point in human history may be widely available at others.

Linked to an analysis of self-reinforcing processes, an investigation of such developing capacities provides a powerful lens for identifying important dimensions of sequencing. In such an analysis, *when* a particular issue or conflict emerges in a society becomes critical for two reasons. First, the resources available to actors at that moment in time help to determine the repertoire of possible responses. Second, once a response is adopted, it may generate self-reinforcing dynamics that put politics on a distinctive long-term path.[16] In Ertman's account, for instance, a crucial historical factor is the gradual spread of literacy. Activities of state building are enduringly shaped by when they occur against the backdrop of this gradual increase in social capacities.

Note that *both* the notion of historically shifting social conditions and the role of self-reinforcing processes are crucial to this line of argument. Without processes of positive feedback, changes in relevant social conditions over time would simply be incorporated into present political processes. Absent a self-reinforcing dynamic, the fact that early state building occurred in a context of limited literacy would leave no lasting impact.

Thus, arguments about sequences involving positive feedback will frequently be based on claims about political space or the historical development of social capacities. In many studies, these two lines of argument are combined. Good examples include Gerschenkron's (1962) classic work on industrialization and Kurth's (1979) examination of the product cycle.[17] Both works emphasize the significance of relative power in contexts where political space is limited and

---

more powerful and independent over the course of American history, but that the institutions and interests surrounding it have as well."

[16]Again, Stinchcombe (1965, p. 153) saw this a long time ago. "The organizational inventions that can be made at a particular time in history depend on the social technology available at the time. Organizations which have purposes that can be efficiently reached with the socially possible organizational forms tend to be founded during the period in which they become possible. Then, both because they can function effectively with those organizational forms and because the forms tend to become institutionalized, the basic structure of the organization tends to remain relatively stable."

[17]Note that Kurth's provocative analysis involves the interaction of two sets of sequences. There are sequences of *products*, which emerge at different historical moments. There are also sequences within each product cycle, from early producers to later producers.

contested. In examining the possibilities of an emerging state one must recognize that it operates in the shadow of earlier industrializers who possess considerable advantages and shape the context in which followers must operate. At the same time, however, both Gerschenkron and Kurth stress that different economic possibilities exist at different historical junctures. Later industrializers will be operating with different social capacities than earlier ones. In Gerschenkron's analysis, processes of late industrialization are distinctive because these countries are trying desperately to "catch up" in a system already containing powerful industrial states, *and* because late industrializers may borrow advanced technology from earlier industrializers, *and* because the crucial sectors for economic growth had shifted with the passage of time (e.g., from cotton and textiles in England to iron, steel, and railroads in Germany).

To take a very different example, Jacob Hacker's (1998) comparative study of the development of health-care systems in Canada, Great Britain, and the United States also stresses path-dependent sequences of both evolving power relations and developing social capacities. In an analysis notably sensitive to the theoretical and methodological issues of comparative historical inquiry, Hacker argues that particular sequences of health policy development produced lasting cross-national differences:

> The emergence of national health insurance programs in advanced industrial democracies should therefore not be seen as a one-time event that occurs because of a particular constellation of political and social factors. Rather, it should be conceived of as an ongoing historical process whose sequence critically determines eventual outcomes. Three questions of sequence are particularly important in determining the path countries eventually take: whether governments fail to enact national health insurance before a sizable portion of the public is enrolled in physician-dominated private insurance plans, whether initial public insurance programs are focused on residual populations . . . and whether efforts to build up the medical industry precede the universalization of access. Countries that do all these things, as the United States did, are left facing virtually insuperable political barriers to the passage of national health insurance. (Hacker 1998, pp. 127–28)

Consolidated physician-dominated private insurance plans created powerful vested interests opposed to national health insurance. At the same time, over the course of the twentieth century the expanding technical capacities of medicine and shifting expectations for health provision have vastly increased the share of national income devoted to health care. The staggering costs associated with a mature "medical-industrial complex" make it much more difficult to shift expenses to public financing after such systems mature than it was to do so earlier. In both these respects, recent advocates of universal health care in the United

States faced not only the natural barriers to radical policy reform inherent in a system of fragmented political institutions (Steinmo and Watts 1995). In a fundamental sense, these reformers were too late.

CONCLUSION: INVESTIGATING TEMPORAL SEQUENCES OF SOCIAL PROCESSES

There are strong theoretical grounds for believing, as Tilly put it, that *when* things happen effects *how* they happen. There is much to be gained by unpacking the various arguments social scientists have advanced about temporal sequences. Sequencing arguments are common, but often less than fully spelled out. The analysis of temporal ordering is central to the claim that "history matters," but this claim will be more convincing and will provide a better foundation for cumulative research if analysts focus more explicitly on where, when, and how causally significant sequences come into play. Social scientists have in fact pointed to the significance of sequences on a range of crucial issues. Yet much of this research has either lacked clear claims about mechanisms that render sequence so crucial, or they have confined their inquiries in ways that needlessly restrict the potential of their arguments.

In this chapter I have suggested that arguments about self-reinforcement provide a focus that can combine analytic precision with substantive breadth. This enterprise draws heavily on the rational choice tradition. Work derived from Arrow has provided the clearest demonstrations of how and why sequences matter, and it has provided a basis for exploring the link between the presence of irreversibilities and the significance of temporal order. And of course, the work of those using the analytic tools of microeconomics has been central to recent study of processes involving positive feedback—which I am suggesting offer an essential building block for discussions of historical sequences in the social sciences. Indeed, the economic historian Douglas North has arguably done more than any other scholar to examine the broad implications of path dependence for social scientists.

The examination of self-reinforcing dynamics can be used to explicitly address issues of timing and sequence, and to investigate the interplay of distinct historical processes. In this sense, there are real affinities between the agenda outlined here and the one suggested by Orren and Skowronek. These arguments share a claim that mechanisms of self-reinforcement can make political outcomes "sticky" or persistent. Yet analysis utilizing such arguments need not suggest an essentially frozen political landscape. Rather, it is *particular aspects* of social relations that become deeply embedded. It therefore matters a great deal when in a broader sequence of development consolidation or institutionalization occurs, and how these embedded aspects interact with more fluid elements of a broader social context (Jervis 1997, chap. 4). Here sequencing becomes a way of identifying the linkages between distinct processes and examining the consequences of the relative timing of those processes. Indeed, it is the very distinctiveness of the domains that permits variation in *relative* timing across cases to generate important divergences. Ertman, for instance, highlights the relative timing of expanded literacy and intensified interstate competition, Shefter that of democratization and state building.

Moreover, many of these arguments about path-dependent sequences focus on broad and lengthy social transformations: industrialization, democratization, state building. These sequencing analyses thus draw our attention to profound macrohistorical processes covering a span of time and range of social action far more sweeping than that incorporated in most contemporary social science—an issue that forms the central subject matter for Chapter Three. Of course, path-dependent sequencing arguments can be applied to more microphenomena. One can fruitfully use such arguments for investigating such things as particular collective action processes or the development of specific public policies. But a focus on path-dependent sequences can be extremely helpful in drawing our attention to social processes that take place on a broad temporal scale, or that involve the interaction of processes operating on different temporal scales (Abbott 1990, pp. 144–46).

Work on sequence-based explanations can make enormous progress by exploiting these arguments more systematically, but to say this is not to minimize what has already been achieved. Quite the contrary. Historically oriented empirical work on sequences can build on a formidable intellectual tradition. Taken as a whole, this literature quite effectively undercuts the claim that the social significance of historical processes can be easily incorporated in the "values" of particular "variables" at a moment in time. Furthermore, the emerging body of theory concerning positive feedback suggests that analysts are now well-placed to develop fruitful claims about when we would expect to see sequencing effects at work in political life.

Chapter Three

LONG-TERM PROCESSES

[W]e must question if the particular moment matters. Political science owes much of its origin to political journalism.
And like political journalism we have an excessive tendency
to concentrate on the here and now, a blindness toward
movements on a grander time scale. Processes are not so
easily captured, but the postulate on which this work must
stand is that they matter more.
—*Edward Carmines and James Stimson (1989)*

Politics is a strong and slow boring of hard boards.
—*Max Weber*

A CORE THEME OF THE PAST TWO CHAPTERS has been the need, as historian Fer-
dinand Braudel famously put it, to remain attentive to the *longue durée*. Many
important social processes take a long time—sometimes an extremely long time—
to unfold. This is a problematic fact for contemporary social science, particularly in areas of inquiry where individual strategic action has become the central
vantage point for framing questions and answers about social life. Especially in
economics and political science, the time horizons of most analysts have become increasingly restricted. Both in what we seek to explain and in our search
for explanations, we focus on the immediate—we look for causes and outcomes
that are both temporally contiguous and rapidly unfolding. In the process, we
miss a lot (Goldstone 1998; Kitschelt 2003). There are important things that we
do not see at all, and what we do see we often misunderstand.

It may help to start out by reviewing briefly four examples from the natural
sciences. Consider first a tornado. Typically, accounts of these storms suggest
that they develop relatively rapidly and that the storm itself lasts for only a short
period. This is a "quick/quick" case: the causal process unfolds over a short time
period, and so does the outcome of interest.

Accounts of an earthquake typically look different. Like the tornado, the outcome of interest—the earthquake itself—takes place in a very short period, a
matter of seconds. The explanation or causal account typically offered, however,
invokes a very slow-moving process: the buildup of pressure on a fault line over
an extended period of time. We would be very unlikely to focus our explanatory
account on what happened in the days or weeks immediately preceding the

earthquake—the last, minuscule increment of pressure that triggers the event. In this case we have a "quick" outcome but a very slow-moving, long-term causal process.

A third example is a cataclysmic ecological event, such as the hypothesized meteorite that hit the Earth 65 million years ago, triggering dramatic climatic change and mass extinctions. A standard account would probably treat this as a "quick/slow" case. Here, a cause (meteor impact) takes place over a short time period, followed by a slowly unfolding outcome (climatic change + extinctions). The outcome can be considered even more "slow moving" if the object of interest is the development of large mammals, which became possible only in the ecological niches vacated by dinosaurs.

A final example is global warming. Models linking the rise in carbon emissions to increased global temperatures suggest that even if emission increases ceased tomorrow, we would nonetheless see a substantial rise in temperatures during the next century. Much of the increase, it seems, is already "in the pipeline"— stored in the ocean, from which it will gradually be released into the atmosphere (Stevens 2000). Thus the outcome (higher temperatures in the Earth's atmosphere) is slow moving, with a considerable temporal lag from the key causal force at work. As in the earthquake example, the causal process itself (gradually rising emission levels) is also slow moving. This, then, is a case of a long-term causal process (increasing emissions) and a long-term outcome (temperature rise).

The "temporal structures" of these explanatory accounts thus reveal substantial diversity, as summarized in table 3.1. The causal processes claimed to generate outcomes of interest may or may not unfold over the short term. The outcomes themselves are equally subject to variation, with some transpiring over a very short time while others work themselves out completely only over a very extended period. In each case, we may refer to the "time horizon" of a variable or cluster of variables—the period of time over which meaningful change occurs (Abbott 1988). To roughly capture this diversity of the time horizons of causes and outcomes in different explanatory accounts, we can divide the possibilities into four quadrants, with one of the natural science examples occupying each quadrant.

As will also be explored in greater depth later in this chapter, it is important to stress that the decision to invoke a particular temporal structure depends on how the analyst frames the research question. In the meteorite example, the duration of the outcome depends in part on whether the object of interest is the extinction of dinosaurs or the emergence of large mammals. Similarly, if one treats the meteorite collision as the entire causal process of interest, it unfolds very rapidly. If one also feels a need to explain how that meteorite came to arrive at that particular point in space at that particular moment, the causal process would unfold over a much longer period. Typically, analysts tackling particular kinds of processes will find one or another temporal structure more helpful and con-

TABLE 3.1
The Time Horizons of Different Causal Accounts

| | | Time Horizon of Outcome | |
		Short	Long
Time	**Short**	I	II
Horizon		(tornado)	(meteorite/extinction)
of Cause	**Long**	III	IV
		(earthquake)	(global warming)

vincing for illuminating problems of interest. The key point for the current discussion is that these causal accounts have diverse temporal structures, and these different structures focus the analyst's attention on different phenomena.

The reason to stress this diversity is that so much of contemporary research in political science seems geared toward Quadrant I. Typically, both causal processes and outcomes are depicted as unfolding entirely over a short period of time. This sort of framework will often be appropriate. There is, however, no reason to think that most political processes, or the most interesting ones, are necessarily best understood by invoking accounts with this kind of temporal structure. In many cases, we will want to extend our temporal field of vision to consider social dynamics that look more like the examples in Quadrants II–IV. In the first part of this chapter, I discuss causal processes that occur gradually over extended periods of time, reviewing some reasons why certain causes are slow moving and offering some examples from social science research. In the next part, I explore the same set of issues for long-term outcomes. The third part moves the discussion beyond the simple framework introduced in table 3.1. It focuses on two types of processes where there may be significant time lags between the onset of a central cause and the initiation of the outcome of interest.

Throughout this discussion, my emphasis is on distinguishing and outlining different types of processes that might operate over extended periods of time. Such distinctions can help provide the foundation for future efforts to integrate long-term processes into theoretical accounts. That is to say, they provide orientations—sources of both questions and potential hypotheses—for empirical research. They also help to highlight and clarify specific methodological challenges facing investigations of long-term processes. Finally, specifying and clarifying different types of long-term processes can serve as an important bridging device for diverse communities of social scientists. It may connect research focused on distinct empirical problems, revealing the extent to which different literatures draw on similar conceptions of causal processes (Hall 2003) and similar analytical techniques for shaping and assessing explanations (Pierson and Skocpol 2002). In the chapter's conclusion, I briefly discuss why much contemporary research in the social sciences seems to gravitate toward Quadrant I, and I summarize some of the main costs of this preoccupation.

Slow-Moving Causal Processes

Social processes take place at different speeds. "Events of equivalent causal importance," as Andrew Abbott has put it, "just don't always take the same amount of time to happen" (Abbott 1988, p. 174). In this section, I focus on causal forces that develop over an extended period of time. There are at least three distinctive types of causal processes that can be described as slow moving. Slow-moving processes may be cumulative, involve threshold effects, or require the unfolding of extended causal chains. I examine each of these possibilities in turn.

Cumulative Causes

The most straightforward type of slow-moving causal process can be termed "incremental" or "cumulative." Here, change in a variable is continuous but extremely gradual. Aspects of technological change provide good examples. Daniel Bell's analysis of postindustrialism (Bell 1974) presents slow technological shifts as key causes of important political changes, a theme recently incorporated into significant work in comparative political economy (Iversen and Wren 1998; Iversen 2001). Similarly, a central causal argument in Robert Putnam's recent argument about declining social capital in the United States concerns the impact of television, which gradually became a more pervasive aspect of American popular culture over the past half-century (Putnam 2000). This change stems from two cumulative processes: the gradual spread of television, and the gradual replacement of earlier generations with those raised in a context where television was ubiquitous. Another important category of cumulative economic processes concerns shifts in relative prices, which often occur very gradually and may have enormous political consequences (Rogowski 1989; North 1990a).

Most of the cumulative causes that I have in mind, however, are "sociological" ones—important social conditions that change dramatically over extended periods of time but at a very slow pace. Demography is an excellent example. Migration, suburbanization, literacy rates (Deutsch 1961; Rokkan 1974; Ertman 1996), language and associated conceptions of nationhood (Gellner 1983), and basic cultural outlooks (Tarrow 1992) are all important social variables that typically change very slowly.

For political scientists, cumulative sociological processes are often linked to long-term shifts in electorates, including their partisan attachments. Key, for example, introduced the concept of "secular realignment"—a movement "from party to party that extends over several presidential elections and appears to be independent of the peculiar factors influencing the vote at individual elections" (Key 1959, p. 199). As Edward Carmines and James Stimson argue, secular realignments can be driven by "such essentially nonpolitical forces as differential birthrates between the party coalitions, interregional migration patterns, or economic-technological transformations" (Carmines and Stimson 1989, p. 143).

It would be hard to deny that contemporary political scientists typically relegate these types of processes to the background, essentially ignoring their potential impact on outcomes of interest. An analyst investigating a short time frame is likely to treat these incremental or cumulative variables as essentially fixed. If such incremental/cumulative factors are on an analyst's radar screen, however, it is possible to incorporate them in either quantitative or qualitative studies that examine longer time horizons. Thus it is crucial that analysts consider theoretical frames that draw attention to the potential impact of cumulative causes.

Threshold Effects

Theory-generated alertness is even more important with a second, closely related type of slow-moving causal process, one that involves *threshold effects*. In many cases, incremental or cumulative forces may not generate incremental changes in outcomes of interest. Instead, these processes have a modest or negligible impact until they reach some critical level, which triggers major changes. The earthquake example presented in the introduction is a clear instance of this kind of process. Another popular example from the physical sciences is the process leading up to an avalanche—a slow buildup of stress leading to a rapid "state change" once some critical level has been reached.

This is precisely the kind of account that Goldstone (1991) offers in his comparative analysis of revolutions. A slow-moving factor (demographic change) is a principal cause of a rapidly unfolding outcome (revolution). In presenting his argument, Goldstone observes that social analysts often have a strong bias against explanations with this kind of structure. "[T]hose tied to linear thinking about historical causation may . . . dismiss the role of population increase. Such increases, after all, were gradual and not enormously large. Events such as revolutions and rebellions are both large and sudden; their very nature seems to call for a different kind of explanation" (p. 32).[1]

[1]Goldstone notes another reason for thinking that the impact of slow-moving processes like demographic change often can be very significant. He points out (1991, p. 33) that population increases "have a particularly nonlinear effect on *marginal* groups—groups that face some sort of boundary conditions, such as peasants who are seeking to gain new lands, or younger sons of elite families who are seeking new elite positions." The social processes at work here are instances of what Fred Hirsch called "positional competition"—settings where the availability of some valued good is essentially fixed (Hirsch 1977). If the number of seats in a game of musical chairs is fixed, adding a few more players may alter the social dynamics dramatically. In Goldstone's demographic account, "increases in total population generally produce a much, much larger increase in marginal populations—that is, in those groups competing for some relatively scarce resource—than in the population as a whole" (1991, p. 33).

There is, however, no reason to exclude the possibility that such slow-moving variables may be tremendously important, even if we are trying to explain outcomes that emerge rapidly. Theorists now suggest that threshold models often make a good deal of sense. Such models have become prominent features in theoretical work on collective action (Granovetter 1978; Marwell and Oliver 1993), including analyses focused on both interest groups (e.g., Baumgartner and Jones 1993) and looser social movements (McAdam 1982) or collectivities such as language communities (Laitin 1998). More generally, threshold dynamics are likely to be prevalent in circumstances where actors face binary choices and where the choices they favor depend in part on their perception of what others are likely to do.

Granovetter's classic article actually invokes a more restricted argument than that suggested here. His focus is on the heterogeneity of *individual* preferences and the resulting differences in their personal thresholds for particular actions (e.g., "I will go to the demonstration if I expect q others to be there with me"). Granovetter's main point is that given significant heterogeneity of individual thresholds, it is possible to generate models in which very small shifts in the thresholds of even a single actor can generate big changes in collective behavior. By contrast, I am interested in collective thresholds, where once a social variable reaches a particular level, it triggers a big effect. The key point is that there are cut points, or tipping points, in many social processes that lead to nonlinearities (Schelling 1978). These processes could, but need not, involve the interplay of heterogeneous preferences that Granovetter has in mind.

Doug McAdam's *Political Process and the Development of Black Insurgency, 1930–1970* (1982) presents a powerful example of a threshold analysis of collective action. Unlike many who present threshold or "critical mass" arguments, however, McAdam is less interested in the striking dynamics that mark a tipping point than in the less dramatic processes that precede it. McAdam places great weight on the role of big, slow-moving processes in establishing the preconditions for successful black mobilization:

> The Montgomery bus boycott of 1955–56 . . . [and] the 1954 Supreme Court decision in the Brown case . . . were landmark events. Nonetheless, to single them out serves . . . to obscure the less dramatic but ultimately more significant historical trends that shaped the prospects for later insurgency. Especially critical . . . were several broad historical processes in the period from 1933 to 1954 that rendered the political establishment more vulnerable to black protest activity while also affording blacks the institutional strength to launch such a challenge. Later events such as the 1954 decision and the Montgomery bus boycott merely served as dramatic (though hardly insignificant) capstones to these processes. (p. 3)

At the heart of McAdam's analysis is the decline of the cotton economy in the quarter-century after 1925. This decline simultaneously diminished the strength of forces opposed to black insurgency and generated patterns of migration that boosted the organizational capacities (e.g., massive expansion of black churches, colleges, and southern chapters of the National Association for the Advancement of Colored People [NAACP]) of a long-oppressed minority. It was these gradual interconnected social processes that created conditions ripe for a set of triggering events.

Although threshold-style arguments have been particularly prominent in the study of collective action, there are good reasons to expect this type of dynamic to be prevalent when social variables of the slow-moving sort operate in established institutional or organizational settings. As I have argued in the preceding chapters, many existing social arrangements are likely to exhibit strongly inertial qualities. These tendencies toward persistence imply that pressures will often build up for some time without generating immediate effects. When some critical level is reached, however, actors may reassess their options or expectations about others' likely actions, leading to relatively rapid change. Change in one institution, furthermore, may quickly undermine others (Baumgartner and Jones 1993). The dynamic of rapid change at this point is similar to those that Granovetter and Schelling outline. Such an analysis may, however, emphasize the long, slow-moving buildup of pressure, rather than the trigger itself or the way in which the ensuing tipping process plays out.

It is worth stressing that the path-dependent or self-reinforcing processes discussed in preceding chapters are all based on threshold models—relatively small movements can push above some critical level, triggering a process of positive feedback that leads to much more dramatic (nonlinear) change. It is important to keep the two arguments distinct, because path-dependent processes need not involve the long, slow buildup of pressure suggested in a model like McAdam's. Invoking a path-dependent process implies nothing about the time horizons of the causal factors that initiate positive feedback. I return to this issue later in this chapter.

Claims about threshold effects play an important role, for example, in Huber and Stephens's analysis of the centrality of *long-term* control of government for explaining welfare state outcomes in advanced industrial societies (Huber and Stephens 2001). In outlining the roots of Social Democratic hegemony in Scandinavia, for instance, they stress that a single election result is unlikely to have a big effect on previously well-institutionalized arrangements. On the other hand, electoral success *over an extended period of time* leads to significant changes, including shifts in the expectations of social actors. At some point, these actors begin to recognize that there is a new status quo, and they adjust their policy preferences to accommodate the new environment. By doing so, they help to propel coordination around these new expectations, reinforcing the new regime.

Similar arguments about threshold effects are central to the critical realignment theories that have played such a prominent role in the study of American electoral politics (Burnham 1970; Brady 1988). David Mayhew has summarized

this line of argument (the quotations in the following passage are from Burnham 1970):

> In brief, what happens in Burnham's account is that political "stress" or
> "tension" build up following the last electoral realignment until they "es-
> calate to a flash point" or a "boiling point," at which time a "triggering
> event" brings on an electoral realignment. . . . To put it more elaborately,
> there exists a "dynamic, even dialectic polarization between long-term in-
> ertia and concentrated bursts of change. . . ." Ordinarily, American institu-
> tions tend toward "underproduction of other than currently 'normal' policy
> outputs. They may tend persistently to ignore, and hence not to aggregate,
> emergent political demand of a mass character until a boiling point of
> some kind is reached." (Mayhew 2002, pp. 17–18)

Mayhew, I should emphasize, is quite critical of this account of American electoral politics. Indeed, he maintains that short-run processes are often of greater
causal significance than realignment theory allows. According to Mayhew, the
"genre's model of stress buildup . . . [has] a tendency to elongate political trou-
bles backwards in time without warrant" (Mayhew 2000, p. 24; cf. Bartels 1998).
He rightly highlights the need to provide evidence for such a gradual buildup of
stress, as well as the need to consider the possibility that short-term processes are
adequate to generate such flashpoints.

Another possible danger of such arguments is that they can present an overly
deterministic picture of social processes. References to a boiling point or threshold can suggest, as McAdam notes, that "[m]ovement emergence is . . . analogous to, and as inexorable as, the process by which water boils" (1982, p. 9). Yet
these models can also be substantially more subtle in the way they combine
long-term and short-term processes. Consider figure 3.1, which looks at the
movement of a particular social variable (say, the organizational resources of a
disadvantaged group) as it approaches a threshold level that triggers a social
movement. During time periods T_1 to T_3 there are fluctuations, but there is also
a gradual trend, resulting from various slow-moving processes, toward the
threshold level that triggers the outcome of interest. As that threshold level is ap-
proached in period T_4, particular fluctuations above the trend line become increasingly likely to act as triggers. An analyst could treat the sources of these
fluctuations as essentially random (Macy 1990). Alternatively, she could seek to
explain these fluctuations as well—which is what McAdam does in his study of
black insurgency. What distinguishes a threshold model of this kind, however, is
that it would not analyze the sources of fluctuations within period T_4 except in
combination with an analysis of the preceding long-term processes that create a
context where these fluctuations can have a major impact.

Particular claims about the role of thresholds in specific contexts must be established with care. Even a critical analyst like Mayhew, however, agrees that such

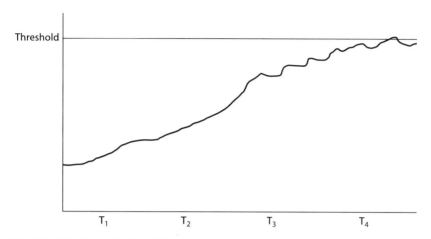

Fig. 3.1. A basic threshold model.

arguments sometimes present a plausible model of social reality that requires attentiveness to significant stretches of time. In this respect, Mayhew's views are in line with considerable theoretical work, as well as substantial empirical research on social movements, institutional change, and regime breakdowns.

Causal Chains

We often think of causal processes involving a straightforward connection where *x* directly yields *y*. Yet in many cases, as I noted in the last chapter, the story runs more like the following: "*x* initiates the sequence *a, b, c*, which yields *y*" (Mahoney 2000). If *a, b,* and *c* take some time to work themselves out, there is likely to be a substantial lag between *x* and *y*. Collier and Collier's influential work on labor incorporation in Latin America presents arguments of this kind, in which the ultimate outcomes of interest reflect a sequence of key developments over extended periods of time (Collier and Collier 1991). As was discussed in the introduction, Daniel Carpenter effectively develops a causal chain argument in his exploration of the roots of bureaucratic autonomy in the United States (Carpenter 2001). This type of claim about long-term, multistage causal processes is often invoked in work on state building (Flora 1999a, 1999b) or democratization (Luebbert 1991; Collier 1999).

Swank (2001) offers a particularly instructive example. In assessing the impact of political institutions on welfare state retrenchment, he criticizes the conventional view that fragmented institutions will be associated with limited cutbacks in social programs. This view holds that institutional fragmentation restricts social policy change by increasing the number of veto points available to defenders of the status quo. Swank accepts that this is true as far as it goes. He notes, however, that the causal chain of long-term indirect effects of institutional fragmentation *runs in the other direction*. Not only does institutional fragmentation limit the initial expansion of the welfare state, but it also reinforces social heterogeneity, inhibits the growth of encompassing interest groups, and weakens cultural commitments to universalism. All of these long-term effects strengthen the welfare state's opponents and weaken its advocates. In short, Swank argues, many of the most important effects of institutional fragmentation work themselves out only indirectly and over extended periods of time. Seeking to analyze the effects of institutions while holding other variables constant, many analysts failed to see that the values of these other variables were themselves in part the long-term consequences of institutional structures. Quadrant I investigations are therefore likely to systematically misinterpret the impact of institutional structures on the contemporary politics of the welfare state.

In assessing the extent and sources of welfare state retrenchment I have advanced a similar causal chain argument (Pierson 1994). To gauge the impact of conservative governments on the welfare state, simply examining their direct efforts to cut social programs ("programmatic retrenchment") is insufficient. Instead, one has to consider the possibility that reforms (e.g., efforts to curtail the flow of tax revenues) will trigger particular causal chains that facilitate program cutbacks later in a sequence ("systemic retrenchment"). In such a case, a conservative government's main impact on the welfare state might be felt a decade or more after it had left office.

Causal chain arguments are typically utilized when key institutional, policy, or organizational outcomes lie some distance in time from initial points of crucial political choice. They are often especially promising in contexts where political actions have *multiple* consequences, and major long-term outcomes are by-products rather than the principal focus of intended actions. Under such circumstances, analysts are easily misled by a focus on the most immediate, highly visible, and clearly intended consequences (Jervis 1997). Yet, as my analysis of conservative retrenchment initiatives shows, causal chain arguments may also focus on intentional, but indirect, strategies that play out only through a sequence of developments over time.

Causal chain arguments raise some tricky issues. A key challenge is to show that the links in such chains are strong ones ("tightly coupled," as Mahoney 2000 puts it). The persuasiveness of a causal chain argument declines quickly if there are many stages or if the probabilities associated with any particular stage are not very high (Fearon 1996; Lieberson 1997). Even if a chain has only three links, and the probability that each link will hold is 80 percent, there is less than a fifty-fifty chance that the entire chain will operate. Thus these arguments are likely to be persuasive only when the chains invoked have a very small number of links and we have solid theoretical or empirical grounds for believing that the links are quite strong.

As suggested in my discussion of the meteorite example, arguments based on causal chains also face an infinite regress problem—what Pascal famously discussed as the Cleopatra's nose problem (Fearon 1996): there is always some earlier link in the chain, so what is to keep one from endlessly seeking that earlier stage? There are three reasonable ways to answer this question. First, analysts may choose to break the chain at "critical junctures" that mark a point at which their cases begin to diverge in significant ways (Mahoney 2001, pp. 7–8). This is the strategy employed by the Colliers, for instance. Second, analysts may break the chain at the point where causal connections become difficult to pin down. If the persuasiveness of arguments about causal chains depends on the demonstration of relatively tight coupling among the links, it makes sense to end the chains where such linkages cannot be firmly established.

The third and perhaps most instructive response for current purposes is to delimit the ends of the causal chain on the basis of the theoretical interests of the analyst. Thus, a sociologist interested in demography might deal with long-term processes that overlap with those of interest to a political scientist. Yet each would investigate a somewhat different causal chain. Consider the following example. Iran has recently undergone significant social turmoil associated with a population boom, triggering overcrowding in schools, the emergence of a large cohort of underemployed young men, and a host of related problems (Hoodfar and Assadpour 2000). This demographic bulge stems partly from strong pro-natalist policies adopted following the 1979 revolution. One result of the current strains has been a striking policy reversal. Iran has now introduced policies facilitating family planning and birth control—the most extensive in the Muslim world (Aghajanian and Merhyar 1999). This example thus involves a set of developments, involving a long-term causal chain, which is of considerable interest to both political scientists and demographers. However, the demographer's chain would probably end with the demographic boom itself (or the more recent rapid decline in fertility rates) and might begin with some other sociological variables (e.g., social responses to the initial set of pro-natalist policies). A political scientist would be most likely to begin and/or end with *political* phenomena: the revolution or pro-natalist policies at the outset, and the social unrest or new family-planning policies at the end of the chain. This example illustrates how the temporal structure of causal accounts depends to a considerable extent on the analyst's intellectual concerns as well as the basic theoretical framework employed. These shape the fashioning of key outcomes to be considered, the time frame covered by the analysis, and the hypotheses that are explored.

All three of these classes of argumentation about causal processes—claims about cumulative processes, threshold effects, and causal chains—require the analyst to gravitate away from Quadrant I. Each raises distinct methodological challenges. Each line of argument is likely to be visible only if an analyst's research design and methods are open to the possibility that such long-term processes are causally significant. There are strong theoretical grounds for believing that each process characterizes a substantial range of social phenomena. Yet this is only part of the story. When we turn to the consideration of outcomes, we also confront considerable temporal diversity.

SLOW-MOVING OUTCOMES

Slow-moving outcomes are ones with long time horizons—that is, processes where meaningful change in the dependent variable occurs only over the long run. Many outcomes of great interest to social scientists take a long time to unfold. The main category of such processes in the social sciences mirrors that in the earlier discussion of cumulative or incremental causes. Just as causes may have a slow, cumulative quality, the same may be true of the outcomes of interest to social scientists. For instance, if a sociologist were seeking to *explain* any of the slow-moving sociological variables discussed in the first part, they would be exploring just such a cumulative outcome. If some factors introduce a shift in, say, birthrates, the impact on population will be realized only over a very extended period of time.

In similar fashion, political outcomes may have a slow-moving, cumulative structure. This will often be the case, for example, if the principal causal mechanism involved is one of *replacement*. Because individual partisan attachments reveal considerable inertia, for instance, when environmental change occurs it usually has its most powerful effects on new voters. Partisan realignment therefore often works through the extremely gradual replacement of political generations, as old members die off and are replaced with new ones who lack the old attachments. Arguments about generational turnover, for example, focus on the exposure of particular age groups to stimuli that have enduring consequences (Mannheim 1952; Putnam 2000). Slow-moving outcomes result from the changing distribution of these generations in the general population over time.

This mechanism of replacement is applicable in a variety of contexts, suggesting a central reason why many political outcomes have a very slow-moving quality. Consider the case of political elites. If occupants of elite positions possess resources that allow them to defend their positions against challenges, major changes in elite composition will often operate through slow-moving processes of replacement. In the U.S. Congress, for instance, incumbents possess tremendous advantages. Incumbent members of Congress are rarely voted out of office. The main mechanism of elite-level restructuring is instead replacement: when particular politicians retire or die, they are succeeded by politicians who better match the current social environment. Thus, even a major change in the fortunes of particular categories of politicians (e.g., declining prospects for moderate Republicans in the Northeast and for Democrats of all stripes in the South after 1960) may take decades to work itself out.

As this language suggests, such arguments may be grounded in theories of evolutionary processes, which posit a selection mechanism operating over extended periods of time (Spruyt 1994; Nelson 1995; Kahler 1999). Firms, politicians, and nation-states may pursue many goals and employ many strategies, but social scientists often argue that over time those pursuing particular goals and employing particular strategies are more likely to survive. Similar analyses are very common in sociology, where there is a robust research program in the field of organizational ecology. Such analyses, with their focus on long-term patterns of birth and death in fairly large populations, have led to the development of distinctive methodological and theoretical strategies (Hannan and Freeman 1989; Carroll and Hannan 2000).

Cumulative outcomes may also be evident in the development of public policy (Rose and Davies 1994). Public expenditure on income transfers, for instance, is an incremental, slowly unfolding outcome of earlier policy choices (Steuerle and Kawai 1996). This is highly relevant for many contemporary studies in political economy, because a great deal of the growth in public expenditure since 1975 reflects these lagged policy commitments rather than the introduction of new, more generous policies. Consider the case of pensions policy.[2] Public pensions account for roughly 40 percent of expenditures on social protection and thus are deeply implicated in the current budgetary stress affecting advanced welfare states. In this policy area there are often *very* long time lags between the enactment of a policy and the realization of its major public expenditure implications. In the case of contributory pensions, it may be *seventy years*—the time it takes for the bulk of the pensioner population to be composed of those who had a full working career under new rules—before policy choices are fully reflected in ongoing expenditures.

Failure to recognize the extent to which public policy outcomes are cumulative and slow moving can easily lead social scientists astray. Presuming that policy changes are quickly translated into expenditure levels (that is, assuming rapidly unfolding outcomes), analysts may mistakenly construct temporally constricted causal accounts. Notably, they may attribute policy changes (inferred from rising spending levels) to social developments (e.g., globalization) that in fact occurred *after* those policy changes took place.

As in the earlier example of elite turnover, this public policy outcome is slow-moving because it operates through a mechanism of replacement. Only cohorts who enter the labor market after the policy change will work their whole lives under the new rules. Thus, it is not until these new workers have completely replaced older workers within the population of pensioners that the new policy's full expenditure implications will be realized. Unlike many arguments based on replacement, this one is not evolutionary in the sense of employing a "selection mechanism" that determines "fitness." Rather, like the generational turnover arguments discussed earlier, it emphasizes that different cohorts will be exposed to different stimuli—which may produce major social effects as these cohorts

---

[2] I draw here on a longer discussion in Pierson 2000. See also Huber and Stephens (2001).

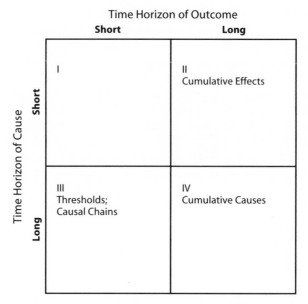

Fig. 3.2. Time horizons in different social science accounts.

move through the life-course. Slow-moving outcomes based on cohort replacement are likely to call for quite different theoretical and methodological strategies
than those based on competitive selection—differences apparent, for instance, in
the distinct analyses of Putnam's study of social capital and generational turnover
and the work of Hannan and others on organizational ecology.

Figure 3.2 summarizes the argument presented so far by overlaying the analysis on the framework presented in table 3.1. It suggests that, as is the case in the
physical sciences, not all processes of interest to social scientists are likely to fit
comfortably in Quadrant I. Many causes and outcomes have long time horizons. Causal chain and threshold arguments invoke independent variables with
long time horizons. Arguments about cumulative effects, by definition, refer to
dependent variables with long time horizons. Arguments about cumulative causes,
unlike threshold arguments, involve linear transformations in which a little
more of (slow-moving) x produces a little more of (slow-moving) y. Thus, cumulative cause arguments imply long time horizons for *both* causes and outcomes.

MOVING BEYOND THE FOCUS ON TIME HORIZONS

So far, I have stressed that social scientists may need to look at extended periods
of time because they wish to consider the role of factors that change only very
gradually. In essence, this argument suggests the need for social scientists to be

attentive to the Braudelian focus on the *longue durée*. Yet there are additional aspects of social processes that may also be missed by a focus on the short term—namely, those in which there is a considerable separation in time between the onset of a cause and the emergence of the main effect. This *temporal separation* is evident in two types of processes that figure prominently in comparative historical analyses: structural explanations and path-dependent explanations.

Structural Determination

Structural accounts constitute a prominent class of arguments about long-term outcomes. Key causal claims are based on the existence of certain broad structures or relationships among structures. Typically, these arguments claim a causal connection between structures and eventual outcomes but are agnostic on issues of timing (Rueschemeyer, Stephens, and Stephens 1992; Skocpol 1979). In these accounts, triggering events are seen as essentially random or incidental to the core causal processes at work. In this respect, they resemble the threshold arguments discussed previously. They differ in that structural arguments need not rely on the gradual buildup of pressures over time. In other words, neither causes nor outcomes need be slow moving. Outcomes, however, may occur at a considerable temporal distance from the appearance of the central cause.

The difference can be seen by contrasting figure 3.3 with figure 3.1's summary of threshold arguments. In figure 3.3, a structural cause (say, the creation of a new institution or the formation of a new alliance) is introduced in Period 3. This moves the pressure on the status quo to a new, much higher level—very close to the threshold level for major political change. From here it is only a matter of time (in this case, until Period 4) before some triggering event precipitates the outcome of interest.

Barrington Moore's account of the origins of dictatorship and democracy offers a classic example of a structural account (Moore 1966). He focuses on macrosocial variables that predispose countries to different regime outcomes. Given particular values of the structural variables, Moore expects certain outcomes to be realized sooner or later. For Moore, triggering events are essentially superficial and should not distract one's attention from the basic causal processes at work.

Structural accounts of social processes can be formalized as instances of "absorbing Markov chains," and a brief explication may clarify the logic of this kind of argument. Over a given period, there is some probability that particular entities (Xs) will be transformed into different entities (Ys) (Stinchcombe 1974; Elster 1983). These processes differ from the causal chains discussed previously. In many cases they involve a single transformation ($x \rightarrow y$) rather than a series with several links. In Markov chains, however, the transformations over any particular time period are probabilistic. In fact, the probability of such a shift in any short

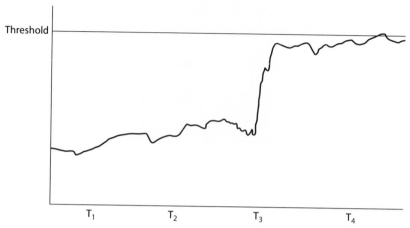

Fig. 3.3. A threshold model with a structural cause.

period may be fairly low. As a result, it is hard to know where things will stand at any particular point in time. There is, however, an attractor (in this case Y). Xs turn into Ys, but Ys don't turn into Xs. Over the long term, the system in question converges on a single outcome.

Cameron (2000) uses the metaphor of a frog hopping from lily pad to lily pad in a pond where one lily pad is coated with superglue. We do not know when the frog will come to a halt on the superglue pad, and it may take quite a long time, but the eventual outcome is fully determined. Nor do such arguments require the strong claim that Ys never turn into Xs. If the probability of x → y transformations is considerably higher than the probability of y → x transformations, we will eventually end up with a population made up almost entirely of Ys.

While this may seem like a fairly artificial construction, it captures the kinds of arguments about causal processes that social scientists often make or should want to make (Lieberson 1985). Przeworski and Limongi (1997), for instance, make an argument of this sort in their analysis of democratization. Once countries reach a certain level of economic development, there is a significant probability that authoritarian governments will turn into democracies but very little chance of transformations in the opposite direction. Over time, we would expect to see fewer and fewer authoritarian governments above that economic threshold level. This structural variable would not, however, explain the timing of particular transitions.

This kind of process suggests the possibility of a substantial temporal lag between the key causal process and the eventual outcome. The "cause" in this case is the structure that generates an absorbing Markov chain dynamic. The chain may take some time to play out, with various quirks influencing the tempo and the particular path taken. The ultimate outcome, however, is not affected by those quirks. The core insight is that temporally constricted analyses may lead to a preoccupation with surface phenomena, while deeper and more fundamental causes are missed.

Path-Dependent or Positive Feedback Processes

As discussed in the previous chapters, a frequent claim in social analysis is that outcomes at a critical juncture induce path-dependent processes. Over time, these processes lead to strikingly divergent outcomes, even from initially similar conditions. In these cases, a fairly modest change induces a feedback loop, which reinforces the initial direction of change. Collective action, for instance, may lead to shifts in expectations and resources that facilitate more collective action; similarly, institutionalization may ease problems of coordination and therefore foster more institutionalization.[3]

A path-dependent causal account employs a particular temporal structure. It highlights the role of what Arthur Stinchcombe has termed "historical causation," in which dynamics triggered by an event or process at one point in time reproduce and reinforce themselves even in the absence of the recurrence of the original event or process (Stinchcombe 1968). Thus, the full outcome of interest may emerge at a considerable distance in time from the critical juncture or "historical cause" because these self-reinforcing processes require substantial time to play out. One could categorize this type of argument as involving a slow-moving cause (with the self-reinforcing processes constituting part of the cause of the eventual outcome to be considered).[4] Treating this as a long-term process involving temporal separation, however, emphasizes the key point of arguments about historical causation. An event or a process may be crucially linked to later outcomes, even if it occurs only once and has ceased to operate long before that final outcome occurs (Lieberson 1985).

As with many of the long-term processes considered here, there are also strong theoretical grounds for believing that path-dependent processes will be prevalent in political life. I have already explored why specific patterns of political mobilization, the institutional "rules of the game," and even citizens' basic ways of thinking about the political world will often generate self-reinforcing dynamics. As noted in previous chapters, arguments with this sort of structure are now widespread in comparative historical work, underpinning such analyses as Shefter's argument about the impact of initial patterns of party mobilization (Shefter 1977), North's analysis of the institutional foundations for economic

---

[3]This suggests another reason why such processes cannot easily be reduced to the dimensions introduced in table 3.1 and figure 3.2. As feedback loops become central to the process that follows a critical juncture, it becomes impossible to delineate clear causes and effects; instead, a set of factors mutually reinforce one another.

[4]This explains the way in which I categorize the time horizons of path-dependent processes in table 3.3.

growth (North 1990a), and Wuthnow's explanation of the rise of modern ideologies (Wuthnow 1989).

Carmines and Stimson's study of "issue evolution" in the U.S. polity investigates
a very different empirical setting, but the analytical structure of their argument is
similar (Carmines and Stimson 1989). Carmines and Stimson are seeking to explain a momentous change in postwar American politics—the shift in the "issue
environment" from one in which the two major parties (and their supporters)
were internally heterogeneous on racial matters to one in which internally homogeneous parties generated far greater partisan polarization around race. They
criticize realignment theory for suggesting a far too rapid "earthquake"-style
change in this outcome. Instead, their analysis stresses a critical juncture of elections (especially 1964 but also 1968) that creates initial partisan differences on
race, followed by a protracted period in which differences in recruitment at both
the mass and elite levels amplify that initial difference. The major political outcome they are interested in develops over the long term: "The initial increase in
mass issue polarization does not complete the process but only begins it by setting
in motion a change that grows over time" (Carmines and Stimson 1989, p. 157).[5]

Thus, social processes may not only be slow moving; they may also take a long
time because of significant temporal separations between a key cause and the outcome of interest. In either case, the full process may not be visible unless the analysis considers a very substantial stretch of time. My discussion of these different
long-term processes is summarized in table 3.2. It highlights a number of distinct
social processes that include at least one of the following features: causal processes
with long time horizons, outcomes with long time horizons, or significant temporal separation between key causes and the outcome of ultimate interest.[6] As
the scholarly literature reviewed in this chapter suggests, the different types of
processes distinguished in table 3.2 encompass a range of arguments that can be
and have been used to illuminate issues of lasting interest to social scientists.

PACKING POLITICS INTO QUADRANT I

How long a time frame should analysts employ in studying social phenomena?
There is no fixed answer to this question. Instead, it depends on the particular
problems that analysts hope to tackle, their assumptions about the nature of the

---

[5]Carmines and Stimson emphasize generational replacement as well as positive feedback in the
growth of partisan differences over time. Thus they combine arguments about cumulative outcomes
and path dependence in explaining their long-term outcome.
[6]It should be emphasized that table 3.2 highlights features of processes that *logically require* examination of extended stretches of time. Other features of these arguments may or may not also call for
attention to long-term processes. Path-dependent arguments, for example, need not rely on a slow-
moving cause to explain the initial event (critical juncture) that triggers a process of positive feedback. In actual applications, however, they often do so.

TABLE 3.2
Categorizing Long-Term Processes

Category	Time Horizons	Temporal Separation	Examples
Cumulative causes	*Long* (causes) *Long* (outcomes)	No	Key; Putnam
Causal chains	*Long* (causes) Short (outcomes)	No	Collier and Collier; Swank
Threshold effects	*Long* (causes) Short (outcomes)	No	Burnham; Goldstone; McAdam
Cumulative outcomes	Short (causes) *Long* (outcomes)	No	Spruyt; Steurle and Kawai
Structural effects (Markov chains)	Short (causes) Short (outcomes)	*Yes*	Moore; Przeworski and Limongi
Path dependence (positive feedback)	Short (for "historical cause") *Long* (for self-reinforcing process)	*Yes* (for "historical cause")	Ertman; Shefter; Carmines and Stimson

Note: *Italics* indicate that a feature logically implies the need to analyze significant stretches of time.

most important processes that might be at work in the area they are studying, and judgments about the feasibility of particular ways of proceeding. As David Lake and Robert Powell have argued, "Methodological approaches, by their very nature, privilege some forms of explanation over others and are, in effect, bets about what will prove to be fruitful ways to attack certain sets of problems" (Lake and Powell 1999, p. 16).

Social scientists are currently placing their bets very heavily on Quadrant I.[7] Just how heavily is suggested by table 3.3, which situates political science research published from 1996 to 2000 in four leading political science journals (*American Political Science Review, American Journal of Political Science, Comparative Politics,* and *World Politics*) within the four quadrants.[8] Of the articles

[7] Although I have argued that the key temporal dimensions of social processes cannot be reduced to the simple typology offered in table 3.1, I use "Quadrant I" as a convenient shorthand reference for studies that are not designed to explore processes that unfold over substantial stretches of time.

[8] Just under one-quarter of the articles were nonclassifiable because they did not focus on a particular causal argument (e.g., political theory articles, replications, discussions of statistical techniques, review articles). An additional 5 percent were "mixed cases" that could not be categorized in a single quadrant—typically because the arguments involved multiple independent or dependent variables with different time horizons. Because of the amount of interpretation required in making the assessments of articles, these results should be seen as suggestive rather than definitive. Details are available from the author upon request. I am grateful to Fiona Barker for her work in compiling and evaluating this data.

TABLE 3.3
Time Horizons in Major Political Science Journals, 1996–2000
(% of articles)

Journal	I	II	III	IV	Mixed	Non-Classifiable
American Political Science Review (n=197)	51.8	4.1	4.1	8.1	2.0	30.0
American Journal of Political Science (n=258)	56.6	3.1	0.0	10.5	2.7	27.1
Comparative Politics (n=98)	49.0	11.2	11.2	9.2	14.3	5.1
World Politics (n=78)	24.4	6.4	14.1	21.8	11.6	21.8
Total (n=631)	49.9	5.1	4.8	10.9	5.4	23.4

making a clear empirical argument where it was possible to assess whether key causes and effects were short or long-term, two-thirds could be categorized as belonging in Quadrant I.

My argument is not that Quadrant I research is of little value. Rather, it is that there is a strong case for diversifying our bets. Choices about the scope of time covered in a particular analysis have profound effects. They lead to substantial shifts in the kinds of theories we employ, the methods we use, the kinds of causal forces we are likely to see at work, and even the very outcomes of interest that we come to identify in the first place. For a social science community largely confined to Quadrant I, a great deal of social life is simply off the radar screen.

Political scientists have not always shown such a decided preference for investigations focused on Quadrant I. From the 1950s through the 1970s, the field of comparative politics was strongly animated by issues of modernization and state building that involved the investigation of precisely the kinds of big, long-term processes discussed here (Deutsch 1961; Huntington 1968; Nordlinger 1968; Flora 1999a). As is well known, much of the modernization literature—or at least a caricature of it—came under attack for exhibiting a rather complacent functionalist and teleological bent that suggested eventual convergence on the model of Western democracies. Yet the collapse of the modernization literature is a clear case of throwing out the baby with the bathwater. The discipline jettisoned an undesirable functionalism and teleology (which, ironically, has often reappeared in a new rationalistic form). Along with it went the discipline's most sustained efforts to think about long-term processes of social and political change.

As the examples considered in this chapter attest, attention to big, long-term processes has remained alive in fields where comparative macrohistorical inquiry has gained a strong foothold, including work on democratization, revolutions, and the development of the welfare state. Yet a number of trends seem to have pushed comparative inquiry toward a focus on short-term processes. One has been the increasing prevalence of statistical analyses using the techniques of multiple regression. I hasten to emphasize that quantitative analyses are by no means incompatible with attentiveness to long-term, slow-moving features of social life. Indeed, they can be well suited to identifying the role of such factors. Some structural arguments, for instance, are easily incorporated in large-N analyses, and well-designed quantitative studies can test for threshold effects as well. Yet in practice, one often finds that the priority on generating high correlations privileges "shallow" (temporally proximate but often near-tautological) accounts over "deep" ones (Rueschemeyer, Stephens, and Stephens 1992; Lieberson 1997; Kitschelt 2003).

A more fundamental problem is that many of the long-term processes outlined here, such as those invoking threshold arguments or multistage causal chains, are unlikely to be incorporated in quantitative studies unless the *theories* that analysts employ point them in this direction. The question, after all, is not just hypothetical capabilities, but how techniques are actually used in practice (Jepperson 1996). Indeed, much in contemporary social science leads precisely in the opposite direction. Jon Elster, among others, has drawn on Hume's insistence that there can be "no action at a distance" to argue forcefully that causal analysis should always strive to identify "local" causes—the more micro, the better (Elster 1983; Hedstrom and Swedberg 1998). For Elster, the drive to identify social mechanisms is precisely a matter of bringing causes as close as possible in time to the outcome to be explained: "The role of mechanisms is twofold. First, they enable us to go from the larger to the smaller: from molecules to atoms, from societies to individuals. Second, and more fundamentally, they reduce the time lag between explanans and explanandum. A mechanism provides a continuous and contiguous chain of causal or intentional links" (Elster 1983, p. 24). It must be stressed, however, that the reasonable desire to create a contiguous chain of causal links up to the present is only one priority, that it runs the risk of pointing us toward the banal or near-tautological, and that it should not come at the price of pushing important dimensions of social processes out of the scope of causal argument.

Probably more important in generating a shift toward Quadrant I accounts, at least among political scientists, has been the increasing prevalence of rational choice analyses. As discussed in Chapter Two, starting from the choices of individuals (or social aggregates treated as strategic actors) strongly encourages the analyst to truncate the investigation in various respects, including the crucial dimension of time. Game-theoretic approaches do not easily stretch over extended spaces (to broad social aggregates) or long time periods without rendering key assumptions of the models implausible.[9]

---

[9]See, for instance, Elster's (2000) forceful critique of the stretching entailed in the recent *Analytic Narratives* volume's application of game theory to macrohistorical phenomena. Elster (1989), Scharpf (1998), and Munck (2001) explore related issues.

It is not that rational choice theory, or even game theory, is simply incompatible with the examination of long-term processes (North 1990a; Axelrod 1997).
"Comparative statics," for instance, offers one way to address some of these liabilities. Here, a game-theoretic model is run with different parameters, allowing
the analyst to ask what happens if a structural variable (such as the age distribution of a population) undergoes a major shift (Weingast 1998). While helpful,
this seems at best to be a very partial solution. It appears capable of addressing at
most a few of the long-term processes discussed in this chapter, and even those
in a quite restricted manner. And of course, as suggested previously, analysts
would need to be thinking along these lines in the first place. Rational choice
imagery, focused on the strategic behavior of actors, may not be the most promising way to generate this type of thinking.

Rational choice theory may contribute to the temporal constriction of analyses in comparative politics in a less direct manner as well. Scholars employing
this approach typically turn to economics for inspiration. This orientation is
likely to make a big difference when it comes to carrying out research. In practice, there appear to be strong elective affinities between the basic theoretical
imageries analysts employ and the hypotheses they choose to evaluate. I have argued that many of the strongest candidates for big, slow-moving causal accounts
are likely to be sociological. Even if in principle some of these processes could
be incorporated into rational choice explanations, they are not the kinds of hypotheses that these analysts typically go looking for.

The pull of Quadrant I is evident not only in quantitative and rational choice
investigations. Qualitative analysts are also likely to gravitate to Quadrant I
unless they make a conscious effort to explore other possibilities. Writing in a
slightly different context, Rueschemeyer et al. (1992, pp. 32–33) summarize the
key problem:

> Studying change within the same society implicitly holds constant those
> structural features of the situation that do not actually change during
> the period of observation. It is for this reason that process-oriented histori-
> cal studies—even if they transcend sheer narrative and are conducted
> with theoretical, explanatory intent—often emphasize the role of volun-
> tary decision and tend to play down—by taking them as givens—structural
> constraints that limit some options of historical actors and encourage
> others.

By adding comparative cases, an analyst may be able to overcome some of the
blind spots associated with structural factors that concern Rueschemeyer et al.
Doing so is unlikely to address the problem of identifying the specific impact of
slow-moving causal processes, however, unless the investigation not only covers
additional cases but also takes in an extended period of time for each of those
cases. As noted previously, this problem appears to mar many recent investigations of transitions to democracy. Even those not grounded in game theory have

often advanced highly voluntaristic or nearly tautological explanations (Kitschelt 2003).

Comparative historical analyses will often do a good job of capturing long-term processes, as suggested by the numerous examples cited in this chapter. These investigations typically examine considerable stretches of time. Equally important, they draw on theoretical traditions, stretching back to the great works of Marx and Weber, which point to hypotheses with this sort of temporal structure. Yet like other methodologies, comparative historical analyses are likely to miss causes and outcomes that are visible only over the long term unless the investigator is sensitive to the need to consider such possibilities in the first place.[10] And, as studies such as Carpenter's demonstrate, the potential for synergies between small-N and quantitative methods for examining such slow-moving processes are likely to be considerable.

Consider Carmines and Stimson's reflections on their efforts to introduce a long-term perspective into the study of American public opinion and elections. Their conclusion provides a telling summary of the core points of this chapter and is worth quoting at length:

> For an evolving process one expects gradual but cumulative changes, so slight at any one time as to appear trivial but capable over the long haul of producing profound transformations. That is what we saw. . . . Consider this evidence in another light, not as a pattern of systematic movement over almost fifty years but as one slice in time (or even fifty separate slices). If this same evidence were decomposed in this fashion—if the question, that is, were subtly changed from how much change does this process produce? to how much of the observed change in a particular variable in a given year is attributable to the process in question?—then inferences drawn by a reasonable analyst would have a strikingly different character. In few cases would the effects in any given year be notable. Only a few would be statistically significant. . . . We would have concluded from such a perspective, indeed the literature on American mass behavior has concluded, that racial changes were crucially important for a few years in the mid-1960s, not very much before or since, and that the issue mattered then, not before and not after. That conclusion would be an appropriate reading of the cross-sectional evidence and, we believe, a profoundly mistaken reading of reality. (Carmines and Stimson 1989, p. 196)

The crowding of researchers into Quadrant I comes at a heavy price. In some cases, the price is that important social outcomes fail to attract significant scholarly

[10]Thus, my argument here points to some difficulties for the recent suggestion that improved process tracing represents an important element in more rigorous qualitative analysis (Bennett and George 2004; Hall 2003). This is an important suggestion, which I return to in the conclusion, but if process tracing is taken to mean the exploration of more micro mechanisms within causal processes, it may have the unintended effect of generating more temporally constricted accounts.

attention. In others, it is that major social forces do not figure into our causal accounts of political life simply because those forces exert their pressures over extended periods of time. Instead, causality is attributed to those factors that operate as triggers—factors that are temporally proximate to outcomes of interest but of relatively minor significance.

The connection between "triggers" and "deeper," more long-term causes suggests that seemingly rival explanations may often be complementary. There may be considerable advantages to combining work in different quadrants. Quadrant I analyses may focus on entrepreneurs who act as catalysts, or strategic interactions that influence the timing or specific outcomes that occur. Long-term investigations can reveal the circumstances that make particular opportunities available, or shape the actors, their preferences, and the payoff structures they confront. Research on transitions to democracy, for instance, may provide opportunities for fruitful combinations. Scholarship based on elite bargaining models (O'Donnell and Schmitter 1986; Przeworski 1991) has, as Charles Tilly puts it, "accelerated the tempo so that at times the transition to democracy looks almost instantaneous: put the pact in gear and go" (Tilly 1995, p. 365). Work outside Quadrant I can give some needed depth to these transition arguments by saying something about the origins of these elite actors and the constraints that factors such as the degree of mobilization put on their negotiations (Collier 1999; Rueschemeyer, Stephens, and Stephens 1992). A number of scholars have begun to explore the prospects for combining the shorter time frames of the "transitology" literature with more structural, long-term influences on patterns of democratization (Huntington 1991; Haggard and Kaufman 1995; Mahoney 2003, pp. 159–63; Mahoney and Snyder 1999).

Yet the accounts generated from alternative temporal frameworks may be competitive as well. In some settings, analysts can be misled about the very character of the outcomes they investigate because they fail to recognize how slowly those outcomes unfold. In others, a focus on correlations at a moment in time can lead to mistaken claims about causation. As Swank's and Carpenter's research shows, it can even lead analysts to highlight claims about short-term causal effects when the long-term causal processes run exactly counter to them. Typically this is because they infer that the actors who appear to possess the greatest political resources at that moment are responsible for outcomes observed at that moment (Hacker and Pierson 2002). The next chapter takes up this particular problem more systematically, since functional arguments of this kind have been especially prevalent in studies that attempt to explain institutional arrangements.

All of these possibilities suggest the crucial contribution of social research that covers considerable stretches of time. "Macrosociology" as Stinchcombe has said, "has to be a sociology of the long pull" (Stinchcombe 1997, p. 406). Both in theory development and in empirical work, we need to stay attentive to the significance of big, long-term processes.

Chapter Four

THE LIMITS OF INSTITUTIONAL DESIGN

> Nations stumble upon establishments, which are indeed the
> result of human action, but not the execution of any human
> design. . . . If Cromwell said, that a man never mounts
> higher, than when he knows not whither he is going;
> it may with more reason be affirmed of communities,
> that they admit of the greatest revolutions where
> no change is intended.
> —*Adam Ferguson, "An Essay on the History
> of Civil Society," p. 122*

> People actually *construct* democracy . . . [but] *construct* has
> the misleading connotation of blueprints and carpenters,
> when over the last few hundred years, the actual formation
> and deformation of democratic regimes has more often
> resembled the erratic evolution of a whole city than the
> purposeful building of a single mansion.
> —*Charles Tilly (1995)*

INSTITUTIONS NOW STAND AT THE HEART of much theorizing and explanation in the social sciences. Analysts working from a variety of perspectives have produced compelling work, emphasizing and explicating the tremendous significance of institutional arrangements for political and social outcomes (Hall and Taylor 1996). By contrast, we have made far less progress in treating institutions as themselves important objects of explanation. The origins of institutions, as well as the sources of institutional change, remain opaque. As David Kreps has observed, the sophisticated economic literature on the effects of institutions "leaves open the question, where did the institutions come from? . . . Having a theory about how institutions arise and evolve could be more informative than theories of equilibrium within the context of a given set of institutions" (Kreps 1990, p. 530). Kreps's observation is now repeated with regularity (Bates, Figueiredo, and Weingast 1998, pp. 604–5; Carey 2000, p. 738; Weingast 2002, p. 661). Analysts starting from the perspectives of rational choice, as well as the sociological and historical variants of institutionalism, have begun to develop relevant arguments about the sources of institutional origins and change. Yet theoretical work on this crucial issue continues to be sketchy at best.

This chapter and the following one take up this problem, exploring how a focus on temporal processes of institutionalization can illuminate this key issue in contemporary social theory and empirical social science. I limit myself to a consideration of formal political institutions—what Carey (2000) has termed "parchment institutions"—which can be defined as the codified rules of political contestation.[1] The central questions are (1) What determines the choice of particular formal institutions? and (2) What determines how institutions, once created, change over time?

It is highly revealing that these questions are usually treated as entirely separable. Rationalist approaches to explaining institutional arrangements, which are the subject of this chapter, concentrate almost exclusively on the first one. They typically adopt a framework I will term *actor-centered functionalism*. Focusing on the choices of individual and collective actors who select political institutions, they fashion explanations through reference to the benefits these actors expect to derive from particular institutional designs. In fact, in most cases they work *backwards* from extant institutional arrangements to develop an account of how these institutions were (or might have been) rationally chosen. These analyses, which focus on moments of institutional choice and link the actions of designers to the anticipated consequences of institutional arrangements, provide key insights into our understanding of institutional origins. Taken alone, however, these arguments are at best incomplete, at worst seriously misleading. In reducing a moving picture to a snapshot, we run the risk of missing crucial aspects of the processes through which formal institutions take shape, as well as the ways in which they either endure or change in social environments that are themselves constantly changing.

This chapter and the one that follows argue for a shift in focus from institutional choice to institutional development. Even taken on their own terms, theories of institutional choice are likely to be highly problematic unless broader issues are addressed. Exploring institutional development brings to the forefront a range of fundamental concerns that actor-centered functionalism typically ignores: the implications of widespread unanticipated consequences in institutional design; the consequences for institutions of ongoing, sometimes rapid and often unpredictable change in surrounding social environments; the capacity of

[1] The discussion thus excludes both informal institutions, such as norms (Jepperson 1991), and individual rules that are nested within the general rules governing political contestation, such as public policies (Pierson 1993). Unless otherwise specified, when I say "institutions" I mean to refer only to formal political institutions. Much of the current discussion would be highly relevant for developing arguments applicable to other types of institutions. The core argument—that we need to think about development as well as choice, and cast a skeptical eye on functionalist claims—would have broad application. Yet analyses focusing on particular types of institutions would require distinctive claims about the mechanisms through which institutional selection and change occur. Discussions that attempt to cover all types of "institutions" run a high risk of overgeneralization and necessarily obscure many features distinctive to the study of formal institutions.

learning or competitive pressures to generate institutional change; and the possible bases of institutional resilience, including those sources of durability that may accumulate with the passage of time. An exploration of these and related dimensions of institutional development over time suggests the necessarily partial insights of any approach to "explaining institutions" concentrated exclusively on the rational design choices of political actors. Theories of institutional origins, which have been the dominant preoccupation of choice-theoretic accounts, are only one important part of what we really want, which is theories of institutional *development.*

The argument in this chapter proceeds in three stages. The first briefly outlines the rational design orientation prominent in much of the work social scientists have done on formal institutions. The second and third explore at length the reasons why one might expect analyses focused on the rational choices of political actors to provide a restricted vantage point for understanding why institutions take the forms that they do. The second section focuses on the reasons why we should expect that substantial gaps will often emerge between the functioning of institutions and the preferences of powerful political actors. The third section explores some of the limitations of two "mechanisms of enhancement"—learning and competition—which rationalists often argue generate functional institutional arrangements over time. This discussion sets the stage for Chapter Five, where I consider a range of factors relevant to the understanding of institutional development.

The Rational Design of Political Institutions

The most prominent mode of theorizing about the rational design of political institutions can be termed *actor-centered functionalism*—that is, the claim that a particular institution exists because it is expected to serve the interests of those who created it. Before I directly address this approach to explaining institutions, two clarifications are necessary. First, I employ the term *actor-centered* to distinguish this line of argument from an alternative, *societal functionalism,* which maintains that a particular institution X exists because it constitutes an effective response to some kind of societal problem. These quite distinct variants need to be clearly distinguished because of the ambiguities that surround the claim that an explanation of a particular institutional arrangement is "functionalist."

Societal functionalist arguments are somewhat less common within the rationalist tradition, since rational choice models generally exhibit skepticism about the extent to which actors concern themselves with the interests of others (Calvert 1995; Knight 1992; Miller 2000).[2] Indeed, rational choice theorists

---

[2] In some cases, however, the interests of powerful actors may be relatively compatible with those of other social actors. For example, developing a state powerful enough to deter potential invaders is

sometimes emphasize the extent to which particular institutions may be functional for powerful actors but quite *dysfunctional* for society as a whole (Miller 2000; Bates 1990; North 1990a).

For current purposes, what is more important is that arguments about societal functionalism will generally rest on quite different mechanisms of institutional development than those suggested in actor-centered functionalism.[3] In particular, societal functionalism emphasizes environmental pressures that "select" for institutional effectiveness over time. Furthermore, they focus on the *actual* effects of institutions rather than the intended ones. As discussed in this chapter, such arguments are sometimes presented in rational choice explanations of institutions (e.g., Weingast 2002, p. 33). These arguments imply both a different kind of functionalism *and* different sources of institutional selection. Indeed, they focus specifically on how institutions may change over time and thus constitute quite distinctive theories of institutional development. Hence, I will defer consideration of such arguments until later in this chapter.

A further ambiguity involves intentions versus results: are we saying that an institution exists because it *does* serve the interests of designers, or that it was chosen because they *thought* that it would? These two alternatives are often conflated (Wendt 2002). As I will discuss later, this distinction becomes extremely important if we have reason to expect that there will often be considerable divergence between the anticipated and actual effects of institutions. Although the distinction is not always explicitly made, in actor-centered functionalism, which focuses on the rational choices of designers, it is the *anticipated* effects of institutions rather than their actual effects that must be regarded as crucial. But such models are typically silent on the issue of what is likely to happen if institutions, once adopted, have effects other than anticipated ones.

Actor-centered functionalism is an obvious starting-point for rational choice theorists, and indeed, for any study of institutional choice. It makes good sense to begin with the prospect that actors choose institutions because they believe that doing so will benefit them. Of course, the manner in which many within the social sciences came to appreciate the role of institutions makes the prevalence of this perspective on institutional origins and change even easier to understand. Having focused primarily on the *effects* of institutions—in particular, the ways in which institutional arrangements might solve a variety of coordination and public-goods problems—analysts turning to the issue of institutional

---

generally in the interests of both institutional designers and most other members of a society; achieving high levels of economic growth may have both concentrated and diffuse benefits. In practice, many actor-centered functionalist arguments do seem to highlight institutional outcomes that have socially desirable features.

[3] For a good discussion of the sloppy ways in which these two variants of functionalism are often conflated in explanations of institutions even though they in fact point to quite different kinds of social processes, see Wendt 2001. He terms the two variants "intentional" and "invisible hand" functionalism.

choice naturally asked if these benefits for institution builders could explain the presence of particular institutions.

Although most scholarly attention has been placed on these institutional effects, not the manner in which the institutions come to exist, actor-centered functionalism appears to underpin most rationalist analyses of institutions. In Barry Weingast's recent survey of rational choice institutionalism, for instance, he reviews a "range of rational choice models that explain why institutions exist and why they take the specific form they do. In brief, the answer is parties often need institutions to help capture gains from cooperation" (2002, p. 670). To take some prominent examples from different subfields of political science: international regimes facilitate agreements through issue linkage and the reduction of monitoring costs (Keohane 1984); congressional committees help prevent cycling among competing legislative proposals (Shepsle 1986), enable gains from "trade" among legislators with different priorities (Weingast and Marshall 1988), or rationalize the flow of scarce information (Krehbiel 1991); the European Court of Justice offers a neutral monitoring and enforcement agency for the European Union's member states (Garrett 1995); and an expanded role for parliament in budgetary matters establishes the credible commitment mechanism a monarch needs to finance large-scale military conflicts (North and Weingast 1989). These works vary in the extent to which they explicitly consider how these institutions originate. In each case, however, one is left with the strong impression that the institutional functions described in large part *explain* the presence of particular institutional arrangements.

Actor-centered functionalism often relies heavily on the new institutional economics, especially Williamson's work on transaction costs (Williamson 1975; Moe 1984). Williamson is quite explicit in arguing that the development of a particular organizational form can be explained as the result of the efforts of rational actors to reduce transaction costs. More generally, actor-centered functionalist arguments take the following form: outcome X (an institution, policy, or organization, for instance) exists because those who design it expect it to serve the function Y.

Perhaps so. If actors are purposive, it will often be the case that the effects of an institution have something—perhaps a lot—to do with an explanation for its emergence, persistence, or change (Keohane 1984). Indeed, rational choice work on institutional effects and institutional design has provided powerful insights into the functioning of institutions. Political institutions can serve to coordinate the expectations and behavior of decentralized actors (Carey 2000), and to facilitate bargaining by creating monitoring bodies, issue linkages, and mechanisms for making credible commitments (Keohane 1984; Weingast 2002). A clearer understanding of these important things that institutions "do" surely helps us to grasp why actors invest considerable energy in the construction and reconstruction of the rules of the game.

The problem, however, is that actor-centered functionalism too often serves as an end-point rather than a starting point for analysis. Rather than directly examining the issue of institutional formation, one simply begins with existing institutions. The idea that these institutions exist in the form that they do *because* they are functional for the social actors who design them is treated as an assumption. The task of the analyst is to lay bare the particular function (generally, the resolution of some sort of collective choice problem) that the institution serves.

Given a reasonable amount of intellectual creativity and a moderately flexible analytical tool kit, this task of unmasking functions often turns out to be a fairly easy one. Rational choice analysts possess just such a tool kit, making it possible to reconcile virtually *any* observed outcome with a functionalist account (Green and Shapiro 1994). If such an account is not readily at hand, one can construct it by incorporating side-payments (Lange 1993), or "nesting" one game inside another (Tsebelis 1990). Yet it is one thing to demonstrate (or, more often, speculate) that an institution is "doing" something for social actors. It is quite another thing to jump to the conclusion that this accounts for the institution's presence. Doing so evades most of the thorniest issues of institutional emergence and change. The crucial question is what happens when we move from an analysis of institutional *effects* to one of institutional *causes*. In explaining the institutional forms we observe in the social world, how much weight can we place on the desire of actors to obtain the main effects of those institutions? How satisfactory is actor-centered functionalism?

The Scope and Limits of Actor-Centered Functionalism

The most straightforward version of rational institutional design focuses on the intentional and farsighted choices of purposive, instrumental actors. By this account, institutional effects should be seen as the intended consequences of their creators' actions—and in that sense as supplying the explanation for why the institution takes the form that it does. All of the key components of this approach to institutional explanation deserve serious interrogation. Actors may be instrumental and farsighted but have such *multiple and diverse goals* that institutional functioning cannot easily be derived from the preferences of designers. Alternatively, actors may not be *instrumental* in the sense implied by this framework. Or they may be instrumental, but not *farsighted*. Perhaps most important, they may in fact have a single, instrumental goal and be farsighted, but major institutional effects may be *unintended*. Finally, actors may make rational design choices, but *change in broader social environments* and/or *in the character of these actors themselves* may markedly worsen the fit between actors and institutional arrangements after they are chosen.

Each of these dimensions exposes a possible limitation on the effectiveness of actors in designing institutions and therefore suggests an important topic for further theoretical and empirical investigation. Each suggests a reason why we might expect significant divergences, or gaps, to emerge over time between the preferences of designers and the functioning of political institutions. To the extent that these gaps are likely to be large, we have good reason to shift our focus from institutional origins to institutional development. We need to give explicit consideration to what happens over time when institutions operate in ways that diverge from the preferences of the powerful social actors who created them.

Limitation 1: Institutions Have Multiple Effects

Specific institutional arrangements invariably have multiple effects.[4] Expanded judicial review in the European Union simultaneously has empowered judges, shifted agenda-setting powers away from the member states toward the European Commission, altered the character of discourse over policy reform, transformed the kinds of policy instruments that decision makers prefer to use, and dramatically changed the value of political resources traditionally employed by interest groups, to name just a few of the most obvious consequences. The centralization of authority structures in Congress may simultaneously advantage the majority party, empower members with more seniority over those with less, and strengthen the hands of Congress as an institution in competition with the Executive (Schickler 2001). For any significant institutional arrangement, political scientists would have little trouble generating a list, often lengthy, of notable consequences. Many of those consequences would be sufficiently visible and important to have made them of real relevance to those who established the institution in the first place.

This multiplicity of effects creates significant complications for the study of institutional design and development. Multiple effects are often mirrored by a multiplicity of motivations among those responsible for the selection of institutions (Schickler 2001). In many cases, as Schickler has argued, institutions are not produced because a single function motivates designers. Instead, institutional innovations constitute "common carriers" for *coalitions* of reformers that support a particular innovation for disparate reasons.[5]

This account of what Schickler terms "disjointed pluralism" has strong affinities with actor-centered functionalism. Here institutional designers are indeed interested in achieving particular goals, and Schickler draws heavily on actor-centered functionalist theories of congressional institutions in developing his arguments about the motivations of reformers. In Schickler's analysis, however, the link between these motivations and institutional outcomes depends on

---

[4]The discussion in this section draws heavily on Eric Schickler's (2001) important study of institutional development in the American Congress.

[5]In Schickler's careful examination of forty-two major institutional innovations in Congress between 1889 and 1980, he was able to identify only six cases where a single institutional effect seemed to provide the clearly dominant motivation for a coalition of reformers (Schickler 2001).

whether diverse groups with distinct, even contradictory motivations can be brought onboard a common carrier. Much thus depends on the strength of disparate factions, and on the availability and skill of entrepreneurs who can craft appropriate appeals to bring a potential coalition to fruition. At the same time, in such a process it is not credible to identify a single institutional effect and, arguing backwards, claim that this effect "explains" the development of the institution in the first place.

Schickler's analysis focuses on a relatively restricted problem in institutional choice—the design of internal rules for a single institution, the American legislature. The problem of multiple actors concerned with multiple effects is likely to be even more intense in the construction of constitutions (Horowitz 2000, 2002). Such basic institutional arrangements necessarily cover many, many functions, and typically involve negotiations among a wide range of actors. A constitution, even more than Schickler's legislative rules, is likely to be a hybrid—a common carrier for the distinctive, perhaps conflicting or even contradictory concerns of many different groups.

Limitation 2: Institutional Designers May Not Act Instrumentally

A more radical critique challenges the common assumption that exclusively instrumental goals guide the behavior of designers. In actor-centered functionalism, institutions are constructed along particular lines because actors expect that particular features will produce specific consequences. Features of institutions are believed to hold significance only to the extent that they help actors achieve these goals.

There is, however, a strong tradition in sociological theory, recently consolidated in sociology's version of "the new institutionalism," which challenges this premise (Meyer and Rowan 1977; March and Olson 1989; Powell and DiMaggio 1991; Jepperson 2001). In structuring institutional arrangements, actors may be motivated more by conceptions of what they believe to be appropriate than by conceptions of what would be effective.[6] Hall and Taylor summarize this line of argument as follows:

> Many of the institutional forms and procedures used by modern organizations were not adopted simply because they were most efficient for the tasks at hand, in line with some transcendent "rationality." Instead, they . . .

---

[6]It is important to be clear about what is meant by noninstrumental action in this context. In a commentary on an earlier version of this chapter, Miller (2000, p. 537) noted that "the most important empirical observations [about political institutions] can be explained *without* resort to the psychotic, neurotic, or normal hormone-driven behavior that is not the result of calculations of our own best self-interest." This is a serious mischaracterization of an extensive and sophisticated literature emphasizing how social processes can give rise to dominant understandings of what "makes sense" for actors to do in particular settings. One can question the scope of purely instrumental reasoning without reference to hormones or psychoses.

should be seen as culturally-specific practices, akin to the myths and cere-
monies devised by many societies, and assimilated into organizations, not
necessarily to enhance their formal means-end efficiency, but as a result of
the kind of processes associated with the transmission of cultural practices
more generally. (1996, pp. 946–47)

Sociologists, for instance, have emphasized the pervasive diffusion of particular
institutional forms, even in widely divergent contexts. Rather than revealing the
focus of actors on efficiency, they suggest that this "institutional isomorphism"
reflects the sensitivity of actors to the need to legitimate their activities.

This is not simply a hypothetical possibility. One significant strand of evidence for the important role of these diffusion processes in institutional selection has been the recent discovery of substantial areas of cultural, spatial, and
temporal cross-national "clustering" in institutional outcomes. If powerful actors were simply adopting the optimal institutions for their own local setting,
there would be little reason to expect such clustering to occur. The only clustering we would see would be functional: countries possessing similar powerful
actors with similar needs would produce similar institutions. Yet Blais and Massicotte's (1997) macroscopic review of legislative electoral formulas around the
world found that the two strongest correlates of electoral systems and rules are
whether or not a country was a British colony and on which continent the country exists. These patterns, they suggest, point to the role of diffusion as a source
of institutional outcomes. Former British colonies were more likely to install
electoral systems and train native elites in their electoral rules, thereby reinforcing such choices within the colonial culture. Noting the preponderance of PR
systems in Latin America, Blais and Massicotte doubt the overriding importance
of strategic considerations, since it would be hard to argue that at the time of institutional creation no powerful actors anywhere in Latin America would have
benefited from a plurality system. Instead, Blais and Massicotte point to the fact
that South American constitutional lawyers were trained in continental Europe
and looked there for models when choosing electoral systems. Donald Horowitz's
review of constitutional design in highly divided societies — arguably the context
where incentives to achieve "rational" design would be the strongest — reaches a
similar conclusion: "Rather than innovate with an explicit view to conciliation,
most states, most of the time, have adhered to institutions associated with their
former colonial power or to institutions that were otherwise familiar to them.
Very few states have learned from the actual experience with ethnic conflict of
any other state" (2000, p. 261).

Although data on the timing of institutional choices is scattered, there appears to
be some evidence of *temporal* clustering as well.[7] Particular ideas for institutional

---

[7]This point, as well as the overall argument of this chapter and the next, highlights the dire need for
a theoretically grounded institutional database that would allow social scientists to systematically
track cross-national patterns of institutional change over extended periods of time.

design may gain appeal during specific periods, resulting in similar institutional outcomes in widely diverse settings. Consider Germany's "mixed" electoral system, adopted in 1949, which combines single-member districts and PR list elections to fill seats in the same chamber. Variants of this previously rare institutional arrangement have recently been adopted in Japan, Italy, Russia, Bulgaria, Mexico, Venezuela, Bolivia, the Philippines, and New Zealand (Carey 2000, p. 741n). As international advice plays more of a role (albeit still limited) in institutional design, constitutional experts operate as what Horowitz calls "provision merchants." "Called in to help design systems in lands far from home," he writes, they "simply bring along their usual tool kits, which were developed for more or less homogeneous societies" (Horowitz 2000, p. 269).

In short, particular arrangements may well be adopted because they are perceived to be appropriate, not because they serve a means-end instrumentality. If so, such arrangements may not work all that well in a particular local context from the perspective of the dominant actors who selected them—or, indeed, for anyone else. They may still be functional in the minimalist sense that they represent equilibria—no actor has an incentive to unilaterally defect. But of course in that sense all institutions, which are by many definitions equilibria, are functionalist. What we cannot do, where the sociologists' claims about cultural effects are correct, is argue that institutions were selected because rational actors chose them to maximize particular institutional results.

The extent to which such "logic of appropriateness" behavior motivates institutional design remains controversial. At a minimum, however, those emphasizing such processes have presented a plausible, theoretically rich alternative account of institutional selection. Furthermore, they have marshaled considerable empirical material casting doubt on the validity of assuming that institutional designers, as a rule, are motivated exclusively or even predominantly by instrumental concerns (Jepperson 2001).

Limitation 3: Institutional Designers May Have Short Time Horizons

The question of actors' time horizons constitutes a central issue for analysts of institutional design. If politicians often have short time-horizons, this has important implications for theories of institutional origins and change. Where designers have short time horizons and the short-term and long-term effects of institutional choices are distinct, it becomes far less likely that institutions will be designed to achieve functional outcomes over the long term. Long-term institutional consequences may be the *by-products* of actions taken for short-term political reasons.

The evolution of the congressional committee system in the United States—an important institutional feature of contemporary American governance—is a good example. As Kenneth Shepsle notes, Henry Clay and his supporters introduced the system to further their immediate goals without regard to long-term consequences: "The lasting effects of this institutional innovation could hardly have been anticipated, much less desired, by Clay. They were by-products (and proved to be the most enduring and important products) of self-interested leadership behavior" (Shepsle 1989, p. 141). In this case, the system's long-term functioning was not the goal of the actors who created it. By the same token, an explanation for the institution's creation cannot be derived from an analysis of its long-term effects.

As was discussed in Chapter One, there are good reasons to believe that this is not an isolated instance.[8] Many of the implications of major institutional reforms only play out in the long run. Yet many political actors, especially politicians in competitive democracies, would often seem most interested in the short-term consequences of their actions; long-term effects may be heavily discounted. They generally will pay attention to long-term consequences only if these become politically salient, or when they have little reason to fear short-term electoral retribution.

It would, however, be as unreasonable to assume that political actors always have short time horizons as to assume that they never do. Considerable work of late has focused on this issue of time horizons, in part because upon reflection it is simply not credible to maintain that political actors always or even usually exhibit short time horizons. A moment's reflection suggests that organizations and political actors often do attend to the long term. Indeed, modern societies would be inconceivable if this were not the case. Governments, for instance, do not generally seek to maximize short-term revenue extraction by engaging in systematic confiscation of private assets. Elected politicians normally do not vote themselves spectacular pay increases. Interest groups generally act as if they care about their reputations—a long-term asset (Hansen 1991). Usually they will not squander their future credibility by lying to legislators they seek to influence.

A number of lines of research have developed to explain why longer time horizons are often evident in politics. If actors are "agents" for principals (such as voters or interest groups) who have long time horizons, then the agents as well may have incentives to give the future its due. The adoption of mechanisms of "credible commitment," in which actors bind themselves within certain structures to force themselves to refrain from exploitive behavior, may orient actions around long-run considerations (North and Weingast 1989; Shepsle 1991; North 1993). Finally, while political actors may be "short-lived," the organizations within which they act persist over extended periods of time and are thus made up of overlapping generations of short-lived actors (Soskice, Bates, and Epstein 1992; Bates and Shepsle 1997). Often these actors are embedded in

[8]Here is another example, concerning the European Union's negotiations over the Maastricht Treaty. There is strong evidence that for immediate electoral reasons, John Major insisted on an opt-out for Britain from the EU's social protocol, rather than an amendment that would have radically watered down the protocol. It was clear at the time that the latter option would have provided a better protection for British sovereignty (Pierson 1996). Indeed, the opt-out did not survive the accession of a Labour government in 1997.

career trajectories where advancement depends on adherence to organizational expectations. In such settings, organizational designs may "transform the ambition for advancement within the institution into constraint, thereby generating enduring regularities in the choices of individuals" (Soskice, Bates, and Epstein 1992, p. 548).

Efforts to lengthen time horizons in politics will, however, often prove ineffective. Especially problematic is the fact that each of the "time-lengthening" devices discussed above relies heavily on the capacity of one set of actors to adequately assess the behavior of others in order to detect opportunistic actions, and then to bring the transgressors to heel. Yet such monitoring behavior is often exceptionally difficult in politics. As was discussed in Chapter One, it is often very hard to establish accountability in political environments. Outcomes themselves are frequently difficult to measure. There are often long lags and complex causal chains connecting political actions to political outcomes. The complexity of the goals of politics, and the loose and diffuse links between actions and outcomes, render politics inherently ambiguous. Even if failures in politics are relatively apparent and the culpability of "agents" can be established, efforts of principals to sanction those agents may be difficult. Many participants in politics (voters, members of interest groups) engage in activities only sporadically. Their tools of action are often crude, such as the blunt instrument of the vote, and their actions may have consequences only when aggregated with those of other actors in circumstances where coordination is difficult or impossible.

Thus, both monitoring and sanctioning difficulties place serious limitations on techniques for lengthening actors' time horizons. It is no accident, for instance, that much of the generally optimistic rational choice discussion of "credible commitments" in politics has focused on relatively transparent *financial* issues (e.g., budget deficits, monetary policy). In these settings, performance indicators are clear and lines of accountability are unambiguous. Hence, behavior is relatively easy to monitor. While these issues are obviously important, it must be stressed that for reasons already noted they are fundamentally atypical of the kinds of matters dealt with in politics.

An additional limitation of these techniques for lengthening time horizons is particularly relevant for the specific issue of institutional design. Even if some of the mechanisms discussed by rational choice theorists are operative in everyday politics, they will often be especially fragile or absent altogether precisely at moments of institutional formation (Horowitz 2000, p. 257). At founding moments, when crucial new rules are put in place, one often cannot count on the operation of well-institutionalized contexts to frame and structure the actions of political decision makers (Elster, Offe, and Preuss 1998).

My point is not that actors always have short time horizons, but that they often do. Where we would expect relatively short time horizons to be operative, functional claims about institutional design become more suspect, and long-term institutional effects may be better treated as by-products rather than goals of institutional designers. Thus, short-term and long-term effects need to be distinguished, and the issue of actor time horizons should be treated as a variable with real implications for questions of institutional origins and change, and therefore a subject deserving serious study.

Limitation 4: Institutional Effects May Be Unanticipated

Even if institutional designers do have singular goals, do act instrumentally, and do focus on the long-term, unanticipated consequences are likely to be widespread. Of all the limitations of the rational design argument, this is perhaps the most significant. Anyone engaged in empirical research in the social sciences knows that the most instrumental and canny of actors still cannot hope to adequately anticipate all the consequences of their actions. Institutions may not be functional because designers make mistakes.

Unanticipated consequences are of tremendous significance in modern polities. Over time, industrial societies have become much more differentiated, involving increased interactions among increasing numbers of people. The historical process has been elegantly summarized by Norbert Elias (1956):

The network of human activities tends to become increasingly complex, far-flung, and closely knit. More and more groups, and with them more and more individuals, tend to become dependent on each other for their security and the satisfaction of their needs which, for the greater part, surpass the comprehension of those involved. It is as if first thousands, then millions, then more and more millions walked through this world with their hands and feet chained together by invisible ties. No one is in charge. No one stands outside. Some want to go this way, others that. They fall upon each other and, vanquishing or defeated, still remain chained to each other.

The profound implications of increasing social complexity need to be underlined. As the number of decisions made and the number of actors involved proliferate, relations of interdependence—among actors, organizations, and institutions—expand geometrically. This growing complexity has two distinct consequences. First, it generates problems of overload. More prevalent and complex political activity places growing demands on decision makers. In this context, time constraints, scarcities of information, and the need to delegate decisions may promote unanticipated effects (March and Olsen 1989; Simon 1957). At the same time, increasing social complexity leads to growing interaction effects. Initiatives often will have important consequences for realms outside those originally intended. As Garret Hardin puts it, "We can never do merely one thing" (Hardin 1963, pp. 79–80). Instead, we should expect that social processes involving large numbers of actors in densely institutionalized societies routinely generate elaborate feedback loops and significant interaction effects. In such settings, decision makers cannot hope to fully anticipate all of the major implications of their actions (Jervis 1997).

Nor is it just that social contexts are extremely complex; the difficulties are exacerbated by the fact that the abilities of individuals to draw inferences and judgments from their experiences have systematic biases.[9] Levitt and March (1988, p. 323) provide an excellent summary:

> [I]ndividual human beings are not perfect statisticians. . . . They make systematic errors in recording the events of history and in making inferences from them. They overestimate the probability of events that actually occur and of events that are available to attention because of their recency or saliency. They are insensitive to sample size. They tend to overattribute events to the intentional actions of individuals. They use simple linear and functional rules, associate causality with spatial and temporal contiguity, and assume that big effects must have big causes. These attributes of individuals as historians all lead to systematic biases in interpretation.[10]

For all these reasons, social activity—even when undertaken by highly knowledgeable and instrumentally motivated actors—should typically give rise to significant unintended effects (Hayek 1973; Hirsch 1977; Schelling 1978; Van Parijs 1982; Perrow 1984; Jervis 1997). Nor is there any reason to exempt the task of institutional design—given the manifold and complex consequences of institutions and the typically volatile circumstances under which major institutional choices are made—from this general tendency. Instead, there are good reasons to be skeptical of theories that place near-exclusive weight on the capacity of decision makers to make extremely accurate assessments of the consequences of institutional choices.

The changing institutional position of state governments in the United States provides a good example (Riker 1955). Because approval of the American constitution required state ratification, the interests of states received considerable attention in the process of institutional design. The framers intended the Senate to serve as a strong support of state interests. State legislatures were to appoint senators, who were expected to serve as delegates representing states in the formation of policy. Over time, however, senators seeking greater autonomy were able to gradually free themselves from state oversight. By the early 1900s, the enactment of the Seventeenth Amendment requiring the popular election of senators only ratified the result of a lengthy erosion of state legislative control.

Examples could easily be multiplied. Many post-Communist systems in Europe adopted independent executives in part to limit party system fragmenta-

---

[9]For an excellent discussion of how "the process of constitutional choice is fraught with the prospect of bias and distortion," see Horowitz 2000.

[10]It is worth noting that many of the cognitive biases highlighted in this passage—overemphasis on intentionality, assumption of linear relationships, emphasis on temporal contiguity in causal accounts—mirror criticisms that I make of major tendencies within contemporary social science.

tion, but in practice this appears to have had the opposite effect (Carey 2000, p. 748; Filippov, Ordeshook, and Shvetsova 1999). The European Court of Justice, expected to play a relatively limited monitoring role over the interactions of powerful member states, worked in collaboration with the national courts of European countries to dramatically expand its authority to exercise judicial review (Burley and Mattli 1993). The simple rule in Section 5 of Article One of the U.S. Constitution, indicating that "each house may determine the rules of its proceedings," gave rise unexpectedly to the Senate filibuster, which, as Gary Miller points out, "has had enormous policy consequences over the twentieth century" (Miller 2000, p. 539). Most students of politics would have no trouble generating many, many additional instances.

Indeed, unintended consequences may be particularly likely in the domain of institutional design, precisely because it typically involves bargained outcomes among competing interests in contexts where multiple issues are simultaneously at stake (see Limitation 1). Horowitz, again, ably summarizes the problem (2000, p. 270):

> Typically, although the setting varies widely, negotiation is the method by which proposals are hammered out. Negotiation has its own exigencies; it entails bargaining, trading and splitting differences. If obstacles arise because the participants have divergent preferences, they may exchange incommensurables to overcome the obstacles, thereby producing a mélange of institutions or even enshrining inconsistent solutions to problems within the same document. With negotiation, one may contrast planning, a process intended to produce internally consistent solutions to problems. Even from a process of planning, of course, perfectly coherent outcomes are unlikely, but in any case, in democratic constitutional design, bargaining and negotiation are the main modalities. Bargaining has much to commend it, but coherence is not among its virtues.

The prevalence of unanticipated institutional effects raises a difficult challenge for social scientists—after all, if savvy social actors cannot anticipate mistakes, why should social scientists expect to do better? Identifying the circumstances that increase the probability of unintended consequences is indeed a formidable task.[11] Fortunately, it is not the fundamental one for those interested in institutional development. The key point is this: the significance of unintended consequences

---

[11]The above discussion, however, points to two productive lines of investigation—both prominent in recent sociological research—that seek to pin down the conditions where unintended consequences are likely to be most significant. The first focuses on problems of cognition—the ways in which we are systematically error prone in our judgments of the social world, in particular those related to questions of cause and effect. For instance, since individuals tend to overweight the significance of recent, highly visible events in their understandings of the social world, we might hypothesize that institutional designers will systematically err in focusing on dramatic "failures" in the immediate past. A second line of analysis would focus on distinctive social contexts. Social settings vary in the

needs to be incorporated into the ways we think about institutional origins and change, *even if we cannot develop theories that can identify the kinds of mistakes that are likely to occur.* Put simply, if designers are extremely proficient in their assessments of institutional effects, then it may make sense to focus only on the moment of institutional choice, without worrying about what happens later.[12] If they are more prone to mistakes, however, then the issue of what happens *after* unanticipated consequences emerge becomes crucial. Under these conditions we need to think about processes of institutional development as well as processes of institutional choice.

In the social sciences, however, the dominant response to the issue of unanticipated consequences has been avoidance. Better altogether if this problem could be made to go away. In practice, analysts have employed three plausible strategies of evasion, which I discuss in ascending order of helpfulness. The most common gambit is to treat unanticipated consequences, perhaps only implicitly, as an "error term" or "noise." In practice this means to ignore the matter. Without at least some further discussion, however, theorists cannot know how serious the issue is that they are skirting—and thus how adequate actor-based functionalism might be for explaining institutional arrangements.

Treating unintended effects as "noise" assumes that such effects will be randomly distributed and will therefore tend to wash out, leaving the systematic, intended effects behind. For some problems and settings, this is a perfectly reasonable way for social scientists to proceed. It may make sense, for instance, in studying certain aggregative social processes involving very large and atomized populations, such as the stock market or public opinion (Page and Shapiro 1992). However, it is a far less helpful approach for the investigation of institutional design and reform. Here, single unintended effects may be quite large. Furthermore, as I will discuss in Chapter Five, if institutions are often very resilient, then we cannot expect accidents to cancel out; instead, early accidents may be self-reinforcing (Arthur 1994).

Dismissing unintended consequences as an "error term" or "noise" provides the justification for an exclusive focus on moments of initial institutional choice. Here, however, we can see a definite limitation of the "cross-sectional" or snapshot view of institutions typical in actor-centered functionalism. Depending on the starting point, either the long-term consequences of institutional choices or the original factors generating the institutional choice will be outside the scope of the analysis. So, of course, will be any recognition of disjunctures between the two. Focusing *either* on institutional origins or on institutional effects—that is, on a

---

extent to which they involve dense and intensive connections among multiple domains (Perrow 1984; Jervis 1997). Such connections generate complexity and multiply the number of consequences flowing from any single intervention. The prevalence of unintended consequences in institutional design should stem in part from this aspect of social contexts.

[12]Of course, one would still have to consider all the other limitations discussed in this chapter.

snapshot of an institution—the issue of unintended consequences simply vanishes from view.

A more helpful, but still limited, response is to acknowledge the high potential for unanticipated consequences and to argue that this fact constitutes a crucial organizing principle of institutional design. As Goodin puts it, "Accidents happen: but the frequency and direction of accidents can be significantly shaped by intentional interventions of social planners. . . . Insofar as the social world is accident-prone, we might want to design around the risk of accidents, seeking robust institutions that can withstand the various shocks that will inevitably befall them" (1996, p. 29).

This is not simply a normative argument about how institutions "should" be designed; the claim is that an awareness of the potential for unintended consequences itself shapes the activities of institutional designers. More broadly, the new institutional economics (and some of its political offshoots) argue that uncertainty—both about the behavior of others and about unforeseen contingencies—plays a major role in shaping the optimal design of institutions (Koremenos, Lipson, and Snidal 2001). An efficient institution should be able to absorb, or adapt to, the predictable (if unspecifiable) bumps in the road.

Yet while this line of argument helpfully incorporates unintended consequences into the discussion of institutional design, it does not directly address the issue of how common such unintended outcomes will be. We are still left wanting to know the extent to which accidents are likely to lead institutions to function in ways at odds with the expectations of designers. Nor does this general resort to "correction-prone" or adaptive design specify what such a design might be, or, crucially, how corrections can be made in reaction to unanticipated consequences. For these problems, one needs to think explicitly about institutional development as a process unfolding over time.

These concerns are addressed in a final response to the problem of unintended consequences, which pushes the analysis away from a focus on the capacities of institutional framers. This line of argument, not inconsistent with those already discussed, suggests various selection mechanisms that will squeeze unanticipated consequences out of institutional settings over time. Claims about *mechanisms of institutional enhancement* are sufficiently interesting and important to warrant separate and extended discussion later in this chapter.

Limitation 5: Institutional Continuity and Environmental Change

The world does not stand still once new institutional arrangements are selected. "Gaps" between the preferences of powerful actors and the functioning of political institutions may also develop over time because of changes within the broader social environment. As was discussed in Chapter Three, frameworks focused on individual or collective choice typically diminish attention to long-term, slow-moving social processes that may be of great significance. In general, such accounts discourage the analyst from concentrating on the broader environments within which choice processes take place (Kahler 1999). Yet major change in these environments inevitably characterizes the long run. These changes may alter the functioning of political institutions, the dominant concerns of powerful social actors, or both.

Consider the development of Canadian institutions (Watts 1987). The designers of the Canadian federation sought a highly centralized form of federalism—in part as a reaction to the ways in which decentralization contributed to the horrors of the American Civil War. Yet the Canadian federation eventually became far less centralized than the American one. Among the reasons: the Canadian federation left the provinces with sole responsibility for many social policy activities that were then considered trivial. Over time, however, economic development fostered growing interdependence, fueling the rise of what came to be known as the welfare state. With the growing role of government in social policy and economic management, responsibilities previously ceded to the provinces turned out to be of tremendous importance. Quite unexpectedly, Canadian federalism developed on a new and far less centralized path.

Political elites facing new concerns as a result of changing circumstances may find that previously desirable institutional effects are now problematic. In Europe in the early twentieth century, elites faced a major political crisis, as majoritarian institutions that had served them well threatened to fall into the hands of increasingly powerful working-class parties (Boix 1999). Under such circumstances, the functioning of political institutions is likely to appear deeply unsatisfactory to powerful political interests.

Limitation 6: The Problem of Actor Discontinuity

Even absent major environmental change, "gaps" may emerge because the actors who inherit institutional arrangements are not the same as those who designed them. Indeed, a major ambiguity in theories of rational institutional design concerns institutional inheritors. What does actor-centered functionalism imply about the benefits of institutions to those who inherit them? Political institutions are typically long lived. Given that institutions will usually outlive the people who create them, we wish to know whether these originally "functional" aspects should be expected to remain in the interests of following generations (e.g., because those followers are much the same sort of actors as the creators).

Typically, actor-centered functionalism seems to rest (although usually only implicitly) on strong assumptions about actor continuity.[13] In the study of international relations, for instance, where there has been a great deal of actor-

---

[13]Some rational choice analyses have addressed aspects of this issue. I have already discussed overlapping generations models, which deal with problems of actor turnover. Some models distinguish the coalitions that enact an institution from the ones inheriting the institution (Moe 1990; Horn

centered functionalist work, this assumption of actor continuity is common. Indeed, it may not be unreasonable since "states" are taken to be the main designers of international institutions—and many international relations scholars argue that the interests of states are quite sharply defined by the structure of the international system. Keohane, for example, writes as follows: "Rational-choice theory . . . assumes that institutions can be accounted for by examining the incentives facing *the actors who created and maintain them.* Institutions exist because they could have reasonably been expected to increase the welfare of their creators" (Keohane 1984, p. 80, emphasis added).

What, however, if there are reasons to question this premise of actor continuity—that is, to consider the possibilities that actors making initial institutional choices may well have quite distinctive preferences from those of their inheritors? This problem is only unimportant if we think that designers' choices will be inherited by actors much like themselves. With the passage of time, however, this assumption becomes more problematic. This will be so especially in settings where the assumption of some stable overarching context that generates a stable pattern of preferences seems implausible. In the context of long-term institutional development the language of "actors" elides a huge amount—who the actors are is often ambiguous. Who, we might ask, are the "inheritors" of the American constitution's framers? Are they "the same" in some clear analytical sense? It is not clear to me that these are answerable questions.

These six limitations provide strong grounds for challenging any presumption that institutional effects will reflect the expectations and desires of institutional designers. As Horowitz (2002, p. 16) concludes, "Constitutions that have been *designed,* as opposed to merely constructed, are difficult to find." The "designers" may be a diverse set of negotiators with multiple goals, making institutional choice a complex and pluralistic outcome; designers may not be thinking primarily in instrumental terms; they may be thinking instrumentally, but be preoccupied by short-term considerations; they may simply make mistakes; they may find that institutions work less well as the surrounding environment changes; and they may be succeeded by actors with distinct preferences. In all these cases, we are likely to see an uneasy tension between institutional arrangements and the preferences of powerful actors. Convincing treatments of institutional development must take all these possibilities into account.

Analyses that seek to explain the presence of formal institutions through reference to institutional effects have made important contributions to social theory. Yet work along these lines also possesses serious limitations. As a result of these ambiguities, problems, and omissions, functionalist explanations of institutions may be *partial,* focusing only on a few of the relevant mechanisms generating

---

1995). These accounts, however, have focused on the implications of this distinction for initial institutional design, not for downstream processes of institutional development.

stability or change in institutions. They may be *nested*, in the sense that their claims are likely to operate only under circumstances that must be established through reference to arguments outside the scope of the theory. In many instances they may simply be wrong. Too often, the argument boils down to something like this: "We know that institutions constitute equilibria. We have propositions that show how such equilibria might be generated. Therefore these propositions *explain* the equilibria that in fact emerge."

The multiple problems with such a framework for explaining institutional outcomes are nicely illustrated in Allison Stanger's recent work (Stanger 2003). As she argues in her detailed comparison of constitutional reforms in eastern Europe, there are important limitations to functional explanations of these outcomes. Political reform movements in eastern Europe carried powerful preconceptions about the character of political life and political activism. These preconceptions, she demonstrates, had profound effects on their approaches to questions of institutional design. Although strategic, goal-oriented behavior is evident, none of the cases she studies exemplify a logic of institutional design in which powerful actors simply incorporate those constitutional features that consolidate their political advantages. Initial results combine rationalist, instrumental elements, with those reflecting the significance of political symbolism. Unintended consequences are manifest—most profoundly in the unraveling of Czechoslovakia, which the constitutional design process greatly accelerated. Ongoing political and social events shaped the reform process in idiosyncratic ways. "Designers" often exhibited short-term orientations rather than long-term visions for mastering these constitutional moments. For all these reasons, as Stanger demonstrates, the downstream process of institutional development becomes just as important a focus of social science inquiry as the initial moment of institutional "selection."

RESCUING FUNCTIONALISM? EVALUATING MECHANISMS OF INSTITUTIONAL ENHANCEMENT

If the arguments just presented have merit, then institutional effects cannot be assumed to derive in a straightforward way from the intentions of farsighted, goal-oriented actors. While this raises significant problems for rationalist explanations of institutions, it is not enough to demonstrate the limits of functionalist reasoning. A second line of functionalist argument focuses on processes of institutional change. It can accept all of the shortcomings in the capacities of rational institutional designers, while nonetheless asserting that functional institutional designs will result over time. Indeed, this line of analysis has been at the center of the (fairly limited) efforts of rational choice theorists to think about institutional change.

That economists have rarely worried about the possibilities of inefficient institutional outcomes stems not only from their faith in the capacities of human designers, but also from a confidence in the potential for institutional enhancement. Winter (1986, p. 244) terms this the "as if" principle: given the presence of certain adaptive mechanisms, one can proceed as if individuals were rational, highly knowledgeable and instrumental actors, because the results over time will be the same. Markets, economists argue, provide two powerful mechanisms for generating efficiency: learning and competition. Learning processes within firms can lead to the gradual enhancement of organizational performance. According to Williamson (1993), one can rely on "the 'far-sighted propensity' or 'rational spirit' that economics ascribes to economic actors. . . . Once the unanticipated consequences are understood, these effects will thereafter be anticipated and the ramifications can be folded back into the organizational design. Unwanted costs will then be mitigated and unanticipated benefits will be enhanced. Better economic performance will ordinarily result" (pp. 116–17). Similarly, competitive pressures in a market society mean that new organizations with more efficient structures will develop, eventually replacing suboptimal organizations (Alchian 1950). I will leave aside the question of whether economists are justified in these confident assertions about economic organizations. The issue is the relevance of these mechanisms to political settings. Potentially, they offer an approach to institutional change that could salvage much of the rationalist approach to explaining institutions. Competition and learning constitute two alternative mechanisms that might account for the elegance of institutional arrangements even in contexts marked by short time horizons, unintended consequences, and so on.

It is crucial to recognize that these arguments about mechanisms of enhancement contain an implicit view of institutions as highly plastic. As Paul DiMaggio and Walter Powell (1991, p. 10) observe, "most public-choice theorists and economists who study institutions view them as provisional, temporary resting places on the way to an efficient equilibrium solution." Although institutions are seen as providing some stability to an otherwise chaotic world, the implicit or explicit claim is generally that major shifts in preferences, power distributions, or information concerning institutional shortcomings should give rise to institutional revision.

This emphasis on the plasticity of institutions was signaled clearly in Riker's classic treatment of institutional effects (Riker 1980). As noted in Chapter Two, Riker was among the first to argue that institutions provided stability by solving the "cycling" problems that are otherwise endemic to collective choice processes. Indeed, this became a key component of rationalist arguments about institutional effects (Shepsle 1989). Riker, however, did not stop there. He noted that institutional arrangements themselves would inherit this same cycling problem. The result, he argued, was that we should expect the rules of the game to be quite fluid over the medium-to-long run: "The only difference between values and institutions is that the revelation of institutional disequilibria is probably a longer process than the revelation of disequilibria of taste. . . . If institutions are congealed tastes and if tastes lack equilibria, then also do institutions, except for short-run events" (Riker 1980, p. 445).[14]

In my view, this assumption of institutional plasticity represents a crucial flaw in standard arguments about institutional enhancement—a claim that I will develop in detail in Chapter Five. At present, however, I wish to explore each of these mechanisms of enhancement on its own terms. To what extent should we expect learning and competition to create substantial pressures for institutional adaptation? In fact, there are good reasons to believe that each of these mechanisms of enhancement, while clearly important, is likely to be less effective when one shifts from Williamson's world of firms in private markets to the world of political institutions (Moe 1984, 1990). At a minimum, clear arguments need to be made concerning the circumstances under which each mechanism is likely to operate.

Enhancement through Learning

I will discuss mechanisms of learning first, since these arguments are more easily linked to an actor-centered functionalist account. Here the central claim would be that powerful actors are able to identify any gaps that might develop between the functioning of institutions and their own preferences. They will then take the necessary corrective steps to redesign institutions so that they operate more effectively. Like many components of actor-centered functionalism, it is hard to deny that this claim is sometimes true. The emergence of the kinds of gaps discussed in the first part of this chapter could be expected to induce powerful actors to search intensively for an improved understanding and plausible responses to institutional shortcomings.

Boix's study of institutional reform in early twentieth-century Europe can illustrate, since it represents perhaps the most persuasive empirical study of institutional enhancement grounded in theories of rational institutional choice (Boix 1999). Boix's empirical puzzle is the following. The electoral systems of European countries were initially organized along majoritarian lines, which suited the interests of powerful political elites. In the late nineteenth and early twentieth centuries, however, these systems came into crisis. A major change in the social environment—namely, the gradual rise of working-class consciousness and organization—led to pressures to expand the suffrage, and to the develop-

---

[14]Indeed, Riker's analysis is so pessimistic about the capacity of politics to generate any enduring structures that he ultimately questions the ability of political scientists to make any general statements about the political world at all—"politics is *the* dismal science because we have learned from it that there are no fundamental equilibria to predict" (1980, p. 443).

ment of strong socialist parties. In this new context, majoritarian institutions came to pose a considerable threat to ruling elites. How did they respond? Boix argues that these elites were able to take this information about new circumstances and use it to refashion institutions along the lines that an actor-based functionalism would expect. Institutional reforms varied depending upon the optimal choices for powerful actors. Where the socialist threat was strong and it was difficult for conservative forces to coordinate around a single party, ruling elites adopted systems of proportional representation.[15] Where the socialist threat was weaker, or coordination around a single conservative party was viable, majoritarian institutions were maintained. Boix's statistical analysis suggests that the historical record provides strong support for his hypothesis.

This account fits well with the Williamson perspective on institutional redesign. Designers (or in this case, their inheritors) rationally assess changed circumstances. Based on their updated understandings of institutional functioning they respond by introducing appropriate modifications to political institutions. The central question is how reliable we should expect this mechanism of institutional enhancement to be. Here I discuss reasons why we might doubt that learning dynamics will generally be very strong. In Chapter Five I will consider reasons why even if there are strong learning processes at work, we might not expect these to be effectively translated into institutional reforms.

The main reason to question the strength of learning processes in political contexts has already been discussed: the great complexity and ambiguity of the political world. As was discussed in Chapter One, the contrast with the market settings analyzed by Williamson is stark. Markets can obviously be highly complex and often confusing. Yet the central clarifying role of prices, the prevalence of repeated interactions, the absence of a need to coordinate many of one's economic decisions with those of large numbers of other actors, and the presence of relatively short causal chains between choices and results make it relatively easy for economic actors to correct mistakes over time. In other words, these features improve the prospects for learning.

Notwithstanding reductionist efforts to make the search for votes the equivalent of the search for dollars, politics lacks anything like the measuring rod of price. Political actors frequently pursue a range of goals. While politicians often will be focused on reelection, others (e.g., bureaucrats, interest groups) have different ambitions. Thus, it is difficult to say what an "effective" political system would look like—what it would optimize—even in theory. Political activity is often intermittent rather than regularly repeated. Causal chains between actions and outcomes are often very long. Politics is simply a far, far murkier environment (North 1990b). This murkiness exacerbates the limitations of human cognition discussed earlier in this chapter.

---

[15]Here Boix relies on Cox's important work on electoral institutions and coordination problems (Cox 1997).

In part because of this opacity, even mistaken understandings of the political world are often self-reinforcing rather than corrective. To return to the concept introduced in Chapter One, our basic conceptions of the political world, of what works and what does not, tend to be "path dependent." Established outlooks on politics, ranging from ideologies to understandings of particular aspects of governments or orientations toward political groups or parties, will often be very resilient. As North has argued, actors operating in contexts of high complexity and opacity are heavily biased in the way they filter information into existing "mental maps" (North 1990a, b; Denzau and North 1994). Confirming information tends to be incorporated, while disconfirming information is filtered out. North's work confirms long-standing views of those studying political culture as well as the recent contributions of cognitive science and organization theory.

Complexity of context and limits of human cognition mean that mistaken understandings in politics often do not get corrected. An additional problem is that institutional revision generally requires "collective learning"—large numbers of people within and across organizations must come to see things in a similar way. As Hannan and Freeman point about, the metaphor of "learning" often applies only awkwardly to collective action processes central to the pursuit of institutional revisions: "When members of an organization have diverse interests, organizational outcomes depend heavily on internal politics, on the balance of power among the constituencies. When such an organization faces an external problem, which action will be taken, if any, depends as much on the coalition structure of the organization as on the contribution of alternative actions to organizational survival or growth. In such situations outcomes cannot easily be matched rationally to changing environments" (Hannan and Freeman 1989, p. 23).

It may be appropriate in some circumstances to argue that politics involves learning processes, in which responses to public problems proceed in a trial-and-error fashion (Lindblom 1959; Heclo 1974; Hall 1993). Indeed, an important subject for further investigation would be to establish the types of political circumstances under which such learning processes seem likely to be effective, as, for example, they appear to have been in the settings explored by Boix. There is little reason, however, to think that learning will constitute a reliable tool of institutional enhancement in politics. Because political reality is so complex and the tasks of evaluating public performance and determining which options would be superior are so formidable, such self-correction is often partial at best.

Enhancement through Competition

The limitations of Williamson's "rational spirit" in politics are even clearer for the second mechanism of institutional enhancement, competition. This mechanism constitutes a form of evolutionary argument for the gradual refinement of institutional design. As Axelrod (1984, p. 169) has noted, "The evolutionary approach is based on a simple principle: whatever is successful is likely to appear more often in the future."

In economics, for instance, Alchian has made the classic argument for organizational refinement through competitive pressure. Alchian accepted that individuals and firms could not be expected to meet the cognitive demands assumed by many microeconomic models. Instead, he employed the "as if" principle: because economic competition effectively selected for superior organizational performance, markets would gradually be made up of firms with rational structures. This would be the case even if such structures were discovered largely by accident. Firms with less efficient structures would either adapt or die; in the long run, it did not really matter much which process was more prevalent. Such arguments are functionalist in the sense that they explain the presence of institutional features through reference to the desirable consequences of those features. Institutional arrangements that serve key social functions are likely to become more widespread over time as a result of selection pressures.

It is important to stress that at this point we leave the realm of "actor-centered functionalism" and turn to a form of what I have termed *societal functionalism.* Arguments based on mechanisms of competition focus less on the intentions of actors than on the ways in which broader environments select for particular kinds of outcomes. It is appropriate to consider these arguments within this discussion of rationalist explanations of institutions, because rational choice scholars have sometimes sought to explain institutional arrangements through resort to mechanisms of this kind. Weingast (2002, pp. 680–81), for example, suggests that democratic institutions designed to secure property rights lead to high economic growth, which enhances political stability—that is, it leads to enhanced regime survival over the long-run.[16] Indeed, given a penchant for working backwards from observed functions of institutions, it is not surprising that a mechanism of this kind would be invoked in many rationalist accounts.

Typically, however, this invocation is not matched by serious investigation of the claim that mechanisms of competitive selection do in fact account for the observed institutional outcome. The plausibility of this view depends on whether or not formal political institutions, like firms, generally confront a dense environment of competing institutions. Will competitors be able to capitalize on inefficient performance, swooping in to carry off an institution's "customers" and drive it into bankruptcy? The answer is sometimes, but usually not. Competitive processes are not irrelevant to the development of political institutions, but there seems little case for giving them the kind of central role that Alchian does in his discussion of the development of firms.

Models of political competition among institutional forms have been most effectively applied in understanding international relations. Tilly, for example,

---

[16]See also Przeworski et al. 2000.

followed Otto Hintze in advancing the classic formulation that "states make war, and war makes states" (Tilly 1975). He argued persuasively that the period of early modern state formation could be understood in Darwinian terms. Hundreds of initial sites of autonomous political authority were winnowed down to roughly two dozen, mostly through ruthless military competition in an environment that "selected" for those state forms most capable of mobilizing for war.

Yet even in the realm of international relations the applicability of functional arguments grounded in competition has evident limits. The extent to which states have needed to "rationalize or die" has varied considerably over time (Kahler 1999). Indeed, even in the harsh environment of early modern European state formation, competition was not the only mechanism at work in selecting survivors (Spruyt 1994). Moreover, the contemporary international environment offers far more extensive niches for weak and/or retrograde state structures to survive (Jepperson 2001). Jackson and Rosberg (1982), for instance, argue that weak states in Africa have remained largely insulated from competition of this kind—protected by an international community that for a variety of reasons seeks to place limits on military contestation between nation-states. Tellingly, the limits of this mechanism of enhancement in the international sphere are clearly acknowledged in Keohane's actor-centered functionalism—the most extended and prominent rationalist analysis of institutional arrangements in the international system. Although he explicitly recognizes that functional outcomes could be generated through this kind of environmental selection, he argues that such mechanisms are too weak in the international system to provide a strong basis for generating functional outcomes. "In world politics," he writes, "states rarely disappear. Thus the functional argument as applied to our subject-matter must rest on the premise of rational anticipation" (Keohane 1984, p. 82).

Once one turns from the international sphere to the domestic one, and specifically to the study of formal political institutions, the case for expecting functional outcomes as a result of competition becomes weaker still. There are some realms of domestic politics where competitive arguments clearly apply. Party systems in democratic polities, for instance, contain an obvious competitive dynamic. One could argue with some justification that parties must adapt their organizational practices and platforms in the face of such competition or confront the prospect of decline. There can be little doubt, however, that domestic political environments are typically more "permissive" than economic ones (Krasner 1989; Powell and DiMaggio 1991).

In most cases, in fact, political institutions are not really subject to direct competition at all.[17] Instead, single institutional arrangements, or sets of rules, typically have a monopoly over a particular part of the political terrain. Consider the two examples of political competition introduced above. Military competition

[17]Thanks to Alan Jacobs for suggesting this line of argumentation.

occurs among nation-states, which are territorial units, each of which contains a wide array of political institutions. Electoral competition occurs among parties, all of which operate under a particular set of electoral rules. While political parties and nation-states may face intense competition, it is not clear that the notion of competition between, say, electoral institutions is a meaningful one. Thus, where competition operates in politics, it often operates "above" (interstate conflict) or "below" (among contending organizations) the level of domestic political institutions. At a minimum, analysts would need to carefully specify the conditions for competitive pressures to generate improvements in institutional design. In practice, such conditions are generally going to be absent or weak in nonmarket settings.

My overall point in this section is not that competition and learning are implausible mechanisms of institutional enhancement. On the contrary, it would be hard to deny that political institutions may be modified and enhanced through each of these processes. Rather, the point is that in the political world each of these mechanisms exhibits considerable limitations. Thus, any tendency toward "evolved functionalism," either actor-centered or societal, should be treated as highly variable. Instead of assuming the efficacy of such mechanisms, political scientists should engage in sustained investigation of the circumstances under which they can be expected to operate reasonably well.

Formidable as these limitations of enhancement mechanisms may be, the problems for functionalist accounts do not stop there. A final problem applicable to both learning and competition needs to be mentioned, and it sets the stage for the next chapter. Even if these mechanisms do operate in a particular setting, we need to know how quickly they operate. As Hannan and Freeman argue, learning enhances "the chance of survival only if the speed of the response is commensurate with the temporal patterns of relevant environments" (Hannan and Freeman 1989, p. 70). If the tempo of such enhancements is slower than the rate of environmental change, these mechanisms will generally be ineffective in restoring some kind of functional equilibrium (Elster 1983, p. 44; March and Olsen 1989, p. 55).

In fact, there are substantial factors that may slow, if not stop, the operation of any mechanisms of enhancement, rendering them relatively ineffective in environments that are also shifting over time. I have just outlined an "internal" critique of arguments about institutional enhancement, emphasizing why these pressures will often be weak. But one also needs to consider an external critique. Assume for a moment that competitive pressures are significant, or learning is considerable. Does it follow that institutional refinement must result? The answer is no. Even where these mechanisms are clearly operative, they face additional hurdles: in Williamson's words, learning or competitive pressures must still be "folded back into the . . . design." For reasons discussed in Chapter Five, this will often be very hard to do.

The Limits of Institutional Design

This initial discussion of rationalist explanations of institutional arrangements suggests that two corrections are called for: (1) functionalist *premises* about institutional origins and change should be replaced by carefully specified functionalist *hypotheses*; and (2) functionalist hypotheses should be supplemented and contrasted with hypotheses stressing the possible nonfunctionalist roots of institutions. We should expect the prevalence of functional outcomes in the construction and reconstruction of political institutions to be highly variable. More subtle theories of institutional origins and change must be built around careful argument about the preconditions for functional outcomes to occur. This requires the specification of where such claims might break down and the circumstances that make the presence of such unfavorable conditions more or less likely.

Rather than assuming that institutions originate and change to meet functional requirements, we need to make this a target for investigation. This is wide-open terrain for systematic research. It may be true, as Nixon said of Keynesianism, that we are all institutionalists now. Yet social scientists have produced relatively little sustained empirical work, organized around clear competing hypotheses, comparing institutional origins and change across different settings. Without this research, we are in no position to evaluate the impact of particular contextual features on institutional outcomes, or even to establish how prevalent such features are in the political world.

The issues discussed in this chapter underscore the importance of examining the intertemporal aspects of politics, rather than taking a "snapshot" view of political processes and outcomes. Functionalist accounts typically are based on the analysis of particular moments—either the moment of institutional origin, or the contemporary functioning of an established institution (deducing origins from current functioning). To see where these accounts might come up short, one must consider dynamic processes that can highlight the implications of short time horizons, the scope of unintended consequences, the efficacy or limitations of learning and competitive mechanisms that play out over time, or the possibly self-reinforcing effects of institutions over extended periods. This requires *genuinely* historical research. By genuinely historical research I mean work that carefully investigates processes unfolding over time, rather than simply mining history for illustrations of essentially static deductive arguments.

Highlighting the benefits of more genuinely historical work implies that the new institutional economics is unlikely to provide a sufficient basis for theories of institutional origins and change in politics. Indeed, I have stressed throughout that efforts to translate theoretical arguments from the economic realm to the political one are more perilous than is often recognized. Such translations need to be done with care, and with an appreciation for the limits of the analogy. This is not to dismiss the "new institutional economics" and its rational choice offshoots in political science. These lines of inquiry have generated fundamental insights. Indeed, much of the current analysis is built around a range of contributions grounded in theories of rational choice. There is little question that insights about institutional functioning must be an important component of our understanding of institutional development. Furthermore, rational choice scholars have made an effort to show how various obstacles to functional dynamics might be overcome.

To emphasize both insights and limitations is not to advocate that we "split the difference" among alternative approaches. It is to recognize that distinct bodies of theory may provide greater leverage for analyzing particular contexts and dynamics. As Jepperson (1996) has put it, seemingly antagonistic "theoretical imageries" may sometimes (but only sometimes) be more complementary and less competitive than we realize. They may cover different aspects of processes, with different theories contributing "modules" that can potentially be linked to produce more complete accounts (Scharpf 1997). They may be discussing discrete phenomena. They may possess poorly articulated boundary conditions (x will hold under conditions a, b, and c, but y will hold under conditions d, e, and f).

All these relationships among theoretical imageries would seem to be relevant here. The most straightforward one concerns boundary conditions. The analysis in this chapter suggests that particular contexts are more favorable to functionalist accounts—namely, those where conditions are such that we can expect initial designers to behave instrumentally, focus on long-term institutional effects, and be relatively accurate in their projections concerning those effects. I would not suggest that political circumstances where these various combinations of favorable conditions hold will be unheard of; indeed, they are probably fairly common. On the other hand, it seems highly unlikely that they will be so common that theorists can safely operate from functionalist assumptions. Functional explanations of institutional origins and change are not wrong headed, but they are radically incomplete. As a consequence, they suggest a world of political institutions that is far more prone to efficiency and continuous refinement, far less encumbered by the preoccupations and mistakes of the past, than the world we actually inhabit.

Social scientists have built their limited inquiries about the origins of institutional arrangements around the study of institutional effects. Rational choice scholars have highlighted some main effects (or "functions") and have based their explanations for institutions around the idea that these functions can be the goals of institutional designers. Without denying this possibility, I will suggest in the next chapter that institutional effects need to be interpreted more broadly. Once in place, institutions have many consequences, particularly over the long run, which reshape political environments. Institutions take on a life of their own and become genuinely independent causal forces in shaping further institutional development. We need to adapt the rich rational choice literature on institutional effects, with its characteristic concentration on immediate polit-ical and policy outcomes, to the distinctive problem of how established institu-tions modify the prospects for further institutional change. Doing so will help us move beyond a focus on moments of institutional choice to the sustained study of institutional development.

Chapter Five

INSTITUTIONAL DEVELOPMENT

> We, too, are interested in equilibrium, but we insist that
> equilibrium can be understood only within a dynamic
> framework that explains how it comes about (if in fact
> it does). Neoclassical economics describes the way the
> world looks once the dust has settled; we are interested
> in how it goes about settling. This is not an idle issue,
> since the business of settling may have considerable
> bearing on how things look afterwards. More important,
> we need to recognize that the dust never really does settle—
> it keeps moving about, buffeted by random currents of air.
> This persistent buffeting by random forces turns out to
> be an essential ingredient in describing how things
> look on average over long periods of time.
> —*H. Peyton Young (1998)*

> Formal political institutions have great capacities
> for eliminating alternatives.
> —*Elisabeth Clemens and James Cook (1999)*

THE ARGUMENTS PRESENTED IN CHAPTER FOUR suggested the need to shift our focus from explaining moments of institutional choice to understanding processes of institutional development. Indeed, the need to do so is increasingly recognized in the social sciences, although efforts in that direction remain halting. In the first two sections of this chapter I review the efforts of historical and sociological institutionalists to explain institutional change. I then draw on the preceding chapters to outline a distinct approach to the subject of institutional development.

Much of the literature I review has focused on why and how particular sets of actors can be catalysts for institutional change. My argument, by contrast, is about how lengthy processes of institutionalization condition the circumstances confronting these reformers. In short, I prefer to talk about institutional development rather than institutional change because the former term encourages us to remain attentive to the ways in which previous institutional outcomes can channel and constrain later efforts at institutional innovation. By now the central themes will be familiar: early steps in a process may fundamentally restrict the range of options available at later ones; identifying the mechanisms that generate such constraints can be a source of powerful insights into the determinants of institutional change; important influences on courses of development may operate only over extended periods of time and are unlikely to be captured by snapshot accounts focused on the choices of particular actors. In combination, these themes suggest some important propositions about processes of institutional development and point to a distinct agenda for future research. In doing so, they demonstrate the substantial advantages that come from addressing these crucial issues of contemporary social theory from a vantage point emphasizing how processes unfold over time.

ALTERNATIVE APPROACHES TO INSTITUTIONAL CHANGE

Choice-theoretic analyses have typically broached the issue of institutional change only implicitly or at the margins. By contrast, other social scientists have addressed the question directly. In this section, I draw on recent work in political science and sociology on institutional change to outline some of the major themes developed in this literature.[1] A number of important claims emerge from these analyses. Yet they, like the choice-theoretic arguments about institutional enhancement reviewed in Chapter Four, can be greatly strengthened by more systematic attention to the ways in which institutional arrangements that are in place for an extended period can structure the conditions for their own revision.

Historical and sociological institutionalists take many of the limits to actor-based functionalism explored in the last chapter as points of departure. Political institutions are depicted as the results of multiple processes, including, but not easily reduced to, the strategic choices of goal-oriented actors. Change in environmental conditions, balances of social power, or unanticipated institutional effects all can facilitate major efforts to generate institutional change. For reasons that I will discuss at the end of this section, it is difficult to discern clear propositions in this literature about the circumstances that are conducive to particular patterns of change in formal institutions. Nonetheless, a number of distinct and interesting lines of argument are discernible.

The Significance of "Critical Junctures"

As Thelen (1999, 2003) has emphasized, historical institutionalists have frequently argued that institutional change typically involves a dynamic of "punctuated equilibrium" (Krasner 1989; Collier and Collier 1991). There are brief

---

[1] For extensive reviews, see Clemens and Cook 1999, and Thelen 1999, 2003. For a very useful contrast of "rational choice," "sociological," and "historical" variants of the "new institutionalism," see Hall and Taylor 1996.

moments in which opportunities for major institutional reforms appear, followed by long stretches of institutional stability. Junctures are "critical" because they place institutional arrangements on paths or trajectories, which are then very difficult to alter.

Arguments about critical junctures were discussed in Chapters One and Two. The branching model employed, with an emphasis on how institutional outcomes at one point in time push social development on distinct tracks, is broadly consistent with the argument I wish to develop in this chapter. As critics have pointed out, however, these analyses often have had a difficult time accounting for institutional change (Thelen 1999, 2003). Critical junctures are often attributed to big, exogenous shocks. In this literature, major events such as war or economic crisis constitute a catalyst for enduring institutional changes. The explanation of change in these moments is thus typically idiosyncratic and post hoc. Furthermore, while the investigation of critical junctures has led to significant insights into the sources of institutional reproduction following the critical juncture (Krasner 1989), these studies have had little to say about downstream processes of further institutional change. Institutions are often seen as stable until the next critical juncture arrives—as Thelen (2003, p. 19) argues, these models "tend to distinguish sharply between periods of institutional creation and periods of 'stasis.'"

The Role of Marginal Groups in Generating Institutional Change

A second major theme in this literature is that previous "losers" are often a catalyst for institutional change (Clemens 1997; Clemens and Cook 1999; Thelen 2003). As Clemens and Cook (1999, p. 452) argue, "Groups marginal to the political system are more likely to tinker with institutions. . . . Denied the social benefits of current institutional configurations, marginal groups have fewer costs associated with deviating from those configurations." In a sense, these authors have followed up on Riker's broad suggestion about institutional malleability.[2] Under the logic suggested by Arrow's impossibility theorem, those on the losing end in the initial round should be able to cobble together an alternative coalition in favor of revision. Yet underlying this focus on the political periphery are a number of critiques of actor-based functionalism: the emphasis on the collective benefits of institutional arrangements rather than their distributional consequences (Knight 1992); the lack of attention to the continuing (often partly submerged) realities of political conflict (Moe 2003); and the

---

[2]Consider Riker (1980, pp. 444–45): "In the end, therefore, institutions are no more than rules and rules are themselves the product of social decisions. Consequently, the rules are also not in equilibrium. One can expect that losers on a series of decisions under a particular set of rules will attempt (often successfully) to change institutions and hence the kind of decisions produced under them." See Shepsle 2003 for a recent discussion of Riker's ideas.

"snapshot" orientation toward the moment of institutional choice, which obscures the possibility that changes in circumstances may lead previously weak actors to effectively challenge institutional arrangements (Thelen 2004).

The Significance of Overlapping Processes

As I noted in Chapter Two, while rationalist accounts generally focus on a single institutional arrangement, others have argued that it is important to examine interaction effects among multiple institutional realms. In Karen Orren and Stephen Skowronek's formulation (1993, p. 321), "The institutions that constitute the polity . . . will abrade against each other and, in the process, drive further change." By pointing to the interplay of multiple institutions as a source of both tensions and opportunities, this discussion of institutional change highlights a possible source of dynamism which studies focused exclusively on a single institution are unlikely to capture.

Melnick's (1994) analysis of the "rights revolution" that has fueled regulatory expansion in the United States provides a good example. Tracing this revolution through multiple venues and over an extended stretch of time, he demonstrates that it must be understood as the result of an interaction between the courts and Congress. Newly emergent citizens' organizations played a crucial role in coupling these distinct institutional sites. Advocates of policy activism in the federal courts and congressional committees have, through interplay between the two branches, been able to advance their agendas beyond what a majority in Congress would have been likely to produce on its own. The development of the rights revolution has, in turn, changed the functioning of all three branches of the federal government in important ways. Innovative groups have been able to exploit the interaction effects among institutions to activate previously dormant possibilities within each institutional setting. Similarly, Baumgartner and Jones (1993) stress how the opening of new political venues can result in rapid institutional change by disrupting or circumventing arenas controlled by previously dominant actors.

The Role of Institutional Entrepreneurs

Accounts of institutional change often highlight the role of "entrepreneurs" (Schickler 2001) or "skilled social actors" (Sweet, Fligstein, and Sandholtz 2001). Mobilization for institutional reform typically creates very difficult collective action problems. Well-situated and creative actors may play a crucial role in framing reform proposals so as to motivate participants and fashion coalitions. If, as Schickler argues, institutional reforms are often "common carriers" for multiple interests (Schickler 2001), then entrepreneurial action may be necessary to craft these solutions and persuade the disparate parties to work together in pursuit of them.

Although stressing the role of human agency in generating institutional change, this literature also highlights certain structural features that facilitate entrepreneurial efforts (Clemens and Cook 1999). Most important is the position of particular actors with respect to multiple social networks (Padgett and Ansell 1993). Because entrepreneurial action requires the construction of coalitions and innovative framing of issues, actors who straddle significant social networks are especially well situated to engage in "skilled social action."

Identifying Typical Processes of Institutional Change

In keeping with themes explored throughout this volume, these analyses have stressed the importance of identifying typical processes of institutional change (Thelen 2003). Recognizing such patterns is viewed as a crucial component in the larger project of developing a persuasive body of theory about the conditions influencing paths of institutional change. Three types of change have received particular attention: layering, functional conversion, and diffusion.

Like the arguments about institutional enhancement discussed in Chapter Four, mechanisms of layering and functional conversion build from the idea that institutions face pressures to adapt to changes in social context. At the same time, they incorporate a recognition that formal political institutions may be difficult to replace wholesale—a theme that I will explore in detail below. As discussed by Thelen (2003, p. 225), *layering* "involves the partial renegotiation of some elements of a given set of institutions while leaving others in place." In some cases, existing institutional arrangements may remain intact, but other institutions are added on—perhaps modifying the functioning of preexisting ones. Schickler (2001, p. 15) suggests that "new coalitions may design novel institutional arrangements but lack the support, or perhaps the inclination, to replace preexisting institutions established to pursue other ends." He points to the evolution of congressional rules for budgeting as an example (p. 16). Reforms in the 1970s, designed to create a more centralized budgeting procedure, were layered on top of existing budgetary arrangements. New budget committees were "superimposed . . . on a decades-old structure of authorization, appropriations, and revenue committees. . . . Too many members had a stake in their existing power bases to allow the dismantling of the old budgetary system."

"Layering" may also involve the creation of "parallel" or potentially "subversive" institutional tracks. Reformers lacking the capacities to overturn existing institutional arrangements may try to nurture new ones, in the hope that over time they will be able to assume more and more prominence. Steven Teles (1998) has pointed to this kind of process in the case of pension reform. Unable to directly challenge existing, well-entrenched systems of public provision, conservative reformers in the United States focused on the establishment of a parallel path—private, funded arrangements backed by public subsidies. In the long run, such layered arrangements can present a successful challenge to the institutional status quo.

What Thelen (2003, p. 226) calls *institutional conversion* refers to situations where "existing institutions are redirected to new purposes, driving changes in the role they perform and/or the functions they serve." Specific institutions potentially may serve many purposes. As a result, what may look like institutional continuity in a formal sense may disguise very considerable changes in institutional functioning. Furthermore, because the meaning of formal rules must be interpreted, and multiple interpretations are often plausible, the substantive role of a set of rules may change even in the absence of formal revision.

As with institutional layering, Thelen argues that conversion may be carried out either by the same sorts of actors who originally created the institution, or by new actors, as a "consequence of the incorporation of groups previously on the margins who turn institutions to new ends." The mechanism of functional conversion thus builds in part on a key claim about the character of institutional environments. As already noted, these environments are often populated with groups who are less than satisfied with existing arrangements and thus eager to exploit opportunities to turn institutions to new purposes. Institutions, Schneiberg and Clemens (forthcoming) argue, "generate grievance (through political exclusion). . . . Actors who are aggrieved but not co-opted are an important source of pressure for institutional change."

A final mechanism of institutional change emphasized in this literature is *diffusion*. Unlike the arguments about layering and conversion, claims about diffusion often suggest the wholesale replacement of institutions. Sociologists in particular have argued that fields of organizational activity often develop a strong consensus on the appropriate institutional technology to be employed for a specific purpose (Meyer and Rowan 1977; DiMaggio and Powell 1991; Jepperson 2001). A number of distinct processes can give rise to this type of consensus, such as the dependence of peripheral actors on more central ones for resources. Particular weight, however, has been placed on the development of clear norms of legitimate behavior in social contexts that are highly rationalized. These "organizational fields" are populated by groups of professionals who are densely networked and have considerable resources and incentives to disseminate models of appropriate action. Where the conditions for such a consensus are present, particular arrangements that are outside the consensus are likely to suffer a decline of legitimacy and face strong pressures to adapt over time. Sociologists emphasize the prevalence of "institutional isomorphism," in which practices within an organizational field exhibit far greater convergence than one would expect based on purely endogenous processes.

Although presented as arguments about institutional change, these claims about isomorphism have generally been applied to quite different sets of practices than the formal political rules under consideration here. Much of the sociological literature focuses on standardized practices, such as norms, rather than on formal institutions. In recent years, however, there was been growing attention to isomorphic processes that would affect the formal institutional properties of nation-states (Meyer et al. 1997). Some sociologists argue that the cultural development of something like a "world society," has accelerated dramatically in recent history—especially after World War II. This is seen as a major source of both institutional convergence, as polities without particular institutional features adopt them, and similar patterns of institutional change across nation-states, as increasingly legitimized norms induce all states to adopt new procedures. The result is "a world in which national states, subject to only modest coercion or control, adopt standard identities and structural forms" (Meyer et al. 1997, p. 174). These accounts emphasize that functionality has little to do with these patterns of institutional development—indeed, what is striking to these observers is the limited impact of local conditions, which would be expected to produce a far greater diversity of institutional forms. As I noted in Chapter Four, Blais and Massicotte have identified spatial and temporal clusters in the structure of formal institutions that are highly suggestive of a diffusion dynamic.

Some Problems

Later in this chapter I will draw in part on the insights in this emerging literature to fashion some propositions about institutional development. At this stage, however, I wish to emphasize three important limitations.[3] The first is the paucity of claims about when we should expect institutional change to occur, or when we should expect to see some patterns of institutional change rather than others. Thelen (2003, p. 37), for instance, concludes by stressing that her essay has focused on conceptual innovation—the identification of modes of institutional change. She acknowledges that identifying "the factors or conditions that facilitate different modes of change" constitutes a "crucial [research] frontier." In this respect it is perhaps telling that I have resorted to a list of "themes" in summarizing this literature. Without minimizing the significance of these contributions, they often leave us in a position similar to some of the "just-so" explanations discussed in Chapter Two: sometimes institutional change looks like this, sometimes like that. From this literature one gets only limited ideas about when, for example, "losers" from previous rounds will be able to press successfully for institutional change, or when we would expect to see mechanisms like functional conversion or layering come into play.[4]

There are important exceptions. Schickler (2001), for instance, develops a number of clear and innovative propositions about the circumstances that should be conducive to particular kinds of institutional change. These are, however, restricted to the specific terrain he examines—institutional arrangements

---

[3]Only the last of these, I hasten to note, applies to arguments about isomorphism.
[4]Clemens and Cook (1999, p. 451), for example, note that dense network ties may "facilitate either containment or diffusion"—that is, either institutional stability or institutional change. Again, this is identified as an important issue for further research.

within the American Congress.[5] Schickler is cautious about drawing broader implications, and rightly so, given the extent to which his imaginative arguments turn on some of the peculiar features of Congress. Indeed, I will suggest later that many of his propositions are unlikely to prove portable beyond the particular setting he explores. This does not diminish his achievement, since clear and persuasive claims about factors influencing institutional development in a single important context are substantial contributions. Yet it remains some distance from a set of plausible claims about the factors influencing diverse paths of institutional development.

This paucity of propositions stems in part from the second problem in these studies, which is the selection biases that emerge from the typical method of inquiry employed in these studies. Essentially, this literature has progressed by building claims from case studies of institutional change. In many respects, this focus has been salutary. As I have emphasized, social scientists miss a great deal if they do not trace institutional arrangements over time. Snapshots hive off important aspects of the problem of institutional development, yielding misleading conclusions. Unintended consequences, for instance, are unlikely to be observed, much less analyzed. It is probably only through the careful tracing of particular historical processes that many of the key theoretical questions about institutional change could even be formulated. And these studies, by identifying and highlighting particular pathways of institutional change, have made a crucial contribution to conceptual development.

By their very nature, however, these studies cannot tell us much about how common particular kinds of institutional change might be. It is hard not to take from them the implicit suggestion that the changes described are fairly frequent—since case studies are often concluded with a set of broad implications to be drawn from them. But in fact, of course, these studies may focus on processes that are quite unusual. And single studies of institutional change, even while usefully pointing to important political phenomena, have distinct liabilities when used as a source of sharp hypotheses about variation in institutional outcomes. Because these are all studies of substantial institutional change, it is difficult to be sure which factors are important in generating the observed outcomes. Factors emphasized—such as the efforts of skilled social actors—may also have been present in other cases where change is not observed.

[5]A few examples: entrepreneurs are more important when some specifiable types of interests are central (e.g., broad congressional interests); dismantling rather than layering of institutions is more likely when a new majority appears after a long period in the minority; efforts to introduce broad Congress-strengthening reforms are more likely during or after wars, and have become increasingly common over the course of the twentieth century; majority party interests are far more likely to motivate institutional reforms in the House than in the Senate; and certain kinds of institutional reform coalitions are more common than others—e.g., those combining majority party interests with broad institutional interests, or minority party interests with the interests of junior members.

A third problem, also related to the reliance on case studies of change, is the tendency to focus on the immediate sources of institutional change—the catalysts. Single case studies will often have a hard time identifying the role of structural factors. These, by their very nature, will typically show little variation within a single case (Rueschemeyer, Stephens, and Stephens 1993, pp. 32–34). As was discussed in Chapter Three, single case studies, unless very carefully designed, are unlikely to highlight structural factors that influence outcomes only with substantial lags, or by restricting the range of possible outcomes. This is especially problematic given the significant role of positive feedback in processes of institutionalization—a topic discussed in detail below. If actors make adaptations and commitments to institutions, institutional equilibria will often deepen over time. Where this happens, a long, slow erosion of the preconditions for institutional reproduction may be a crucial factor in generating institutional change. What may seem like a relatively rapid process of reform is in fact only the final stage of a process that has in fact been underway for an extended period.

Instead, case studies of institutional change will often be drawn to the study of "triggers." Broad, structural features, as well as long, slow-moving processes, which may be crucial preconditions for institutional change, recede from view. In part because such studies make it possible to examine moments of institutional change in fine detail, the role of particular actors in initiating such movements is likely to be highlighted. Yet these studies have greater difficulty in identifying those features that facilitate, impede, or channel entrepreneurial activity.

In short, it is probably not accidental that this literature has placed heavy weight on the role of particular kinds of actors—entrepreneurs, "skilled social actors," and "losers"—in generating change. By contrast, there has been much less emphasis on the types of circumstances that make those kinds of efforts more or less likely to succeed, or that constrain the direction of successful reform efforts. The characteristic blind spots of single studies of institutional change, it must be emphasized, become especially problematic when these inquiries are being used to foster conceptual development and generate hypotheses, as has been the case in the study of institutional change. The biases contained in these accounts will be transferred to the development of concepts and hypotheses employed in broader studies of institutional change.

The final problem is a preoccupation with the sources of pressure for change. This literature is not only overly preoccupied with studying the contributions of institutional reformers; it is more generally focused on the factors that lead to *demands* for change. This is true even for more structural accounts, such as the sociologists' arguments about institutional diffusion and isomorphism and the emphasis historical institutionalists have placed on "critical junctures." Why is this a problem? Because understanding the preconditions for particular types of institutional change requires attentiveness not only to the pressures for reform but also to the character and extent of *resistance* to such pressures. Change and stability are two sides of the same coin. The successful generation of grievances against particular institutional arrangements must be understood as partly a breakdown in the factors reinforcing the status quo. An adequate theory of institutional development must pay sustained attention to the issue of institutional resilience.[6]

INSTITUTIONAL RESILIENCE AND INSTITUTIONAL DEVELOPMENT

Absent a consideration of the sources of institutional resilience, we cannot assess the effectiveness of the mechanisms of institutional enhancement emphasized in rationalist accounts, or the mechanisms of institutional change identified by historical and sociological institutionalists. As institutional resilience increases, the effectiveness of these mechanisms declines. Equally important, where we can establish the features of a particular setting that increase resilience, we gain insights into the factors that facilitate particular kinds of institutional change. Because resilience is a variable, and because its effects may be to channel rather than simply prevent institutional reform, a careful exploration of its roots can help us to think more clearly about the prospects for "bounded" institutional innovation (Thelen 1999, 2003, 2004).

I will argue below that many of the key concepts for an understanding of institutional resilience can be found in work of rational choice scholars. Yet for the most part rationalist theories of institutional choice have not regarded this dimension of institutional development as particularly important. The reasons for this oversight are clear. Rationalist accounts are generally optimistic about the capacities of designers. At the same time, they have typically emphasized institutional plasticity and the capacity of reformers or selection processes to enhance institutional performance over time.

The argument I develop in the remainder of this section, however, is that there are strong theoretical grounds for holding that institutional resilience in many settings is likely to be considerable—far more pervasive than Riker's analysis of institutional cycling suggested. Four major obstacles to revision need to be distinguished: coordination problems, veto points, asset specificity, and positive feedback. Together, these factors often make revision quite difficult. Equally important, they influence the conditions under which revisions will be possible and favor certain kinds of revisions over others. They therefore constitute fundamental building blocks for an understanding of institutional change.

---

[6]I should emphasize that these arguments about institutional resilience represent potential complements, rather than competitors, to arguments about institutional development that focus on catalysts for change. Each approach is likely to capture important aspects of the issue. Later in the chapter I point to instances where there are particularly direct synergies between these lines of argument.

Coordination Problems

Much in recent rationalist theorizing has emphasized how institutions solve co-ordination problems for actors. In these models, actors are better off if they have reliable expectations about the behavior of others. Institutional choice is seen as primarily a matter of actors converging on a focal point that solves their coordination problems (Cox 1997; Carey 2000; Calvert 1995; Hardin 1989; Miller 2000). These actors may disagree about the "best" outcome, but they are eager to reach a shared understanding. Even coordination around some less-desired outcome is better than no coordination at all. In these models, expectations about what others will choose to do are crucial in driving behavior toward a co-ordinated outcome.[7]

Institutions constitute equilibria; once actors have coordinated on one, they have no incentive to unilaterally alter their behavior. Furthermore, an emphasis on coordination and adaptive expectations suggests, as John Carey has argued, "that institutional equilibria are sticky, even in the face of changes in the surrounding political environment" (Carey 2000, p. 754). The formidable difficulties involved in coordinating multiple actors around some possible institutional alternative hamper the prospects for revision (Hardin 1989).

In this sense, actor-centered functionalism does highlight an important source of institutional resilience. Yet here again the equilibria in question seem very fragile—if actors can coordinate around some alternative, even a radically different one, the institution in question should quickly give way. In Carey's lucid account, for instance, the only thing giving greater stability to *formal* political institutions is the fact that they are written down ("parchment" institutions). This makes them stronger focal points. To date, there has been little analysis of just how much stability coordination problems induce. Alexander (2001) has suggested an important limitation—echoing the work of Clemens, Schickler, and Thelen on "losers" or actors marginalized by the status quo. Because groups that already exist, such as social movements or political parties, will often champion revision efforts, the most formidable coordination problems may already have been solved.

Furthermore, coordination models often say little about what is likely to happen if a particular institutional equilibrium does give way. In many cases, these

---

[7]In its emphasis on solving coordination problems, this institutions-as-equilibria approach is a variant of actor-centered functionalism, but a weaker one. Actors benefit from the solution to their co-ordination problem, but a particular institution can be an equilibrium even though all the actors involved might have preferred some other outcome. In other words, institutional choice can constitute a prisoner's dilemma. Coordination models have some other interesting characteristics. Because these models emphasize the presence of multiple equilibria, they suggest that power relationships may be very important in determining which equilibrium is reached (Knight 1992; Krasner 1991). Because actors will generally prefer some institution to no institution, the typical struggle is over which institution to settle on, and here political resources become crucial (Carey 2000).

models suggest that any new equilibrium may be as likely as any other, regardless of how different it is from the old status quo. In other words, these models are not very helpful for thinking about the paths of likely reform over time for any particular institutional arrangement.[8]

Coordination difficulties do indeed constitute a potential barrier to institutional revision, but they represent a very partial treatment of the sources of institutional resilience. If we are interested in institutional development rather than simply initial institutional choices, we wish to know how fragile particular institutional equilibria might be, what kinds of challenges they may be most vulnerable to, and what kinds of revisions are most likely if challenges do in fact emerge.[9]

In addition to coordination problems, three additional sources of institutional resilience need to be considered: veto points, asset specificity, and positive feedback. These factors are likely to operate even in contexts where learning effects, competitive pressures, challenges from below, or isomorphic processes may be significant. They confer substantial resilience to formal political institutions, extending well beyond the stickiness stemming from coordination problems. This resilience may be sufficient to block institutional change entirely. It may also play a crucial role in channeling efforts at revision along particular paths, making reform in highly institutionalized settings an overwhelmingly incremental process.

Veto Points

Institutional arrangements in politics are typically hard to change. As Goodin (1996, p. 23) puts it, stability and predictability are achieved through "a system of 'nested rules,' with rules at each successive level in the hierarchy being increasingly costly to change." Thus, in many national settings "nested rules" created by ordinary legislation must pass through multiple veto points, often requiring broad supermajorities. In other political settings, such as the European Union, hurdles to change are even greater. And in most polities, efforts to change rules higher in the hierarchy (e.g., constitutions) require even greater levels of consensus. Indeed, many constitutions effectively prohibit—short of a revolutionary rejection of the existing regime—certain types of revision altogether.

As I noted in Chapter One, there are two broad reasons why political institutions tend to be designed to be change resistant. First, in many cases, designers seek to constrain themselves. The key insight of the "credible commitments" literature is that actors can solve the "time inconsistency" problem that otherwise bedevils collective agreements if they remove certain alternatives from their future menu of options. Like Ulysses preparing for the Sirens, political actors

---

[8]Carey (2000) argues to the contrary, but it is not clear on what grounds.
[9]The importance of examining the fragility of institutional equilibria is a central theme in Young 1998.

often bind themselves, restricting their own freedom in order to achieve some greater goal.

Second, those who design institutions and policies may wish to bind their successors. Moe terms this the problem of "political uncertainty" (Moe 1990). Unlike economic actors, political actors lack property rights. Designers know that continuous control over institutions is unlikely. This lack of continuous control has implications both for how institutions are designed and for the prospect of changing institutions once they are created. In particular, those designing institutions must consider the possibility that their political rivals will one day be in power, and will be eager to overturn their designs, or to turn the institutions they create to other purposes. To protect themselves, these actors will often introduce rules that make preexisting arrangements hard to reverse. As Moe (1990, p. 125) puts it, designers "do not want 'their' agencies to fall under the control of opponents. And given the way public authority is allocated and exercised in a democracy, they often can only shut out their opponents by shutting themselves out too. In many cases, then, they purposely create structures that even they cannot control." This is perfectly sensible. Confronting the twin problems of time inconsistency and political uncertainty, designers may reasonably decide to make political institutions change resistant. Nonetheless, this characteristic of political institutions has clear implications for the analysis of institutional change. When actors at a later time attempt to make institutional reforms, they will often face considerable obstacles.

Of course, there is now an extensive political science literature on veto points—a literature to which rational choice scholarship has made extensive contributions (Scharpf 1988; Immergut 1992; Tsebelis 1995, 2000). This literature, however, focuses overwhelmingly on policy change rather than institutional change—largely, perhaps, because the issue of institutional change has until recently been such a peripheral concern for political scientists. Yet the presence of veto points clearly has major implications for both the likelihood of institutional reform and for the kinds of institutional reform that will be most plausible in particular settings.

For the study of institutional development, a crucial issue is not just the number of veto points but their *structure*. Specifically, some institutional veto points are what Gary Miller has called "self-referencing"—the actors protected by them control the process of institutional revision (Miller 2000, p. 539). Not all veto points are self-referencing, and those that are will be self-referencing only with respect to certain kinds of reforms. Sometimes institutional reforms may be introduced by referenda, which can weaken the capacity of political elites to block changes damaging to their interests.[10] In some cases (e.g., Russia in 1993), a president has the legal authority to implement institutional reforms by decrees

---

[10]For example, Italy's major reallocation of political authority to the regions, which passed in a popular vote in October 2001.

that alter electoral laws or diminish the power of the legislature (Cox 1997, p. 18n).

On the other hand, many institutional arrangements are self-referencing because key actors are often very concerned to build such protections into institutional designs. Where the same set of actors who would lose influence as the result of an institutional reform must agree to any revision one would naturally expect a higher level of institutional resilience. In the United States, for example, the 2000 election, in which the person who received the most votes for president was not elected, might have been expected to give rise to strenuous demands for reform or abolition of the Electoral College. Yet no such movement developed. Part of the explanation must be that this feature of the American Constitution is self-referencing: any of the established routes for institutional revision would require the agreement of small states, which would stand to lose influence as the result of a switch to a straightforward popular vote. The same point applies to the United States Senate, which also vastly overrepresents small states. Thus attention to the structure as well as scope of institutional veto points can generate important insights into both the degree of resilience of existing institutions and the most probable pathways of institutional reform.

Alexander's (2001) recent comparative analysis of institutional reforms in Europe suggests the significance of both the scope and structure of veto points. He does not highlight this point—indeed, he wishes to argue that veto points are not particularly important and that institutional revision is generally easy.[11] Yet his empirical discussion (pp. 263–64) of attempts at institutional revision in established European democracies supports the argument presented here. Attempts at major insitutional reform appear to have been much more common, although still relatively rare, in contexts where veto points were minimal (e.g., the French Fourth Republic) or not self-referencing (e.g., the repeated use of referenda in Ireland and Italy).

---

[11]Although I strongly disagree with Alexander's conclusion, which largely discounts the sources of institutional resilience explored here, his article is an important contribution to the emerging discussion of institutional development. He raises a number of important points about the circumstances when institutional revision is likely to be more common—and thus supports the core claim presented here, which is that resilience should be treated as a variable. His sweeping conclusion about the absence of resilience stems, I think, from two sources: his focus on initial periods of democratic consolidation, and his depiction of serious efforts to pursue even incremental institutional reforms as evidence that institutions are not resilient. Yet the approach advanced here also implies that formal institutions are likely to be most prone to major revision during the initial consolidation phase, and it would anticipate that *bounded* innovation (as well as occasional more radical disjunctures) would continue. What it tries to do is establish some of the key factors that make different patterns of revision more prevalent. As I note at several points in this chapter, Alexander's evidence actually seems to support my core claims about the factors that inhibit and channel institutional reform.

Asset Specificity and Positive Feedback

Resilience stems not only from the fact that coordination problems and the presence of veto points may make particular institutional revisions *difficult*. Even more important, individual and organizational adaptations to existing arrangements may also make reversal *unattractive*. Over time, actors may adapt to the new rules of the game by making extensive commitments based on the expectation that these rules will continue. Where such adaptations occur, these actions shift, perhaps radically, the costs and benefits of alternative courses of institutional development. Rather than reflecting the (functional) benefits of institutionalized exchange, institutional continuity (or strong tendencies toward only incremental adjustment) may reflect the rising costs of adopting previously available alternatives.

These commitments, I wish to argue, are extensive and diverse. Equally important, they are likely to accumulate with the passage of time. Thus an implication of a more developmental perspective on institutions would be the following proposition: *all other things being equal, an institution will be more resilient, and any revisions more incremental in nature, the longer the institution has been in place.*[12] This may seem a less than striking assertion, but it contrasts sharply with most coordination models, which would seem to imply that revision of an institution would be little different after it had been in place for twenty years than it would be after twenty minutes. Any difference would be a matter only of changes in the strength of actors' *expectations*, not a change in their preferences for different institutional arrangements. In fact, largely because of developing commitments, we should expect the preferences of actors for different institutional arrangements to be dynamic rather than stable.[13] As I will demonstrate later in this chapter, this has major implications for how we should think about processes of institutional revision.

It is possible, and indeed analytically crucial (Thelen 1999), to say much more about the circumstances that can produce such self-reinforcing processes.

---

[12]In essence, this is an institutional variant of Stinchcombe's famous "liability of newness" argument about social organizations (Stinchcombe 1965).

[13]Avner Greif and David Laitin (2002) have usefully summarized this line of argument as involving an emphasis on what they call "quasi-parameters" and a shift from the "self-enforcing" conception of institutions common in coordination models to a recognition that institutions can be not just self-enforcing but *reinforcing*. "If an institution reinforces itself, more individuals in more situations would find it best to adhere to the behavior associated with it. In particular, exogenous changes in the underlying situation that otherwise would have led an institution to change would fail to have this effect. An institution would be self-enforcing in a wider range of parameters." This paper represents an interesting effort to work from a game-theoretic foundation toward a more sustained consideration of historical dynamics. Tellingly, however, Greif and Laitin conclude (pp. 33–34) that "the standard repeated stage game associated with self-enforcing equilibria is not appropriate for modelling quasi-parameters ... furthering the analysis of self-reinforcement will benefit from a more explicitly dynamic analytical framework."

The following discussion is intended to highlight the nature of the diverse commitments that can result from particular institutional arrangements and the kinds of processes that are likely to generate them. The issue has received surprisingly little attention in political science. This is ironic, since the problem essentially requires the analyst to focus on institutional *effects*—precisely the area that has been at the heart of institutionalist theory. Yet theorists have focused on the effects of institutions on political processes and policy outcomes; rarely have they examined the closely linked question of how an institution's effects on the social and political environment alter in turn the prospects for further institutional revision. One can, however, adapt several insights from institutional theories to address this issue.

What are the important implications that flow from the adoption of a particular institution? The key claim of institutional analyses of various stripes is that this adoption matters—that it has major consequences for future political action. Here our interest is narrower: to what extent do particular institutional adoptions set in motion a set of effects that change actors' calculations of the costs and benefits of alternative institutional arrangements? A useful place to begin is with the concept of *asset specificity*.[14] An extensive body of work in political economy emphasizes variation in the extent to which the value of assets are specific to a particular setting or use, rather than being easily reallocated to some other activity (Alt et al. 1996; Lake 1999). To the extent that their assets are specific, actors are likely to become more committed to the continuation of the activity where those assets are applied. Joskow (1988), drawing on Williamson, distinguishes *site specificity* (where value is based on location), *physical specificity* (where value depends on the type of transaction), *human specificity* (where value depends on specialized knowledge and special relationships or developed trust), and *dedicated assets* (where the value of the assets in question derives from continuing specific exchange).

As Peter Gourevitch has suggested, this argument has tremendous relevance for the study of institutional development:

> Political actors develop investments, "specific assets," in a particular arrangement—relationships, expectations, privileges, knowledge of procedures, all tied to the institution at work. Where investments in the specific assets of an institution are high, actors will find the cost of any institutional change that endangers these assets to be quite high; indeed, actors in this situation may be reluctant to run risks of any change at all. . . . Investment of specific assets helps to explain institutional persistence. As actors in each society invest in a particular institutional arrangement, they have incentives to protect their investment by opposing change. (Gourevitch 2000, pp. 144–45)

[14]The following discussion draws heavily on ideas suggested by Shannon O'Neil Trowbridge, and to joint work in progress.

There are in fact strong political analogues to all the types of asset specificity listed above, which stem from the consequences that flow from particular kinds of institutional arrangements. Individual politicians, political organizations such as parties, interest groups, and even ordinary citizens will, over time, develop assets that may be specific to a political institution (or set of institutions). In a federal system such as that of the United States, for example, where "all politics is local," politicians and political organizations will develop site-specific assets—campaign headquarters, investments of time in traveling through specified areas and talking with geographically concentrated voters, and the development of expertise and reputations associated with particular issues that are important largely within a specific geographic area. Institutional arrangements may encourage investment in specific physical assets, such as particular kinds of party organizations or mobilizing strategies, that would be of far less value under alternative institutional arrangements (Strom and Muller 1999). This is undoubtedly one of the reasons why the organization of political interests often looks remarkably different in different institutional settings (Schmitter and Lehmbruch 1979). Full-time political participants such as politicians and lobbyists also develop extensive specific human assets—namely, their skills in operating effectively within a particular institutional environment and their relationships with actors empowered by those arrangements. Finally, political actors will develop dedicated assets, engaging in implicit or explicit long-term contracts with other actors (e.g., those with more seniority within their organization) where the payoffs to those with less seniority depend on the continuation of institutional arrangements (Bates and Shepsle 1997).

Political scientists have noted in broad terms that political institutions can encourage specific types of investments (Lake 1999; Alt et al. 1996). Yet that observation is usually only used to account for the distinct policy preferences and mobilizational strategies employed in different institutional contexts. What has been missed is the crucial implication that these investments will alter actors' assessments of the benefits of institutional change. Although this important research agenda has been left largely unexplored, the large literature on institutional effects and the relatively well-developed theoretical work on asset specificity could facilitate rapid progress.

Careful readers of Chapter One will note that the discussion of institutional resilience so far stresses some of the key features described there as sources of *positive feedback*—which in turn generates path-dependent development. In such a process, moves in a particular direction can be self-reinforcing, making it increasingly difficult over time to reverse course. Adaptive expectations, particularly in settings where actors have strong incentives to coordinate, generate positive feedback. So does the accumulation of individual and organizational commitments, as emphasized in work on asset specificity. Yet these factors fail to capture the full range of positive feedback effects that accompany processes of institutionalization, and it is important to consider these other effects as well.

Perhaps most important is the development of strong interlinkages among institutional arrangements over time. Once established, formal political institutions become an essential part of the infrastructure on which other, less foundational institutional arrangements are constructed. By "less foundational institutional arrangements" I particularly have in mind public policies. Major public policies represent very substantial extensions of political authority that further alter the incentives and resources of political actors—often dramatically (Weir and Skocpol 1985; Pierson 1993; Hacker 2002; Pierson and Skocpol 2002). Much recent research in comparative political economy (Hall and Soskice 2001a; Kitschelt et al. 1999) and comparative public policy (Esping-Andersen 1990; Huber and Stephens 2001; Pierson 2001) emphasizes the extent to which policy packages in particular countries can be characterized as "regimes"—interlocking pieces that are, in broad terms, complementary. Where complementarities exist, the value of each component is enhanced by the presence of the others. By implication, the removal of one component may diminish the benefits of others. This potential damage to complementary institutions may constitute a major cost of institutional revision.

The role of particular political institutions in underpinning these policy regimes awaits systematic exploration. There is, however, a widespread consensus that the design of institutions has large effects on patterns of interest mobilization, the structure of political cleavages, the distribution of political authority and the capacity of actors to commit to particular kinds of bargains. Thus, we should expect political institutions to be key components in the development of complementary policy arrangements. Indeed, recent research strongly suggests that institutional arrangements are likely to play an important role in generating and sustaining particular policy regimes (Wood 1997; Gourevitch 2000; Swank 2001). To the extent that these regimes are valued, so will be the institutions that support them.

Established institutions thus may create powerful inducements that reinforce their own stability. The costs of particular kinds of institutional revision are likely to increase markedly over time. Arguments about asset specificity can be modified to capture part of this process. Yet in their focus on the individual and organizational level they miss the ways in which formal political institutions and sets of public policies will tend to become interwoven over time. "Political institutions," as March and Olsen stressed, "form a complicated ecology of interconnected rules" (1989, p. 170). Douglas North similarly emphasizes this developing interrelatedness: "In short," he concludes, "the interdependent web of an institutional matrix produces massive increasing returns," making path dependence a common feature of institutional evolution (1990a, p. 95). Once institutions are in place, they facilitate the adoption of other, complementary institutions. All these arrangements place pressure on actors to adjust, often in fundamental ways, to a new context.

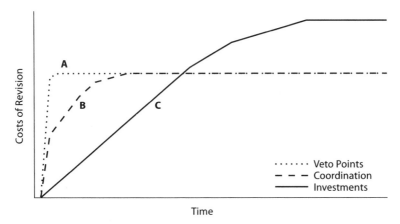

Fig. 5.1. Sources of resilience over time.

Figure 5.1 illustrates some of the implications of this line of argument for the examination of institutional resilience. Curve A indicates the costs of revising institutions when only the structure of veto points is taken into account. These costs are generated as soon as the institution is adopted, and thereafter remain constant over time. Curve B tracks the costs associated with coordination difficulties. The bulk of these costs also appear quite rapidly, although perhaps they will increase moderately as actors' expectations of institutional continuity increase. Curve C displays the costs that we would expect to develop over time as actors and organizations invest in the status quo and develop complementary institutions and policies. In short, while arguments about vetoes and (to a lesser extent) coordination imply stable costs of institutional revision over time, arguments about investments and positive feedback see these costs as dynamic: institutions are typically not only self-enforcing but self-reenforcing.

Theories of institutional development need to pay careful attention to the sources of institutional resilience, both to check any tendency to see institutional revision as a straightforward process and to give us a stronger sense of what kinds of conditions make what kinds of revisions possible. Williamson's confident assertion that learning or competition allow firms to adjust to unanticipated consequences applies far less well to an analysis of politics, and especially to the study of formal political institutions. Learning from past events may lead actors to act differently in launching new initiatives. Recapturing ground in previously institutionalized fields of activity, however, will often be quite difficult. Actors do not inherit a blank slate that they can remake at will when their preferences shift or unintended consequences become visible.

Instead, actors find that the dead weight of previous institutional choices often seriously limits their room to maneuver. Coordination around alternatives may be difficult, and veto points may present formidable obstacles. More fundamentally, the depth and interrelatedness of accumulated investments may make the adoption of previously plausible alternatives prohibitively costly—especially if the institution in question has been in place for some time. Thus, even if the learning and competitive mechanisms emphasized by rationalists are present, it is far from self-evident that these pressures will translate into institutional enhancement. The same applies to arguments of historical and sociological institutionalists about exogenous shocks, diffusion processes, and other potential catalysts of institutional change. Any revisions that do occur will often be powerfully constrained and channeled by previous institutional choices and the processes those choices unleash.

We do not have, and sorely need, systematic data about institutional development that would allow us to subject these broad claims to careful scrutiny. Yet there is at least sketchy evidence to suggest a high level of long-term institutional stability in many settings. Lijphart, a leading expert on comparative political institutions, concludes that "drastic changes in electoral systems and shifts from presidentialism to parliamentarism . . . are extremely rare in established democracies" (Lijphart 1992, p. 208). Colomer (2001, p. 242) divided democratic regimes into three categories: parliamentary/majoritarian, parliamentary/proportional representation, and presidential and semipresidential. In all, he finds only *five* changes in regime type in the absence of democratic breakdown—three parliamentary regime shifts from majoritarian to proportional representation or mixed formulas (Switzerland in 1918, New Zealand in 1993, and Japan in 1994) and two shifts from parliamentary regimes to presidentialist formulas (France in 1958 and Israel in 1996). This suggests a level of institutional stability that provides a strong answer to Riker's pessimism and underscores the broad and deep underpinnings of established institutions. Institutions themselves shape the parameters of future institutional development.

The emphasis placed here on the downstream social and political consequences of formal institutions thus contains a double irony for functionalist accounts. First, it suggests that the idea that social environments "select" for certain outcomes rather than others may often be plausible, but that societal functionalism has the causal arrow backwards. Rather than competitive environments selecting institutions that fit the needs of social actors, institutions, once in place, may "select" actors. This would occur through two processes, familiar to those interested in evolutionary arguments. First, actors adapt to institutional environments by adopting new agendas, strategies, and mobilizing techniques. In the long run, actors' very identities may be powerfully shaped by institutional arrangements. Second, individual and collective actors who do not adapt will often be less likely to survive. Through processes of adaptation and selection, actors whose strategies do not "fit" well in a particular institutional context may become less common over the long haul.

The second and broader irony is that a snapshot view of such a process will mistakenly be viewed as a confirmation of actor-based functionalism. When an analyst cuts into a process of institutional development at any moment in time she may indeed see a relatively nice "fit" between the preferences of powerful actors and the functioning of institutions. This might seem to suggest that we are in the realm of rational institutional design, but in fact such an assertion would get the causality exactly backwards. Rather than these powerful actors generating the institution, the institutional arrangements may have played a powerful role in generating the properties of the actors.

UNDERSTANDING INSTITUTIONAL DEVELOPMENT

All of this could be read to suggest that once institutions are adopted they become "frozen" or "locked in"—in short, as a denial of the possibility of institutional change. Because this is a common assertion of those who see this line of argument as excessively static, it is essential to be clear. The arguments advanced here about resilience do not suggest that formal political institutions, once established, will never change, or that institutional reform will always be incremental, or that only the factors that contribute to resilience are relevant in assessing the prospects for institutional revision. Large-scale social transformations may in fact generate intense pressure for more fundamental reform. In some cases they may overwhelm the factors discussed here (Alexander 2001; Thelen 2003). Riker's discussion of the unexpected development of direct elections for senators in the United States, described in Chapter Four, offers a good example. Over time, the growing social pressures for a more democratic selection process, combined with a changing balance of political power, led to fundamental institutional change. The broad cultural, economic, and social trends fueling processes of democratization have often overwhelmed sources of stability in institutional arrangements (Alexander 2001; Colomer 2001; Rueschemeyer, Stephens, and Stephens 1992).

What the current analysis suggests is that institutions will generally be far from plastic, and that when institutions have been in place for a long time *most* changes will be incremental. Colomer's (2001) study cited above, for example, notes that while the broad contours of democratic regimes have been quite stable over time, more incremental adjustments are fairly common. While institutional stability is often a striking feature of political life, the arguments developed above suggest that we can say quite a bit about what circumstances affect the prospects for making institutional revisions, and about the specific kinds of revisions that will be more or less likely in particular settings.

Consider some of the themes explored by historical and sociological institutionalists. A number of recent analyses have emphasized that a key factor in institutional change is the role of "losers" from previous rounds of institutional selection (Alexander 2001; Clemens and Cook 1999; Schickler 2001; Thelen 2003). Losers may lie low, waiting for an opportunity to pursue their own institutional agenda. Schickler's study of Congress provides substantial empirical support for this possibility in one institutional setting. As discussed above, Thelen has explored some general processes, "functional conversion" and "layering," through which these institutional revisions might occur.

The key issue is whether we can say something systematic about the conditions that facilitate or impede these kinds of revisions. If, as Schneiberg and Clemens suggest, "actors who are aggrieved but not co-opted are important sources of pressures for institutional change," we want to know the circumstances that allow groups to retain organizational strength without being co-opted. In fact, there is reason to think that this is a theoretically tractable question. All the dimensions of resilience discussed above would be relevant to an evaluation of the prospect that losers will be able to stick around and engineer favorable revisions at a later date. How difficult are the coordination problems they face? What is the scope and structure of institutional veto points? Probably most important, how much pressure do they (or their potential supporters) face to adjust to the new institutional status quo?

The answers to these questions are likely to vary, depending on circumstances that we can reasonably aspire to specify. Exploration of the sources of this variation should be a core component of a research agenda on institutional development. Schickler's study of congressional institutions can be used to illustrate the broader point. The answer to the question of how much pressure losers face to adapt *in this particular setting* is "not all that much." In the terms introduced in Chapter Four, this is a context where one can anticipate a fair amount of actor continuity over time. Members of Congress who lost in one round of institutional formation were nonetheless assured of a seat at the table for future revisions. In most cases these changes in the internal rules of Congress had only marginal effects on their prospects for political survival. As a result, this political setting is one where "cycling" dynamics among institutional arrangements are likely to be prevalent, and strong path-dependent effects will be modest—which is exactly what Schickler demonstrates.

As Schickler acknowledges, however, the assurances of actor continuity institutionalized in Congress are hardly typical. In suggesting that his argument is relevant where "members have diverse goals and can each influence [an organization's] structure and processes," Schickler proposes extensions to such settings as "universities, professional associations, national parties made up of semiautonomous state or local units, and governmental agencies charged with multiple and technically complex missions" (2001, p. 268). But he does not consider whether the kind of actor continuity over time built in to core features of

Congress applies in these other settings, and there are grounds for skepticism on this key point.

By contrast, institutional arrangements governing, say, electoral rules, legislative/ executive relations, and the role of the judiciary may put considerable pressure on actors to adapt. In these institutional settings, "losers" may in fact not be around to seek revisions. Even if they are, they may find that the dynamic effects of institutions foster such extensive adaptations among potential supporters that they have little choice but to adapt themselves and limit their ambitions to incremental reform.

Arguments about the sources of institutional resilience also have significant implications for recent claims about the role of political entrepreneurs as drivers of institutional change. Understanding what makes institutional change costly may provide greater clarity about the kinds of circumstances under which such entrepreneurial efforts have a chance of success—something that I have stressed is very difficult to discern when one only examines instances of institutional reform. By making it possible for analysts to specify which aspects of existing arrangements powerful actors are deeply invested in, arguments about resilience may also highlight the kinds of moves that might be available to entrepreneurs. In similar fashion, an examination of these commitments can make it easier to identify which participants a "skilled social actor" could potentially recruit for a reform alliance.

Jacob Hacker (forthcoming) has recently offered a nice formulation of how we might connect the themes highlighted in this literature with an appreciation for the ways in which arrangements may become institutionalized over time. His focus is on policy change rather than institutional change, but the structure of the argument would be identical if one substituted "institution" where he says "policy":

> A set of actors is opposed to the ends of an existing policy. In the starkest calculation, they must decide whether to "work within" this extant policy framework to achieve their ends or "work outside" it by eliminating or replacing it. Seen this way, it becomes clear that two questions loom large. First, how easily can these actors achieve their aims through the existing policy framework? And, second, how costly would it be to replace it with a policy more closely tailored to the ends they desire? If the answer to the first question is "very easily," then the actors may pass up challenging even a policy that would be relatively costless to change. If the answer to the second question is "very costly," then they may try to work within even a policy framework that is heavily biased against the ends they seek (Hacker, forthcoming, p. 9).

The implications are summarized in Figure 5.2, which is modified from Hacker's presentation. In determining their best strategy, reformers must think about the costs and benefits of pursuing "replacement" or "conversion." Depending

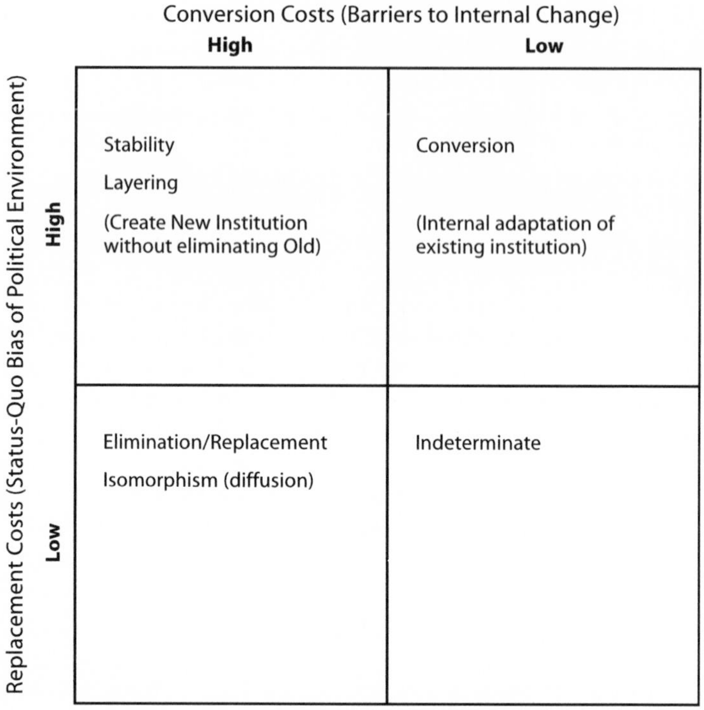

Conversion Costs (Barriers to Internal Change)

	High	**Low**
High	Stability Layering (Create New Institution without eliminating Old)	Conversion (Internal adaptation of existing institution)
Low	Elimination/Replacement Isomorphism (diffusion)	Indeterminate

Replacement Costs (Status-Quo Bias of Political Environment)

Fig. 5.2. Conversion costs, replacement costs, and institutional change.

on these parameters, actors may be encouraged to seek reform from within, replacement of the existing institution, the layering of a new arrangement on top of the old one, or acquiesce to the institutional status quo. Much of the analysis of the costs and benefits of alternative courses of action could be derived from the discussion presented so far in this chapter.

These suggestions for linkages to the research agendas of historical and sociological institutionalists underscore my central point—that to understand institutional development we need to think seriously about institutional resilience. Hannan and Freeman made this key observation in their path-breaking work on organizational ecology, although their focus was on organizations rather than institutions: "Structures that adapt swiftly and effortlessly are unlikely to shape processes of historical change. Another way of putting this is that if organizations are the building blocks of modern societies . . . inertia is what gives them this quality. If organizations are plastic, then only the intentions of organizational elites matter" (Hannan and Freeman 1989, p. 33). Institutions, I have argued, are typically not plastic. They do not adapt swiftly and effortlessly. They are subject to change, but the multiple sources of resilience suggest that in many circumstances they will exhibit very substantial inertia. It is this inertial quality that makes them important contributors to an understanding of long-term processes of institutional development.

An Agenda for the Study of Institutional Development

The central theme of the discussion so far has been that a focus on institutional effects can give us substantial leverage for thinking about institutional development through time. It provides crucial insights, for example, into the important question of whether, and if so, how, "losers" from previous rounds of institutional selection can push for substantial institutional revisions. Yet the line of argument developed so far in this chapter does not simply contribute to themes developed in previous theoretical work on institutional change. In addition, there are important research frontiers concerning institutional development that can be derived specifically from a focus on the downstream effects of institutions and are unlikely to be recognized otherwise. In the remainder of this section I would like to sketch out five lines of inquiry—potential research agendas—that follow from a focus on institutional development rather than institutional choice: deep equilibria, menus of institutional change, institutional coupling, slow-moving processes of institutional change, and policy development.

Deep Equilibria

In Tom Stoppard's *Arcadia*, the precocious young Thomasina asks her tutor "why you can stir jam into pudding, but you cannot stir it out." The first extension I would propose concerns the effort to identify what can be termed *deep equilibria* in paths of institutional development. I have emphasized that a central issue in thinking about institutional arrangements is not simply whether they constitute equilibria, but how stable those equilibria are likely to be in light of changing conditions (Young 1998). A deep equilibrium occurs when the various factors contributing to the resilience of a particular institution or set of institutions are so considerable that once arrangements settle on that point they are highly likely to endure for an extended period of time. The line of argument here is thus a version of the absorbing Markov chain dynamic, which I introduced in Chapter Three with the example of a frog hopping across lily pads.

Let me offer three brief but widely disparate examples: PR electoral systems, separatism, and judicialization.[15] My comments are only meant to be sugges-

[15]Colomer (2001, p. 242) suggests that direct presidential election constitutes another deep equilibrium: "Empirical observation in a broad long-term perspective suggests that once installed, direct presidential elections are not easily abandoned. There have been a few instances of reverse moves, such as Germany after Nazism. But in almost all cases, further redemocratization after an authoritarian period has been followed by a reinstatement of direct presidential elections."

tive, but they indicate the range of potential applications of this line of inquiry. Proportional representation is perhaps the most obvious example—indeed, because it is so straightforward it usefully highlights the phenomenon of a deep equilibrium and makes it relatively easy to specify the mechanisms involved in producing it. Political scientists have long observed that PR systems are rarely overturned short of a change in the entire political regime. Although the mechanisms involved were not clearly specified,[16] the adoption of PR played a crucial role in Lipset and Rokkan's famous argument about "frozen" party systems in twentieth-century European political development. The deep equilibrium of PR systems would appear to have several sources. Most important, small parties that are allowed to emerge or survive because of such rules have an intense interest in institutional continuity. Since the support of these parties will almost always be required to form a governing majority, they can effectively block change. At the same time, such political arrangements can contribute to the development of interest organizations, and, in many cases, patterns of political cleavage that reinforce demands for the continuation of PR.

At least within the context of democratic polities, separatism constitutes a second potential candidate for a "deep" equilibrium. If a distinct region is able to vote for separatism, this vote is unlikely to be reversed, even given a pretty wide range of changes in future conditions. Consider the case of Canada, where Quebec has held several recent referenda on sovereignty. The federalists have won each of these votes, but some of them have been very close. This suggests an important counterfactual: what would happen if separatists were to win one of these votes? Two important effects seem highly probable: first, ascendant separatists would move quickly to adopt institutional arrangements that made it extremely difficult to reverse the decision; and second, there would be massive exit of Anglophones to the rest of Canada. Each of these two effects would reinforce the other, creating a deep equilibrium. There is, in short, a fundamental asymmetry to the ongoing saga of Canadian federalism. Outcomes of the referenda have favored federalists by small but consistent margins. Yet federalists must win every round to sustain the status quo, while their opponents need win only once. Here there are two equilibria, but one appears to be much deeper than the other.[17]

Judicialization offers a third possibility of a deep institutional equilibrium. Polities vary dramatically in the extent to which they are subject to dispute resolution by a relatively independent judiciary. In some countries, courts represent a very weak site of political power within the broader constellation of institutional arrangements, while in other countries the judiciary is extremely powerful. There is also considerable variation in the degree of judicialization across

[16]Bartolini and Mair (1990, p. 57) observe that "the reasons for such persistence or 'freezing' are complex and neither the Lipset-Rokkan essay nor Rokkan's subsequent work found the necessary scope to explore this aspect more fully."
[17]To be clear, I am not arguing that Quebec separatism is the more likely outcome. I am discussing the likely implications of a separatist victory in a referendum if one were to occur.

different sectors of a particular polity. What is notable, however, is the extent to which judicialization seems to be virtually a one-way street. The direction of change over time is overwhelmingly toward expansion. Lijphart (1999, p. 226), for instance, developed a four-point scale measuring the strength of judicial review in thirty-six democracies over the period 1945–1996. Countries are spread out across his scale, and the majority actually have either no judicial review or only weak judicial review. He codes five countries (Belgium, Canada, Colombia, France, and Italy) as having shifted from one category to another, however, and all five moved in the direction of stronger judicial review. You can stir the courts into democratic politics but you cannot stir them out.

There are a number of mechanisms that appear to make expansions of court power virtually irreversible.[18] The emergence of courts as the site of political and legal dispute resolution generates a rapid expansion of law-centered actors who have a considerable stake in preserving and expanding the use of these procedures, as well as substantial resources (the authority to make binding decisions) that greatly facilitate their pursuit of these goals (Epps 1998). Once particular social environments have been judicialized, other actors involved in those domains face powerful incentives to adapt. Judicial procedures become a key part of the rules of the game. Actors thus need to develop the organizational structures and strategic repertoires that make it possible to operate effectively in this context. As different groups make such adaptations, perhaps grudgingly, their investments will increase their support for judicial procedures and reinforce the pressures on other groups to do the same.

The example of judicialization also highlights the significance of long-term processes emphasized by sociologists in explaining the production and reproduction of institutional arrangements. Repeated employment of judicial procedures over an extended period of time is likely to generate profound changes in norms. These methods of dispute resolution obtain a "taken-for-granted" quality (March and Olsen 1989). Everyday practices "chronically reproduce" these institutional arrangements without any conscious effort on the part of the actors involved (Jepperson 1991). Thus, multiple mechanisms operating in a mutually reinforcing fashion make judicialized politics, like PR and separatism, a deep equilibrium.

All else being equal, we would expect arrangements that constitute deep equilibria to become more prevalent over the long run. We would also anticipate that the politics of institutional change would be different in such contexts — namely, overwhelmingly incremental in character. Finally, it seems plausible to suggest that the presence of deep equilibria, if understood by the actors involved, will have consequences for political struggles over institutional reform. Knowing that separatists need to win only one referendum, for instance, could

---

[18]Many of the path-dependent mechanisms outlined briefly here are explored in depth in Stone Sweet 2000, 2002, Hathaway 2001. In the international arena, where "legalization" is less far reaching but still notable, see Goldstein et al. 2001.

have significant effects on the tactics and long-term strategies of both sides in the conflict. In short, it seems extremely fruitful for social scientists interested in institutional development to identify potentially deep equilibria. And the discussion here suggests many of the factors that should in fact be expected to generate such outcomes.

Menus of Institutional Change

For many of the key institutional components of modern polities, there are likely to be a limited number of plausible broad arrangements (although infinite variety in the details). The existence of relatively clear typologies of electoral systems, varieties of legislative-executive relations, central-local relations, and other institutional features of developed democracies suggests that there are often fairly restricted repertoires of institutional moves. Yet those considering institutional reforms are not all selecting from the same menu. Given particular starting points, particular "moves" or paths of development may be much more probable than others. Thus, if the point about deep equilibria is that sometimes $A \rightarrow B$ moves are much more likely than $B \rightarrow A$ moves, the point here is that from institutional arrangement C the likeliest moves are to E or F, while from D the likeliest moves may be to H or I. In other words, we might think of paths of institutional development as being analogous to careers. In professional careers, some sequences appear repeatedly while others are extremely uncommon. It can be highly instructive to try to identify these patterns and specify the structural features that encourage the appearances of some sequences and seem to virtually rule out others (Abbott 1990).

The arguments developed earlier in this chapter offer considerable theoretical resources for thinking about institutional change in this fashion. In pointing to the numerous sources of institutional resilience, I have repeatedly emphasized that this does not imply the absence of institutional change. Understanding the factors that provide the "glue" for a particular institutional arrangement can be extremely helpful for identifying likely paths of institutional reform. If we know, for example, which elements of institutional arrangements constitute important investments for which sets of actors, we are more likely to be able to identify which kinds of revisions they would consider more acceptable and which would be considered more problematic. Similarly, if we know which institutional arrangements are self-referencing, we will have a better idea which paths of potential institutional development are likely to be unreachable from a particular starting point.

A policy example can illustrate this kind of argument: the reform of deeply institutionalized public pension systems in mature welfare states (Myles and Pierson 2001). Most of these pension systems became very well institutionalized by 1980. Yet a series of profound social, economic, and political changes has generated a climate of austerity in which virtually all national pension systems are undergoing substantial revisions. Because different national systems are starting from very different points of departure, with greatly differing degrees of institutionalization, the menu of options available to reformers varies dramatically. Where generous, earnings-related pay-as-you-go pension systems have been in place for a substantial stretch of time, established precommitments make a shift to a funded, individualized system of retirement accounts virtually impossible. Instead, policymakers have pursued reforms designed to control costs and link contributions more closely to benefits. In systems without mature pay-as-you-go plans, more radical reform options remain on the table, and have in fact been implemented in some cases (e.g., the United Kingdom). In short, a clear understanding of where countries are in a course of institutional development give us a much sharper sense of what kinds of reform are most plausible.

Colomer (2001) has advanced an ambitious argument of this sort for formal political institutions. As noted before, he observes tremendous stability in the broad regime characteristics of established democracies—majoritarian, PR, and presidentialist systems are rarely replaced by one of the other models. In all these settings, however, he argues that there are significant political pressures for increasing inclusiveness and pluralism over time. In presidentialist systems, this means shifting to majority runoff or qualified plurality rules in presidential elections, as well as efforts to heighten presidential accountability and create a more balanced division of powers. In parliamentary systems, there have been clear trends toward greater proportionality in electoral systems (Lijphart 1999). In short, countries with different broad institutional regimes are unlikely to switch paths. Thus, in contemplating reform they are effectively choosing from different menus. Within each regime type, however, the list of plausible reforms is likely to be limited.

Inquiries focused on menus of reform options may not produce clear-cut expectations of positive outcomes (i.e., "given institutional arrangement x, we should expect to witness institutional development y"). Rather, the claims will be more along the lines of "you can't get there from here," or "y and z are plausible developments from the starting point x, but q is extremely unlikely." Because social scientists are routinely taught to strive for "if x then y" statements this may seem like a modest achievement. However, if it is reasonable to argue that there is often a limited repertoire of plausible institutional arrangements to begin with, then being able to assign very low probabilities to one or two of those possibilities constitutes a significant contribution to knowledge. As I suggested in Chapter Four, it is arguably much more informative than our efforts to "explain" a single instance of institutional change by working backwards from a single observed outcome. Andrew Abbott has put the central point forcefully:

Imagine if we could tell a policy maker not just, "Well, if you put x amount of money on that problem the problem will grow .15 less than it otherwise would have next year." But suppose we could say, "Well, if you put x amount of money on the problem, then *a* and *b* might happen, and if *a* happens then perhaps *c*, but if both *a* and *b*, then *c* is quite unlikely, and, since *c* is necessary to *d* where you want to go, then you can't solve your problem by this approach, unless you can avoid *b*." Imagine if that were not just a thought experiment that we all can do in interpreting regression results, but were a direct result of standard methods applied to data on policy experiences. That would be policy science indeed. (Abbott 1997, pp. 1168–69)

Institutional Coupling

A third promising line of argument for exploring institutional development would examine interaction effects among multiple institutions. In many cases, we can expect paths of institutional development to be shaped by key relationships among institutions—the focus of inquiry should be on this meso-institutional level, rather than on dynamics purely internal to a single institution taken in isolation (Pierson and Skocpol 2002). This, one may recall, is a central claim in Orren and Skowronek's work on historical processes of development involving multiple, overlapping institutions. Because the current discussion has been more focused on identifying the circumstances producing particular kinds of institutional effects, however, it leads to specific suggestions about likely institutional interactions and their implications for paths of institutional development.

At least two broad possible types of interactions seem particularly relevant—although this list could no doubt be expanded. The first, already discussed in this chapter, is the possibility that there may be quite substantial complementarities among distinct institutions—that is, two or more institutional arrangements are mutually reinforcing. The existence of complementarities among institutions would carry a number of significant implications for patterns of institutional development. Where such complementarities are substantial, we should expect to observe distinct clusterings of institutional arrangements. If institution X is present, we will be more likely to see the development of institution Y, all other things being equal. Indeed, there *is* evidence of such clustering (Gourevitch 2002).[19] Where complementarities are present, we would also expect the presence of each institution to have a positive effect on the durability of the other institution—again, all else being equal. Finally, substantial reform of one institution would be expected to increase the probability of change in complementary institutions.

---

[19]Clustering, of course, could have other sources than mutual reinforcement resulting from complementarities. Most obviously, the same factors (e.g., a particular set of powerful actors) that gave rise to one institution could give rise to the other. Empirical research exploring institutional development over time can establish the role of mutual reinforcement in generating observed patterns of institutional clustering (Thelen 2004).

If institutional development may be influenced by tight coupling or complementarities, there are likely to be significant consequences of specific forms of
"loose coupling" as well. The form of loose coupling among institutions that I
refer to is one where there are substantial ambiguities about the allocation of authority among them. The notion of ambiguity is suggested in Richard Neustadt's
famous description of the United States as not a separation-of-powers system but
one of "separate institutions sharing power" (Neustadt 1990). These ambiguities
create opportunities, especially for those unhappy with the status quo.

The core suggestion here builds on the insight of E. E. Schattschneider that
different institutional settings constitute distinct "venues" in which political organizations can seek to pursue their goals (Schattschneider 1960). Since each
venue is structured differently, each presents different constraints, risks, and opportunities for political actors, and requires distinctive strategies. Thus, actors
who are disadvantaged in one institutional venue often have strong incentives to
pursue a shift in political activity to alternative venues, if the relationships
among institutions make this possible. Institutional interaction may involve
arrangements that are potential alternatives rather than complements.

Arguments about the role of multiple institutional venues have become a sta-
ple in treatments of policy development, at least in the United States (Baumgartner and Jones 1993; Melnick 1994). Little attention, however, has been
given to the implications of loose institutional coupling for patterns of institutional development. There are good reasons to suspect that such loose coupling
will present opportunities for venue-shopping among institutional reformers as
well. Here again, there are potentially strong synergies with some of the significant themes sociological and historical institutionalists have developed about
catalysts for institutional change. Both the role of entrepreneurs and previously
marginal actors are likely to be quite distinctive in settings involving loosely coupled institutions, where they may have access to a number of relatively well understood political strategies. The availability of such venue-shopping strategies
also suggests that there is a plausible link between the presence of loosely coupled institutions and the prevalence of unintended consequences in institutional development. Where demarcations of authority are ambiguous, original
designers may be less capable of sustaining control over long-term paths of institutional development.

Two types of institutional configurations offer clear instances of loose institutional coupling: federalism and executive-judicial relations. There is significant
variation, both cross-nationally and over time, in the extent to which institutional roles and responsibilities are ambiguous in these settings. Yet in practice,
wide stretches of ambiguity are typically prevalent in each. Although we lack the
systematic data that would allow a serious assessment of this issue, a casual review of qualitative work on institutional development suggests that further work
on the implications of such loosely coupled institutional arrangements would

be fruitful. The literatures on both court development (Ackerman 1999; Burley and Mattli 1993; Epps 1998; Melnick 1994; Lijphart 1999, pp. 223–30) and federalism (Watts 1987; Gibson and Faletti 2000; Riker 1955) are replete with cases of dramatic and unexpected changes in institutional relationships over time.

There is also a striking difference between the two settings, however, which suggests important linkages among the research agendas I have just outlined. As already discussed, in the case of judicial-executive relations, unanticipated consequences seem to run almost entirely in one direction: an expanded role for courts.[20] In the case of federalism, there is no such unidirectionality. Sometimes federal systems become more decentralized over time (e.g., Canada) and sometimes they become more centralized (e.g., the United States). In Gibson and Faletti's account, Argentine federalism shifts unexpectedly from an instrument through which the state of Buenos Aires was able to dominate weaker states to one which served as "their deliverer from that domination" (Gibson and Faletti 2000, p. 19).

Long-Term Processes of Institutional Change

I have emphasized how the downstream effects of institutional choices may substantially increase the costs of pursuing various institutional reforms. As actors adapt to institutional arrangements, the status quo gains additional support, making it stable under a broader range of circumstances than was initially the case. An important implication of this claim is that effective challenges to the institutional status quo will often require substantial time to emerge (Hacker 2002; Thelen 2004). Developments unfavorable to institutional reproduction must reach a critical threshold level that makes reform possible. The moment of institutional innovation will often follow a long buildup of pressure. Agents of change may play the starring role in the dramatic conclusion, but their appearance in the final chapter is often heavily dependent on preceding developments occurring over an extended period.

In short, because sources of resilience will often accumulate over time, the topic of institutional change is an excellent candidate for the range of themes explored in Chapter Three. Long-term processes, which are typically invisible in "snapshot" studies of political phenomena, will often be crucial in creating the preconditions for institutional reform. These processes might operate mainly to gradually diminish the benefits associated with a particular institutional arrange-

---

[20]Lijphart's (1999, p. 228) comparative analysis of judicial review arrangements is telling: "countries with centralized judicial review tend to have stronger judicial review than countries with decentralized systems: six of the seven centralized systems are in the top two categories. This is a rather surprising conclusion because centralized review was originally developed as a compromise between not having judicial review at all and the decentralized type of it. The explanation must be that, if a special body is created for the express and exclusive purpose of reviewing the constitutionality of legislation, it is very likely to carry out this task with some vigor."

ment, or they might have the effect of reducing the costs of mobilizing for institutional change. While I have emphasized the difficulty of evaluating institutional performance, it remains plausible that extended periods of disappointing results attributed to a particular institutional arrangement may lead actors to reassess the benefits derived from the status quo (Thelen 2004). Some institutions are, in fact, sufficiently dysfunctional in an evolving social context that one might anticipate a gradual decline in perceptions of the status quo's benefits over time.

Equally valuable would be efforts to examine long-term processes that diminish the costs of carrying out institutional reforms. McAdam's (1982) analysis of the rise of the civil rights movement and the collapse of Jim Crow, discussed in Chapter Three, illustrates this possibility. He identifies profound long-term changes in the southern political economy and in the social resources available to civil rights activists, which made a challenge to the institutional status quo possible. When it came, institutional reform appeared to take place relatively quickly—but only if one focused on the catalysts rather than the deeper changes in opportunity structures that made these challenges to the institutional status quo viable.

From Institutional Development to Policy Development

A final significant research frontier would be to extend the line of argument developed in this chapter from explanations of formal political institutions to the study of public policy. Following North's definition of institutions as "the rules of the game in a society or, more generally . . . the humanly devised constraints that shape human interaction" (1990a, p. 3), it makes good sense to think of major public policies as important institutions (Pierson 1993; Pierson, forthcoming). For the individuals and social organizations that make up civil society, public policies are clearly very central rules governing their interactions. These rules specify rewards and punishments associated with particular behaviors, ranging from eligibility for specific forms of government largesse on the one hand to large fines, incarceration, or even death on the other. Leaving aside the formal institutions typically explored by sociologists, the institutions that impinge on the modern citizen most directly and intensively as she goes about her daily life are in fact public policies, *not* the formal political institutions that have preoccupied political scientists.

I have argued that there are advantages to thinking about institutional development as well as institutional choice. Similarly, and for many of the same reasons, there are strong arguments for thinking about policy development as something distinct from the ways in which powerful political actors *select* policies at a moment in time to serve their needs. Indeed, some of the most interesting recent discussions of institutional change have in fact focused on policy development over extended periods of time (Hacker, forthcoming; Patashnik

2003; Thelen 2004). The preoccupation with moments of policy choice can often direct our attention towards the dramatic and away from the important. Policies that start small may, if conditions are right for self-reinforcement or if unintended consequences are large, end up being extremely significant (Howard 1997; Hacker 2002). Policies that make a grand entrance may erode over time, unless they possess characteristics that generate not just initial success but substantial resilience (Patashnik 2003). "Fit" between powerful actors and policy arrangements may reflect the former's adaptation to the latter rather than the success of those actors in enacting these policies in the first place (Hacker and Pierson 2002). As the frequent references to policy development in this chapter attest, a great deal of the critique in the past two chapters concerning the study of formal political institutions, as well as the agendas I have suggested, would apply equally well to the study of public policy.

In sum, examining processes of institutionalization and the downstream consequences of institutional choices opens up a number of promising lines of inquiry for enhancing our understanding of institutional stability and institutional change. The perspective advanced here highlights the importance of considering not only whether an institutional arrangement constitutes an equilibrium, but exploring the depth and character of that equilibrium as well. It points to the need to determine plausible sequences or paths of institutional revision. It stresses the need to consider big, slow-moving social processes as potentially crucial elements in understanding when and how reforms might occur. All of these dimensions provide important complements, as well as partial correctives, to the emerging literature on institutional change, which has focused on the actors or catalysts that may trigger institutional reform. If institutional development is understood as an unfolding historical process, it is simply a mistake to juxtapose theories of institutional stability and theories of institutional change. One cannot have one without the other.

More broadly, the last two chapters have offered an extended application of this book's main argument to some core issues in contemporary theory. Institutional development is a *process* unfolding over extended periods of time. Snapshots focused on moments of institutional choice or institutional reform can capture parts of such processes, but they can also be highly misleading. Attention to the dynamic quality of institutional development can expose some of these blind spots, identifying both places where these arguments go astray and a wide range of important issues that are simply ignored. It can also generate exciting new ways of understanding why societies come to have the institutional arrangements they do, and for discovering the particular range of possibilities that they confront in the present.

Conclusion

TEMPORAL CONTEXT IN SOCIAL SCIENCE INQUIRY

> [R]esearch is a game against nature in which nature coun-
> ters with a strategy of concealment. . . . Obviously, the effec-
> tiveness of a given strategy of discovery will depend on
> nature's strategy of concealment, and conversely, the effec-
> tiveness of the laws of nature as a strategy of concealment
> will depend on the strategy chosen by research workers. . . .
> [A] rather simple strategy of concealment may be quite
> effective given a certain strategy of discovery. As a first step
> we may ask, what *is* the favorite strategy of sociologists? It is
> a marked characteristic of sociological research that it is
> preoccupied with cross-sectional study of small
> units, often individuals.
> —*Gøsta Carlsson (1972)*

MY GOALS IN THIS BOOK HAVE BEEN TO IDENTIFY and explore a range of frequently occurring causal processes that exhibit strong temporal dimensions.
Sensitivity to these temporal dimensions can help social scientists bring their
practices more in line with the way the social world actually works. As in the passage from Gøsta Carlsson, I have suggested that much that is important about
the social world is likely to remain concealed if our inquiries are grounded, as
they too often are, in efforts to examine only a moment in time. If we think, instead, of how social processes unfold over time we will ask questions that we
might not otherwise ask, identify flaws in possible explanations that we would
otherwise not see, and find answers that we otherwise would not find.

This claim has considerable implications for both the theories and methods
employed in contemporary social science. Taking a step back from the arguments presented here, I wish to briefly highlight some of those implications. A
useful place to start is with the idea of context. Placing social analysis in time implies recognizing that any particular moment is situated in some sort of temporal context—it is part of an unfolding social process. Now "context" has become,
for many in the social sciences, a bad word—a synonym for thick description,
and an obstacle to social-scientific analysis. Indeed, over the past few decades,
much of the social sciences has undergone what could rightly be called a decontextual revolution.

This decontextual revolution has been apparent in major developments in both methods and theory. Many social scientists have gravitated toward methodologies such as regression analysis that are typically radically decontextualizing (Abbott 1988, 1997; Ragin 1987). This is not a necessary feature of such techniques. On the contrary, statisticians often possess formidable tools for considering interaction effects (Franzese 2003) and for examining complex temporal relationships in their data sets (Beck, Katz, and Tucker 1998; Jackson 1996). But these potential capacities frequently go unexploited. There are often considerable costs of employing such techniques (loss of "degrees of freedom," the sacrifice of otherwise-appealing data sets that cannot provide the necessary information, and the need to undertake time-consuming efforts to assemble more appropriate data and/or learn more appropriate techniques). Typically, these costs are not paid in contemporary social science because quantitative researchers generally hear reassuring messages that they do not need to be.

For on the theoretical plane, as well, the trend has been toward decontextualization. This is the orientation of most rational choice analysis, which is by far the dominant form of theorizing in economics and widely utilized in contemporary political science as well. Most rational choice analysts place priority on combining the greatest degree of parsimony and the greatest capacity for generalization. This leads to a presumption that compelling hypotheses involve little in the way of "local" information. In political science, rational choice analyses typically focus on variable-entities such as "voters," "interest groups," and a whole range of institutions (central banks, legislatures, federalism, courts) that are taken to be similar units, with similar effects, in widely divergent settings. The building blocks for theory are maximizing individuals, typically treated in a highly atomized way and portrayed as possessing core traits that are largely separable from any particular context. Theorizing grounded in rational choice analysis typically has an ambitious agenda of establishing claims that should apply, at least on average, across a wide range of settings whenever a few crucial conditions hold.

In the midst of these strong decontextualizing trends, historically oriented analysis in the social sciences has often been criticized as a particularly egregious instance of backward thinking (Bates 1997; Geddes 1990). Preoccupied with contexts that are taken to be unique, historical analyses are seen as antithetical to the identification of patterns and the development of generalizations. These approaches to inquiry are dismissed as "traditional" and contrasted, unfavorably, with the "modern."

Yet there is, as Andrew Abbott (1997, p. 1171) has argued eloquently, another way to think about it: "'Context' has two senses. . . . The strict sense . . . denotes those things that environ and thereby define a thing of interest. The loose sense simply denotes detail. The acute reader will note that these correspond nicely to the two judgments of the scientific worth of contextual information. If decontextualization is merely the removal of excess detail, then it's a fine thing, scientifically. On the other hand, if it is the removal of defining locational information, it is a scientific disaster." It is Abbott's strict sense of context that animates this volume. Particular social contexts constrain and enable political actors, and indeed may shape those actors' very understandings of who they are and what they want to do.

The standard objection to this line of argument is that an emphasis on context means falling back to thick descriptions of single cases—to "just-so" accounts, or Goldstone's "Seussian" explanations where "it just happened that this happened first, then this, then that, and is not likely to happen that way again" (Goldstone 1998, p. 833). Alternatively, it is argued that the call for thicker, more contextualized explanations can lead to reliance on simple paired comparisons of complex cases that raise potentially insuperable methodological difficulties (Geddes 1990; Lieberson 1997; King, Keohane, and Verba 1994).

I do not believe the trade-offs that social scientists face are so stark. In advancing that view, this analysis constitutes part of a wave of recent work—methodological, theoretical, and empirical—that seeks to combine sensitivity to causal complexity and contextual effects with aspirations to draw out implications about social processes that transcend a single social setting.[1] It is an exciting and challenging agenda—raising the prospect of social analyses that capture more of the richness of actually lived histories while still speaking to the social scientific goal of generating usable knowledge.

To be clear, the point is not that we need to know everything about the context of a particular phenomenon—which is not just a practical but a logical impossibility (Gaddis 2002). The point is that what is too easily dismissed as "context" may in fact be absolutely crucial to understanding important social processes. Too often, contemporary social science simply drops out a huge range of crucial factors and processes, either because our methods and theories make it difficult to incorporate them, or because they simply lead us not to see them in the first place. And, as I have emphasized throughout, the profoundly important temporal dimensions of social interactions are often the first to go.

Making Temporal Context Explicit

Two distinct but compatible analytical moves exemplify the core orientations of this more contextualized approach to social science inquiry. The first and most straightforward move is the introduction of explicit temporal (and/or spatial) *boundary conditions* on the hypotheses that an analyst wishes to advance. This is not a move that I have discussed in any detail in this book, but it is one for which

[1] This literature is vast, but a good point of entry is the collection of essays in Mahoney and Rueschemeyer 2003. On the methodological issues involved, see Brady and Collier 2003; Mahoney 2001; Bennett and George 2004; Ragin 2000; and Hall 2003. On recent theoretical developments, especially focused on the temporal dimensions of social processes, see Abbott 2001, Mahoney 2000, and Thelen 1999. For excellent empirical analyses, see Carpenter 2001, Huber and Stephens 2001, Mahoney 2001, Schickler 2001, Thelen 2004, and Waldner 1999.

the book's core arguments are relevant. The posture of adopting strict boundary conditions represents a strategic retreat from the universalist aspirations of large segments of the social sciences. To establish such boundary conditions forgoes, or at least postpones, the search for relationships among variables that one would expect to hold across a wide range of settings. Instead, the expectation is that strong contextual effects (if you will, background variables that strongly influence the effects of other factors) will play a major role in determining how particular features are related to one another in a particular setting. *Ceteris paribus* clauses are considered plausible only across a restricted range of time or space.

One can see the character of this more cautious position by contrasting it with a methodological technique that has become increasingly popular in variable-oriented comparative research: regression analysis based on pooled time-series (Shalev 1999). Pooling has gained prominence because it hurdles the biggest obstacle to statistical analysis in many areas of social-scientific inquiry: the limited number of available observations (Abbott 2001). If each "country-year" can be treated as a separate observation, time series data can be used to vastly expand the relatively small number of "country-cases." The "n" for statistical analysis can be increased twenty or thirtyfold, allowing the investigator to consider more complex hypotheses and generate more reliable results.

For those who question the decontextual revolution, however, the assumptions underpinning the move to pooled time series elicit tremendous skepticism. Can we really assume that the causal relationship between two variables—say, economic openness and labor-union density—was the same in 1965 that it was in 1995? Pooling represents an attempt to deal with one kind of causal complexity by wishing away another—namely, the fact that relationships among variables of interest are likely to change as broader background conditions change over time or across space (Shalev 1999; Hall 2003). As I suggested in the introduction, this same objection would apply equally well to a common strategy in qualitatively oriented historical research that focuses on a single case in the past, or a small number of cases drawn from different time periods, where the (usually implicit) assumption is that the broad shifts in background conditions over time pose no major problems for causal inference (Bartolini 1993; Lieberman 2001).

The opposite presumption—that the effects of such background conditions are likely to be strong—leads to the organization of research around more bounded social entities. Typically, the boundaries are temporal, spatial, or both.[2] For example, the powerful comparative historical analyses of state building by Anderson, Tilly, Ertman, Mann, Downing, and others did not seek to present general propositions about state building. They focused on developing

---

[2] At least initially. As Thelen has argued, one can and arguably should strive to replace boundary conditions defined in temporal or spatial terms with ones that are defined analytically (Thelen 2000). More on this below.

explanations applicable to European experiences during a particular (albeit lengthy) historical period. Greg Luebbert's impressive study of the development of liberal, fascist, and social-democratic regimes fashioned explanations applicable to *interwar Europe* (Luebbert 1991). He did not claim that the same factors could account, without serious modification, for regime outcomes in, say, contemporary South America.[3]

Analytical and methodological choices in the social sciences inevitably involve trade-offs, and it is important to make these explicit whenever we can. The setting of temporal and spatial scope conditions, like other choices, comes at a price. The first cost, as critics have forcefully argued, is that restricting our arguments to a small number of cases raises major problems of causal inference (Geddes 1990; King, Keohane, and Verba 1994). Limited samples raise the dangers of selection bias and increase the likelihood that we will end up with more variables under consideration than we have empirical observations to use in assessing causal claims. The second is that the application of such scope conditions seems to surrender one of the chief aspirations of most social scientists—namely, to identify causal factors that can "travel" across a range of settings.

It is precisely these weaknesses that suggest why the decision to bound empirical inquiries and theoretical claims is increasingly coupled with a second analytical strategy: the development of theory and methods that are explicitly tailored to address key aspects of context. If the option of setting boundary conditions seems a cautious one, embracing a strategic retreat in the face of causal complexity, it becomes much less so when combined with this second strategy. Analysts seek to explore which aspects of context, or the "embeddedness" of social interactions, can be specified in terms that can potentially be applied in multiple settings. To employ Abbott's language, the goal is to specify the features of a particular setting that "environ and thus define a thing of interest." As I will explore shortly, the beauty of this strategy is that it simultaneously copes with many of the weaknesses of the decontextual revolution and addresses the concern of many social scientists that the imposition of relatively narrow spatial and temporal boundary conditions make powerful social science impossible.

Thinking about context means thinking about relationships. Indeed, the focus of recent theoretical work has been on the character of spatial and temporal relationships. Particular actors, organizations, or institutions are shaped in part by their spatial relationships to other aspects of a social setting. Similarly, a particular moment in time is part of broader temporal processes. Events are parts of various sequences of events. Their place in those sequences may play a critical role in determining their meaning. Thus, these theoretical works explore

---

[3]It should be noted that comparative historical work typically employs scope conditions for an additional reason. The motivation for these analyses has typically been a concern with specific real-world outcomes. Luebbert, for instance, was particularly interested in understanding the replacement of democracy with fascism in some, but not all, European cases. On the role of this problem-driven focus in comparative historical analysis, see Pierson and Skocpol 2002.

the spatial and temporal settings that provide crucial elements of context for any object of social inquiry.

One could easily imagine—and some have pursued—an agenda focused on spatial contexts (Abbott 1997; Herbst 2000; Kopstein and Reilly 2000). Here, instead, I have explored some of the theoretically important dimensions of temporal context. A viable effort to explain key features of the remarkable and highly varied social world we inhabit, I have argued, will often require an appreciation of how social activities are embedded in time. Arguments about path dependence focus on chains of events or processes stemming from some initial "critical juncture," emphasizing, for instance, the potentially self-reinforcing effects of early outcomes. Discussions of sequencing reveal the consequences of differences in the temporal ordering of both macroprocesses and microinteractions. Attention to long-term processes highlights the markedly different rates at which distinct causal processes and outcomes in the social world may unfold. Finally, I have stressed the importance of looking beyond moments of institutional selection to examine processes of institutional development—to explore how and why institutional arrangements adapt, or fail to adapt, to a variety of pressures for amendment or replacement occurring over an extended period of time.

As I have emphasized throughout, the formulations offered in this book draw heavily on a growing body of work engaged with issues of temporal context. The goal of this research, as Kathleen Thelen has nicely put it, is to "capture the impact of time in as timeless a way as possible" (Thelen 2000, p. 101n). That is, it seeks to specify common characteristics of temporal relationships that would allow one to use more general analytical tools to make sense of particular empirical settings. In this emerging literature "context" takes on a particular meaning. It becomes a point of entry for thinking about how events and processes are related to each other in social dynamics that unfold over extended periods of time. It is decidedly not a matter of treating each social setting as unique and infinitely complex. Instead, these inquiries urge us to recognize that any event or process is environed by its temporal location, its place within a sequence of occurrences, and by its interactions with various processes unfolding at different speeds. Especially when we are attempting to understand broad social transformations, these relationships constitute a central subject of social-scientific inquiry. We need to know not just "what" (i.e., the value on some variable), but "when." This, I would suggest, has significant implications for the social sciences—both for the ways in which we design research and for the theories we employ to make sense of the social world.

Methods and Research Design

Emphasizing the temporal dimensions of social processes in no way involves a wholesale rejection of the typical methods of variable-centered analysis. Hypotheses about temporal relations, if clearly specified, may be translated into the language of variables. If appropriate data are available, they may be subjected to statistical test. For example, claims about path dependence are often grounded in the scale of commitments resulting from previous institutional, organizational, or policy outcomes. In principle, these commitments can and should be specified and measured. As noted above, modern statistics involves a range of tools for investigating temporal relationships within large data sets. Techniques like event history analysis (Box-Steffensmeier and Jones 1997), for instance, can be extremely useful for investigating many of the long-term processes discussed in this book.

In many cases, however, we currently lack the data that would facilitate the use of such tools. If the core themes of this book have merit, then they are highly suggestive about distinct kinds of data that we will need to generate to explore some important issues in the social sciences. For instance, quantitative investigations of many of the arguments about institutional development explored in Chapters Four and Five would require richer longitudinal data sets than we currently possess. Similar efforts are urgently needed in a range of areas, such as the development of important public policies and political organizations.

Moreover, the appropriate data for statistical testing will not always be available, even in principle. For many issues of interest to social scientists, the number of observed instances may be quite small. In the real world, large stretches of the hypothetically available data space are simply empty (Abbott 2001). As I suggested above, even where the number of instances may seem larger, scholars pursuing contextualized analysis are generally suspicious of the often heroic assumptions about the nature of causal relationships and the homogeneity of units like "democracies" or "interest groups" that are required to generate "large Ns" (Ragin 2000; Hall 2003; Keohane 2003).

In the presence of these difficulties, the richer theories of causal process connected to recent work on temporal effects provide a substantial advantage for the rigorous investigation of hypotheses. This is by no means obvious. The "many variables, few cases" problem that has recently received renewed attention in political science is in some respect worsened by the arguments about temporal context explored here. Path-dependent arguments, for example, can require that one examine not just correlations among variables but evaluate sequences of variables over time. This might not pose particularly acute problems for studying outcomes where it is possible to generate many cases (e.g., the formation of interest groups). Thus, studies of collective action and the development of actors' mental maps of politics would seem to be promising areas of study. The "few cases, many variables" problem would, however, appear to pose serious difficulties for positive feedback arguments that operate at a more aggregated level (Geddes 1997).

Again, the conclusion that this is an intractable problem is mistaken. It stems from the view that a study of, say, two or three revolutions means than an analyst can gain leverage from only two or three observations. This might well be true for the typically "thin" theories prevalent in decontextualized research. Drawing heavily on statistical associations, these theories are often silent, or nearly so, about the processes or mechanisms that connect their variables to outcomes. By contrast, emerging arguments about temporal relationships are much more attentive to mechanisms. They therefore provide a basis for thicker theories that can generate many more observable implications within each broad "case" subjected to empirical scrutiny.

Much of the recent work on process tracing (Bennett and George 2004; Hall 2003; King, Keohane, and Verba 1994; Rueschemeyer and Stephens 1997) stresses that a clearly developed theory is likely to have numerous additional implications beyond the suggested correlation between dependent and independent variable. If, for instance, our theory suggests that a policy adopted at time T induces specific kinds of positive feedback (e.g., changes in patterns of political organization, or the distribution of actors, or the policy preferences of voters), then we should expect to see not only reinforcement of the policy at time $T + 1$ but also the expected changes in patterns of political organization and other intermediate outcomes. Furthermore, we should expect these intermediate outcomes to come about in specifiable and often observable ways. Analysts can utilize our increasing theoretical understanding of path-dependent processes to generate many observable implications in what at first glance appears to be a study of only a few cases (Hacker 2002; Hacker and Pierson 2002; Thelen 2003). If in fact we do observe these other implications, our confidence in the theory is likely to be greater than if we observe only the single correlation suggested by a less fully articulated theory. Recent advances in theorizing thus provide one important answer to the methodological concerns that have been raised about inquiries sensitive to context yet committed to the generation of usable knowledge. Richer theories increase the prospects for surmounting, or at least diminishing, the "many variables, few cases" problem.

As James Mahoney and Dietrich Rueschemeyer have recently emphasized, additional leverage can be gained through collaborative research, or by a more decentralized research program involving the overlapping efforts of numerous scholars (Mahoney and Rueschemeyer 2003). *Multiple* research efforts, if properly coordinated (through communication rather than centralized control), can explore many, many observations, significantly enhancing the prospects for substantial accumulation of findings (Mahoney 2003). This highlights the importance of developing coherent, clearly specified research programs involving a substantial community of scholars. Here again, the current inquiry has considerable relevance for the conduct of research. Recent explorations on a host of issues related to the temporal dimensions of social processes, including path dependence (Hacker 2002; Mahoney 2001; Myles and Pierson 2001) and institutional development (Hacker, forthcoming; Schickler 2001; Thelen 2004; Patashnik 2003), have drawn on common conceptual and theoretical frameworks. This makes it far easier for analysts working on distinctive empirical terrain to recognize their shared theoretical interests, and to formulate their inquiries in ways that facilitate cross-fertilization and an accumulation of findings.

The arguments about temporal relationships explored here also point to other interesting methodological possibilities. One is the need to reassess existing statistical techniques that have fallen into disuse as multiple regression has become almost hegemonic, but may be well suited for exploring temporal relationships (Shalev 1999; Braumoeller 2000). There are new methods as well. Agent-based modeling, which allows analysts to create virtual worlds where histories can be run thousands of times, offers exciting new opportunities to explore temporal relationships (Cederman 1997; Axelrod 1997). Andrew Abbott (1990, 2001) has written extensively about a range of techniques for exploring narrative sequences and temporal patterns. And there is growing interest in combining multiple techniques, quantitative and qualitative, that exploit complementary strengths. "Bridging" or "nesting" designs can compensate for blind spots or limitations associated with a particular methodological tool (Brady and Collier 2003; Lieberman 2003). Some of the best recent empirical work emphasizing temporal dynamics has incorporated precisely this kind of effort to employ multiple methods that have complementary strengths (Carpenter 2001; Huber and Stephens 2001; Schickler 2001).

In short, the techniques exist for wide-ranging and diverse explanations of the issues explored in this volume. I have stressed throughout, however, that it is one thing to say that analysts can, in principle, do something. It is quite another thing for them to make it a regular practice. Above all, this depends on the theories we develop and our underlying assumptions about the way the social world works (Hall 2003). These orientations lead to the posing of certain kinds of questions rather than others, as well as to a concentration on particular promising answers that warrant intensive investigation. Methodological possibilities are likely to remain untapped unless the theories we employ encourage us to think seriously about the temporal dimensions of social processes.

Theory

The arguments about temporal processes explored in this book have not advanced any particular theory of any specific political or social phenomena. Instead, I have drawn on many claims by social scientists working in various theoretical traditions to illustrate promising approaches to a wide range of political and social outcomes that utilize, or could utilize, the arguments presented here. These illustrations were intended to demonstrate how the theoretical claims we make about a host of important issues can be improved by a better appreciation of temporal processes.

The considerable progress we have made in understanding temporal relationships has involved a shift from a focus on "causal laws"—implying highly consistent relationships among particular variables across a wide range of settings—to the explication of particular social mechanisms—or "frequently observed ways in which things happen," as Jon Elster has put it (Elster 1989, p. viii). Analysts working on many of the theoretical issues outlined above have sought to explore how distinct mechanisms operate, when they are most likely to occur, and with what implications. Even if the specific claims we wish to make about the social world will often be temporally or spatially bounded, these insights about mechanisms are likely to be portable across a range of settings. For instance, recent applications of arguments about positive feedback to social processes involve empirical settings as diverse as the development of American social welfare policies (Hacker 2002), emerging patterns of Latin American federalism (Faletti, in process), and the formation of distinctive national profiles of sports culture (Markovits and Hellerman 2001). A social science sensitive to temporal context can thus strike a fruitful balance between the particular and the general. To a greater degree than traditional studies of a single case, it can both draw on and contribute to the broader social-scientific enterprise of generating usable, portable knowledge. Yet it can do so precisely by embracing and exploring the specific spatial and temporal relationships that environ and thus define particular processes that are of interest.

The pluralistic implications of my argument deserve emphasis. Identifying and exploring distinct mechanisms that generate striking temporal relationships—whether these involve positive feedback, sequencing, or slow-moving causes and outcomes—can make important contributions to a wide range of theoretical traditions. There are considerable insights to be derived from a focus on the temporal dimensions of social processes, irrespective of the specific claims an analyst may want to advance about the major "drivers" of social outcomes. Committed "rationalists" or "constructivists" may benefit from thinking clearly about when, why, and how much the temporal sequence of events or processes might effect the likely impact of variables they consider to be of greatest theoretical significance, as well as the ultimate outcomes that interest them. Analysts with radically divergent theoretical orientations can profit from considering what potential questions and answers they miss when they focus only on particular moments stripped of temporal context.

This agnostic stance on grand theoretical divides may elicit more frustration than it should. The frustration is encouraged by the aggressive posturing and jousting that often occurs in the social sciences with respect to distinct theoretical traditions, demanding of each of us that we pick sides. This combative stance, while common, is simplistic. As I observed in Chapter Four, it greatly exaggerates the extent to which what Jepperson has called "theoretical imageries" (Jepperson 1996; see also Jepperson, Wendt, and Katzenstein 1996, pp. 78–82) are internally coherent, all encompassing, and mutually exclusive. As Jepperson demonstrates, there are many plausible relationships among theoretical imageries. They may possess poorly articulated boundary conditions (x will hold under conditions a, b, and c, but y will hold under conditions d, e, and f). They may be saying the same thing in different ways. They may address different phenomena, or ask different questions. They may focus on different aspects of important phenomena. In such cases, as Scharpf has argued, different theories might contribute distinct "modules" that can potentially be linked to produce more complete accounts (Scharpf 1997). For example, to employ the terminology I used in Chapter Three, one can easily imagine different theoretical imageries being used in combination to link a "Quadrant I" explanation to a "Quadrant II" account.

Distinct bodies of theory may provide greater leverage for analyzing particular aspects of social reality. To briefly consider one prominent example, I have argued throughout that rational choice analysis has characteristic strengths and weaknesses for the exploration of temporal dimensions of social processes. By now, an appreciation of the strengths should be evident. Arrow and Riker's analyses of collective choice and cycling provide powerful insights into the consequences of temporal ordering. The "rational design" literature, which I have termed "actor-based functionalism," has developed many of our most intriguing hypotheses about the determinants of institutional selection. Economists such as Arthur, David, and North have produced crucial breakthroughs in our exploration of path dependence.

Yet there are blind spots as well, characteristic of an imagery that rests, at its core, on the investigation of strategic interaction among individuals. Many of these blind spots emerge clearly once one turns one's systematic attention to temporal processes. Sequencing arguments have been narrowly applied, generating important findings but with much of their enormous potential left unexploited. Despite the huge contributions of economists to the literature on path dependence, its implications are largely ignored in contemporary rational choice scholarship. Focusing on the "moves" of "actors," rational choice analyses have been far less attentive to slow-moving, long-term processes that clearly must play an important role in our understanding of the social world. And a focus on moments of institutional choice has been matched by inattentiveness to problems of institutional development—problems that generate fundamental challenges to conceptions of the social world that privilege rational design. The current argument suggests that practitioners of rational choice could benefit from greater awareness of, and attentiveness to, these blind spots. They should also consider drawing on potentially complementary imageries that may be better equipped to address them.

The development of theoretical discussions of path dependence within economics and sociology makes an interesting and revealing contrast. Economists did an excellent job of exploring the core properties of dynamics involving self-reinforcement. They identified some (but only some, as James Mahoney has forcefully argued) of the key mechanisms at work, and deduced some fundamental implications. From the vantage point of organization theory the sociologist Arthur Stinchcombe identified the same central issues in the 1960s (Stinchcombe

1965, 1968). He and later sociologists came at the problem with a focus on organizations rather than individual actors, and with a core interest in how a "field" consisting of many organizations interacted with its environment over time. These sociologists, working both within the sociological variant of "new institutionalism" (Powell and DiMaggio 1991) and through the developing imagery of "organizational ecology" (Hannan and Freeman 1989), persuasively identified additional mechanisms (related to both cultural practices and the distribution of power) that can generate self-reinforcement. Moreover, they have produced a rich literature on organizational *development* that explored the implications of organizational inertia in a context marked by multiple, interacting (not just competitive) organizations, operating in environments that were changing over time. Taking the same basic insights about self-reinforcing dynamics, these theoretical imageries have produced rich contributions to our understanding of the social world, but those insights have been strikingly different.

To emphasize that different imageries entail different strengths and weaknesses, that they can generate distinctive insights as well as possess distinctive limitations, is not a plea that we "split the difference" among alternative approaches. It is, however, a plea for pluralism, for an acknowledgment that all angles of vision create distortions. In studying the social world, we need to adopt multiple angles, or be willing to rely on the help of others, to see more clearly.

We are beginning to recapture one angle of vision that was deeply threatened by the decontextual revolution—a threat that raised the prospect of seriously distorting our understandings of social life. We are beginning, again, to place politics in time. Doing so will not be a panacea. Inquiries that adopt a more explicitly temporal focus will inevitably have blind spots, and introduce distortions, of their own. Yet this shift in focus offers exciting opportunities for correcting common mistakes and silences in contemporary social science. It will enable us to strike a more effective and satisfying balance between explaining the general and comprehending the specific. It offers new possibilities for understanding our extraordinarily complex and ever-changing social world.

BIBLIOGRAPHY

Abbott, Andrew (1983). "Sequences of Social Events: Concepts and Methods for the Analysis of Order in Social Processes," *Historical Methods*, Vol. 16, No. 4, Fall, pp. 129–47.

——— (1988). "Transcending General Linear Reality," *Sociological Theory*, Vol. 6, pp.169–86.

——— (1990). "Conceptions of Time and Events in Social Science Methods: Causal and Narrative Approaches," *Historical Methods*, Fall 1990, Vol. 23, No. 4, pp. 140–50.

——— (1997). "Of Time and Space," *Social Forces*, Vol. 75, pp. 1149-82.

——— (2001). *Time Matters: On Theory and Method.* Chicago: University of Chicago Press.

Ackerman, Bruce. (1999). "Revolution on a Human Scale," *Yale Law Journal*, Vol. 108, No. 8, pp. 2279–2349.

Aghajanian, Akbar, and Amir H. Merhyar (1999). "Fertility, Contraceptive Use and Family Planning Program Activity in the Islamic Republic of Iran," *International Family Planning Perspectives*, Vol. 25, No. 2, June, pp. 98–102.

Alchian, Armen A. (1950). "Uncertainty, Evolution and Economic Theory," *Journal of Political Economy*, Vol. 58, pp. 211-21.

Aldrich, John H. (1995). *Why Parties? The Origin and Transformation of Party Politics in America.* Chicago: University of Chicago Press.

Alexander, Gerard (2001). "Institutions, Path Dependence, and Democratic Consolidation," *Journal of Theoretical Politics*, Vol. 13, No. 3, pp. 249–70.

Alt, James E., Jeffery Frieden, Michael J. Gilligan, Dani Rodrik, and Ronald Rogowski (1996). "The Political Economy of International Trade: Enduring Puzzles and an Agenda for Inquiry," *Comparative Political Studies*, Vol. 29, No. 6, pp. 689–717.

Aminzade, Roy (1992). "Historical Sociology and Time," *Sociological Methods and Research*, Vol. 20, pp. 456–80.

Anderson, Perry (1974) *Lineages of the Absolutist State.* London: Verso.

Aron, Raymond (1961). *Introduction to the Philosophy of History* (Boston: Beacon Press).

Arrow, Kenneth J. (1963). *Social Choice and Individual Values*, 2d ed. New Haven: Yale University Press.

Arthur, W. Brian (1994). *Increasing Returns and Path Dependence in the Economy.* Ann Arbor: University of Michigan Press.

Axelrod, Robert (1984). *The Evolution of Cooperation.* New York: Basic Books.

——— (1997). *The Complexity of Cooperation.* Princeton: Princeton University Press.

Bachrach, Peter, and Morton S. Baratz (1962). "The Two Faces of Power," *American Political Science Review*, Vol. 56, pp. 947–52.

Bartels, Larry M. (1998). "Electoral Continuity and Change, 1868–1996," *Electoral Studies*, Vol. 17, pp. 301–26.

Bartolini, Stefano (1993). "On Time and Comparative Research," *Journal of Theoretical Politics*, Vol. 5, No. 2, pp. 131–67.

Bartolini, Stefano, and Peter Mair (1990). *Identity, Competition and Electoral Availability.* Cambridge: Cambridge University Press.

Bates, Robert (1990). "Macropolitical Economy in the Field of Development," in James E. Alt and Kenneth A. Shepsle, eds., *Perspectives on Political Economy*, pp. 31–54. Cambridge: Cambridge University Press.

——— (1997). "Area Studies and the Discipline: A Useful Controversy?" *PS*, June.

Bates, Robert, and Kenneth Shepsle (1997). "Intertemporal Institutions," in John Drobak and John Nye, eds., *The Frontiers of New Institutional Economics*. New York: Academic Press.

Bates, Robert, et al. (1998). *Analytic Narratives*. Cambridge: Cambridge University Press.

Bates, Robert, R., P. de Figueiredo, Jr., and Barry R. Weingast (1998). "The Politics of Interpretation: Rationality, Culture, and Transition," *Politics and Society*, Vol. 26, No. 4, pp. 221–35.

Baumgartner, Frank R., and Bryan D. Jones (1993). *Agendas and Instability in American Politics*. Chicago: University of Chicago Press.

Beck, Nathaniel, Jonathan N. Katz, and Richard Tucker (1998). "Taking Time Seriously: Time-Series-Cross-Section Analysis with a Binary Dependent Variable," *American Journal of Political Science*, Vol. 42, No. 4, pp. 1260–88.

Bell, Daniel (1974). *The Coming of Postindustrial Society*. New York: Basic Books.

Bennett, Andrew, and Alexander George (2004). *Case Studies and Theory Development*. Cambridge, Mass.: MIT Press.

Berger, Suzanne, and Ronald Dore, eds. (1996). *National Diversity and Global Capitalism*. Ithaca, N.Y.: Cornell University Press.

Berman, Sheri (1998). *The Social Democratic Moment: Ideas and Politics in the Making of Interwar Europe*. Princeton: Princeton University Press.

Berman, Sheri (2003). "Islamism, Revolution, and Civil Society," *Perspectives on Politics*, Vol. 1, No. 2, pp. 257–72.

Blais, Andre, and Louis Massicotte (1997). "Electoral Formulas: A Macroscopic Perspective," *European Journal of Political Research*, Vol. 32, pp. 107–29.

Blyth, Mark (2002). *Great Transformations: Economic Ideas and Institutional Change in the Twentieth Century*. Cambridge: Cambridge University Press.

Boix, Carles (1999). "Setting the Rules of the Game: The Choice of Electoral Systems in Advanced Democracies," *American Political Science Review*, September, 609–24.

Box-Steffensmeier, Janet M., and Jones, Bradford S. (1997). "Time Is of the Essence: Event History Models in Political Science," *American Journal of Political Science*, Vol. 41, pp. 1414–61.

Brady, David W. (1988). *Critical Elections and Congressional Policy Making*. Stanford, Calif.: Stanford University Press.

Brady, Henry E., and David Collier, eds. (2003). *Rethinking Social Inquiry: Diverse Tools, Shared Standards*. Boulder, Colo., and Berkeley: Roman and Littlefield, and Berkeley Public Policy Press.

Braumoeller, Bear F. (2000). "Causal Complexity and the Study of Politics," unpublished manuscript, Harvard University, Cambridge, Mass.

Burley, Anne-Marie, and Walter Mattli (1993). "Europe before the Court: A Political Theory of Legal Integration," *International Organization*, Vol. 47, No. 1, pp. 41–76.

Burnham, Walter D. (1970). *Critical Elections and the Mainsprings of American Politics*. New York: W. W. Norton.

Calvert, Randall L. (1995). "Rational Actors, Equilibrium, and Social Institutions," in

Jack Knight and Itai Sened, eds., *Explaining Social Institutions*, pp. 57–93. Ann Arbor: University of Michigan Press.

Cameron, Charles (2000). "Congress Constructs the Judiciary, 1789–2000." Memo prepared for Russell Sage Foundation Conference on History and Politics, April 2000.

Carey, John M. (2000). "Parchment, Equilibria, and Institutions," *Comparative Political Studies*, Vol. 33, Nos. 6–7, pp. 735–61.

Carlsson, Gøsta (1972). "Lagged Structures and Cross-Sectional Methods," *Acta Sociologica*, Vol. 15, pp. 323–41.

Carmines, Edward G., and James A. Stimson (1989). *Issue Evolution: Race and the Transformation of American Politics*. Princeton: Princeton University Press.

Carpenter, Daniel P. (2001). *The Forging of Bureaucratic Autonomy: Reputations, Networks, and Policy Innovation in Executive Agencies, 1862-1928*. Princeton: Princeton University Press.

Carroll, Glenn R., and Michael T. Hannan (2000). *The Demography of Corporations and Industries*. Princeton: Princeton University Press.

Cederman, Lars-Erik (1997). *Emergent Actors in World Politics: How States and Nations Develop and Dissolve*. Princeton: Princeton University Press.

Clemens, Elisabeth (1997). *The People's Lobby: Organizational Innovation and the Rise of Interest Group Politics in the United States, 1890–1925*. Chicago: University of Chicago Press.

Clemens, Elisabeth (2002). "Invention, Innovation, Proliferation: Explaining Organizational Genesis and Change," in Michael Lounsbury and Marc Ventresca, eds., *Social Structure and Organizations Revisited: Research in the Sociology of Organizations*, vol. 19. New York: Elsevier.

Clemens, Elisabeth S., and James M. Cook (1999). "Politics and Institutionalism: Explaining Durability and Change," *Annual Review of Sociology*, Vol. 25, pp. 441–66.

Collier, Ruth Berins (1999). *Paths Toward Democracy: The Working Class and Elites in Western Europe and South America*. Cambridge: Cambridge University Press.

Collier, Ruth Berins, and David Collier (1991). *Shaping the Political Arena: Critical Junctures, The Labor Movement, and Regime Dynamics in Latin America*. Princeton: Princeton University Press.

Colomer, Josep M. (2001). "Disequilibrium Institutions and Pluralist Democracy," *Journal of Theoretical Politics*, Vol. 13, No. 3, pp. 235–47.

Converse, Philip E. (1991). "Popular Representation and the Distribution of Information," in John Ferejohn and James Kuklinski, eds., *Information and Democratic Processes*, pp. 369–88. Urbana: University of Illinois Press.

Cornes, Richard, and Todd Sandler (1996). *The Theory of Externalities, Public Goods and Club Goods*, 2d ed. Cambridge: Cambridge University Press.

Cox, Gary (1997). *Making Votes Count: Strategic Coordination in the World's Electoral Systems*. Cambridge: Cambridge University Press.

Crouch, Colin (1986). "Sharing Public Space: States and Organized Interests in Western Europe," in John Hall, ed., *States in History*, pp. 177–210. Oxford: Basil Blackwell.

David, Paul (1985). "Clio and the Economics of QWERTY," *American Economic Review*, Vol. 75, pp. 332–37.

——— (1994). "Why Are Institutions the 'Carriers of History'? Path Dependence and the Evolution of Conventions, Organizations, and Institutions," *Structural Change and Economic Dynamics*, Vol. 5, No. 2, pp. 205–20.

——— (2000). "Path Dependence, Its Critics, and the Quest for 'Historical Economics,'" in P. Garrouste and S. Ioannides, eds., *Evolution and Path Dependence in Economic Ideas: Past and Present.* Cheltenham, U.K.: Edward Elgar.

Denzau, Arthur D., and Douglass C. North (1994). "Shared Mental Models: Ideologies and Institutions," *Kyklos,* Vol. 47, No. 1, pp. 3–31.

Deutsch, Karl (1961). "Social Mobilization and Political Development," *American Political Science Review,* Vol. 55, No. 3, pp. 493–514.

Diamond, Jared (1997). *Guns, Germs and Steel: The Fates of Human Societies.* New York: W. W. Norton.

DiMaggio, Paul J., and Walter W. Powell (1991). "Introduction," in Walter W. Powell and Paul J. DiMaggio, eds., *The New Institutionalism in Organizational Analysis,* pp. 1–38. Chicago: University of Chicago Press.

Elias, Norbert (1956). "Involvement and Detachment," *British Journal of Sociology,* Vol. 7, No. 3, pp. 226–52.

Elster, Jon (1983). *Explaining Technical Change.* Cambridge: Cambridge University Press.

——— (1989). *Solomonic Judgments.* Cambridge: Cambridge University Press.

——— (2000). "Rational Choice History: A Case of Excessive Ambition," *American Political Science Review,* Vol. 94, No. 3, September, pp. 685–95.

Elster, Jon, Claus Offe, and Ulrich K. Preuss (1998). *Institutional Design in Post-Communist Societies: Rebuilding the Ship at Sea.* Cambridge: Cambridge University Press.

Epps, Charles R. (1998). *The Rights Revolution: Lawyers, Activists, and Supreme Courts in Comparative Perspective.* Chicago: University of Chicago Press.

Ertman, Thomas (1997). *Birth of the Leviathan: Building States and Regimes in Medieval and Early Modern Europe.* Cambridge: Cambridge University Press.

Esping-Andersen, Gøsta (1990). *Three Worlds of Welfare Capitalism.* Princeton: Princeton University Press.

Fearon, James (1996). "Causes and Counterfactuals in Social Science: Exploring an Analogy between Cellular Automata and Historical Processes," in Philip E. Tetlock and Aaron Belkin, eds., *Counterfactual Thought Experiments in World Politics: Logical, Methodological, and Psychological Perspectives,* pp. 39–67. Princeton: Princeton University Press.

Ferejohn, John, Morris Fiorina, and Richard McKelvey (1987). "Sophisticated Voting and Agenda Independence in the Distributive Politics Setting," *American Journal of Political Science,* Vol. 31.

Filippov, Mikhail G., Peter C. Ordeshook, and Olga V. Shvetsova (1999). "Party Fragmentation and Presidential Elections in Post-Communist Democracies," *Constitutional Political Economy,* Vol. 10, pp. 3–26.

Flora, Peter (1999a). "Introduction and Interpretation," in Peter Flora, ed., *State Formation, Nation-Building, and Mass Politics in Europe: The Theory of Stein Rokkan.* Oxford: Oxford University Press.

———, ed. (1999b). *State Formation, Nation-Building, and Mass Politics in Europe: The Theory of Stein Rokkan.* Oxford: Oxford University Press.

Franzese, Robert (2003). "Quantitative Empirical Methods and Context Conditionality," *APSA-CP Newsletter,* Vol. 14, No. 1, pp. 20–24.

Gaddis, John Lewis (2002). *The Landscape of History: How Historians Map the Past.* Oxford: Oxford University Press.

Garrett, Geoffrey (1995). "The Politics of Legal Integration in the European Union," *International Organization,* Vol. 49, pp. 171–81.

Gaventa, John (1980). *Power and Powerlessness: Quiescence and Rebellion in an Appalachian Valley*. Urbana: University of Illinois Press.

Geddes, Barbara (1990). "How the Cases You Choose Affect the Answers You Get: Selection Bias in Comparative Politics," in James A. Stimson, ed., *Political Analysis*, Vol. 2, pp. 131–50. Ann Arbor: University of Michigan Press.

——— (1997). "The Use of Case Studies in Path Dependent Arguments," unpublished manuscript, Department of Political Science, University of California at Los Angeles.

Gellner, Ernst (1983). *Nations and Nationalism*. Ithaca, N.Y.: Cornell University Press.

Gerschenkron, Alexander (1962). *Economic Backwardness in Historical Perspective*. Cambridge, Mass.: Harvard University Press.

Gibson, Edward, and Tulia Faletti (2000). "Unity by the Stick: Regional Conflict and the Origins of Argentine Federalism," unpublished manuscript.

Goldstein, Judith L., Miles Kahler, Robert O. Keohane, and Anne-Marie Slaughter (2001). *Legalization and World Politics*. Cambridge, Mass.: MIT Press.

Goldstone, Jack A. (1991). *Revolution and Rebellion in the Early Modern World*. Berkeley: University of California Press.

Goldstone, Jack A. (1998). "Initial Conditions, General Laws, Path Dependence and Explanation in Historical Sociology," *American Journal of Sociology*, Vol. 104, No. 3, pp. 829–45.

Goodin, Robert E. (1996). "Institutions and Their Design," in Robert E. Goodin, eds., *The Theory of Institutional Design*, pp. 1–53. Cambridge: Cambridge University Press.

Gourevitch, Peter Alexis (2000). "The Governance Problem in International Relations," in David Lake and Robert Powell, eds., *Strategic Choice and International Relations*, pp. 137–64. Princeton: Princeton University Press.

Gourevitch, Peter, and Michael Hawes (2001). "Political Institutions and National Production Systems in the Globalized Economy," paper presented at the Conference on Varieties of Capitalism, University of North Carolina.

Granovetter, Mark (1978). "Threshold Models of Collective Behavior," *American Journal of Sociology*, Vol. 83, pp. 1420–43.

Green, Donald, and Shapiro, Ian (1994). *Pathologies of Rational Choice Theory: A Critique of Applications in Political Science*. New Haven: Yale University Press.

Greider, William (1982). *The Education of David Stockman and Other Americans*. New York: Dutton.

Greif, Avner, and David Laitin (2002). "How Do Self-enforcing Institutions Endogenously Change? Institutional Reinforcement and Quasi-Parameters," unpublished manuscript, Palo Alto, Calif.

Hacker, Jacob (1998). "The Historical Logic of National Health Insurance: Structure and Sequence in the Development of British, Canadian, and U.S. Medical Policy," *Studies in American Political Development*, Vol. 12, No. 1, pp. 57–130.

——— (2002). *The Divided Welfare State: The Battle over Public and Private Social Benefits in the United States*. Cambridge: Cambridge University Press.

——— (forthcoming). "Privatizing Risk without Privatizing Benefits: U.S. Welfare State Reform in Comparative Perspective," *American Political Science Review*.

Hacker, Jacob, and Paul Pierson (2002). "Business Power and Social Policy: Employers and the Formation of the American Welfare State," *Politics and Society*, Vol. 30, No. 2, pp. 277–325.

Haggard, Stephan, and Robert R. Kaufman (1995). *The Political Economy of Democratic Transitions*. Princeton: Princeton University Press.

Hall, Peter A. (1993). "Policy Paradigms, Social Learning, and the State: The Case of Economic Policymaking in Britain," *Comparative Politics*, April, pp. 275–96.

——— (1999). "The Political Economy of Europe in an Era of Interdependence," in Herbert Kitschelt et al., eds., *Change and Continuity in Contemporary Capitalism*, pp. 135–63. Cambridge: Cambridge University Press.

——— (2003). "Aligning Ontology and Methodology in Comparative Research," in James Mahoney and Dietrich Rueschemeyer, eds., *Comparative Historical Analysis in the Social Sciences*, pp. 373–404. Princeton: Princeton University Press.

Hall, Peter A., and David Soskice (2001a). *Varieties of Capitalism*. Oxford: Oxford University Press.

——— (2001b). "An Introduction to Varieties of Capitalism," in Peter A. Hall and David Soskice, eds., *Varieties of Capitalism*. Oxford: Oxford University Press.

Hall, Peter A., and Rosemary C. R. Taylor (1996). "Political Science and the Three New Institutionalisms," *Political Studies*, Vol. 44, pp. 936–57.

Hannan, Michael T., and Freeman, John (1989). *Organizational Ecology*. Cambridge, Mass.: Harvard University Press.

Hansen, John Mark (1991). *Gaining Access: Congress and the Farm Lobby, 1919–1981*. Chicago: University of Chicago Press.

Hardin, Garrett (1963). "The Cybernetics of Competition," *Perspectives in Biology and Medicine*, Vol. 7, pp. 58–84.

Hardin, Russell (1989). "Why a Constitution?" in Bernard Grofman and Donald Wittman, eds., *The Federalist Papers and the New Institutionalism*. New York: Agathon.

Harsanyi, John C. (1960). "Explanation and Comparative Dynamics in Social Science," *Behavior Science*, No. 5, pp. 136–45.

Hathaway, Oona (2001). "The Path Dependence of the Law: The Course and Pattern of Legal Change in a Common Law System," *Iowa Law Review*, Vol. 86, pp. 601–65.

Hayek, Friedrich (1973). *Law, Legislation, and Liberty: Rules and Order*. London: Routledge.

Heclo, Hugh (1974). *Modern Social Politics in Britain and Sweden*. New Haven: Yale University Press.

Hedstrom, Peter, and Richard Swedborg, eds. (1998). *Social Mechanisms: An Analytical Approach to Social Theory*. New York: Cambridge University Press.

Herbst, Jeffrey (2000). *States and Power in Africa: Comparative Lessons in Authority and Control*. Princeton: Princeton University Press.

Hill, Greg (1997). "History, Necessity, and Rational Choice Theory," *Rationality and Society*, Vol. 9, No. 2, pp. 189–213.

Hirsch, Fred (1977). *The Social Limits to Growth*. Cambridge, Mass.: Harvard University Press.

Hollingsworth, J. Rogers, and Robert Boyer (1997). *Contemporary Capitalism: The Embeddedness of Institutions*. Cambridge: Cambridge University Press.

Homans, George (1967). *The Nature of Social Science*. New York: Harcourt, Brace and World.

Hoodfar, Homa, and Samad Assadpour (2000). "The Politics of Population Policy in the Islamic Republic of Iran," *Studies in Family Planning*, Vol. 31, No. 1, March, pp. 19–34.

Horn, Murray J. (1995). *The Political Economy of Public Administration: Institutional Choice in the Public Sector*. Cambridge: Cambridge University Press.

Horowitz, Donald L. (2000). "Constitutional Design: An Oxymoron?" *Nomos*, Vol. 42, pp. 253–84.

——— (2002). "Constitutional Design: Proposals versus Processes," in Andrew Reynolds, ed., *The Architecture of Democracy: Constitutional Design, Conflict Management, and Democracy*, pp. 15–36. Oxford: Oxford University Press.

Howard, Christopher (1997). *The Hidden Welfare State*. Princeton: Princeton University Press.

Huber, Evelyn, and John Stephens (2001). *Development and Crisis of the Welfare State: Parties and Policies in Global Markets*. Chicago: University of Chicago Press.

Huntington, Samuel (1968). *Political Order in Changing Societies*. New Haven: Yale University Press.

——— (1991). *The Third Wave: Democratization in the Late Twentieth Century*. Norman: University of Oklahoma Press.

Ikenberry, John (1994). "History's Heavy Hand: Institutions and the Politics of the State," unpublished manuscript.

Immergut, Ellen (1992). *Health Politics*. Cambridge: Cambridge University Press.

Iversen, Torben (2001). "The Dynamics of Welfare State Expansion: Trade Openness, De-industrialization, and Partisan Politics," in Paul Pierson, ed., *The New Politics of the Welfare State*, pp. 45–79. Oxford: Oxford University Press.

Iversen, Torben, and Anne Wren (1998). "Equality, Employment and Budgetary Restraint: The Trilemma of the Service Economy," *World Politics*, Vol. 50, pp. 507–46.

Jackson, John E. (1996). "Political Methodology: An Overview," in Robert E. Goodin and Hans-Dieter Klingemann, *Handbook of Political Science*, pp. 717–48. Oxford: Oxford University Press.

Jackson, Robert H., and Carl G. Rosberg (1982). "Why Africa's Weak States Persist: The Empirical and the Juridical in Statehood," *World Politics*, Vol. 35, No. 1, pp. 1–24.

Jepperson, Ronald (1991). "Institutions, Institutional Effects, and Institutionalism," in Walter W. Powell and Paul DiMaggio, eds., *The New Institutionalism in Organizational Analysis*, pp. 143–63. Chicago: University of Chicago Press.

Jepperson, Ronald L. (1996). "Relations between Different Theoretical Imageries (With Application to Institutionalism)," unpublished manuscript.

——— (2001). "The Development and Application of Sociological Neoinstitutionalism," RSC No. 2001/5, European Forum Series, European University Institute, Florence.

Jepperson, Ronald L., Alexander Wendt, and Peter J. Katzenstein (1996). "Norms, Identity, and Culture in National Security," in Peter J. Katzenstein, ed., *The Culture of National Security: Norms and Identity in World Politics*, pp. 33–75. New York: Columbia University Press.

Jervis, Robert (1997). *System Effects: Complexity in Political and Social Life*. Princeton: Princeton University Press.

——— (2000). "Timing and Interaction in Politics: A Comment on Pierson," *Studies in American Political Development*, Vol. 14, pp. 93–100.

Joskow, Paul (1988). "Asset Specificity and the Structure of Vertical Relationships: Empirical Evidence," *Journal of Law, Economics, and Organization*, Vol. 4, pp. 95–117.

Kahler, Miles (1999). "Evolution, Choice, and International Change," in David A. Lake and Robert Powell, eds., *Strategic Choice and International Relations*, pp. 165–96. Princeton: Princeton University Press.

Karl, Terry Lynn (1997). *The Paradox of Plenty: Oil Booms and Petro-States.* Berkeley: University of California Press.

Katznelson, Ira (1997). "Structure and Configuration in Comparative Politics," in Mark Irving Lichbach and Alan S. Zuckerman, eds., *Comparative Politics: Rationality, Culture, and Structure*, pp. 81–112. Cambridge: Cambridge University Press.

———— (2003). "Periodization and Preferences: Reflections on Purposive Action in Comparative Historical Social Science," in James Mahoney and Dietrich Rueschemeyer, eds., *Comparative Historical Analysis in the Social Sciences*, pp. 270–301. Princeton: Princeton University Press.

Keohane, Robert O. (1984). *After Hegemony: Cooperation and Discord in the World Political Economy.* Princeton: Princeton University Press.

———— (2003). "Disciplinary Schizophrenia: Implications for Graduate Education in Political Science," *Qualitative Methods.* (Newsletter of the American Political Science Association Organized Section on Qualitative Methods), Vol. 1, No. 1, pp. 9–12.

Key, V. O. (1959). "Secular Realignment and the Party System," *Journal of Politics*, Vol. 21, pp. 198–210.

Keyssar, Alexander (2000). *The Right to Vote: The Contested History of Democracy in the United States.* New York: Basic Books.

King, Gary, Robert Keohane, and Sidney Verba (1994). *Designing Social Inquiry.* Princeton: Princeton University Press.

Kitschelt, Herbert (2003). "Accounting for Postcommunist Regime Diversity: What Counts as a Good Cause?" in Grzegorz Ekiert and Stephen E. Hanson, eds., *Capitalism and Democracy in Central and Eastern Europe: Assessing the Legacy of Communist Rule*, pp. 49–86. Cambridge: Cambridge University Press.

Kitschelt, Herbert, Peter Lange, Gary Marks, and John D. Stephens, eds. (1999). *Continuity and Change in Contemporary Capitalism.* Cambridge: Cambridge University Press.

Knapp, Peter (1983). "Can Social Theory Escape from History? Views of History in Social Science," *History and Theory*, Vol. 23, pp. 34–52.

Knight, Jack (1992). *Institutions and Social Conflict.* Cambridge: Cambridge University Press.

———— (1995). "Models, Interpretations, and Theories: Constructing Explanations of Institutional Emergence and Change," in Jack Knight and Itai Sened, ed., *Explaining Social Institutions*, pp. 95–119. Ann Arbor: University of Michigan Press.

Kopstein, Jeffrey, and David A. Reilly (2000). "Geographic Diffusion and the Transformation of the Postcommunist World," *World Politics*, Vol. 53, No. 1, pp. 1–37.

Koremenos, Barbara, Charles Lipson, and Duncan Snidal (2001). "The Rational Design of International Institutions," *International Organization*, Vol. 55, No. 4, pp. 761–99.

Krasner, Stephen (1989). "Sovereignty: An Institutional Perspective," in James A. Caporaso, ed., *The Elusive State: International and Comparative Perspectives.* Newbury Park, Calif.: Sage.

———— (1991). "Global Communcations and National Power: Life on the Pareto Frontier," *World Politics*, Vol. 43, pp. 336–66.

Krehbiel, Keith (1991). *Information and Legislative Organization.* Ann Arbor: University of Michigan Press.

Kreps, David (1990). *A Course in Microeconomic Theory.* New York: Harvester Wheatsheaf.

Krugman, Paul (1991). "History and Industry Location: The Case of the Manufacturing Belt," *American Economic Review*, Vol. 81, No. 2, pp. 80–83.

——— (1996). *Pop Internationalism.* Cambridge, Mass.: MIT Press.

Kurth, James (1979). "Political Consequences of the Product Cycle," *International Organization*, Vol. 33, pp. 1–34.

Laitin, David (1998). *Identity in Formation: The Russian-Speaking Populations in the Near Abroad.* Ithaca, N.Y.: Cornell University Press.

Lake, David A. (1999). *Entangling Relations: American Foreign Policy in Its Century.* Princeton: Princeton University Press.

Lake, David A., and Robert Powell (1999). "International Relations: A Strategic Choice Approach," in David Lake and Robert Powell, eds., *Strategic Choice and International Relations*, pp. 1–38. Princeton: Princeton University Press.

Lange, Peter (1993). "The Maastricht Social Protocol: Why Did They Do It?" *Politics and Society*, Vol. 21, pp. 5–36.

Levi, Margaret (1997). "A Model, a Method, and a Map: Rational Choice in Comparative and Historical Analysis," in Mark I. Lichbach and Alan S. Zuckerman, eds., *Comparative Politics: Rationality, Culture, and Structure*, pp. 19–41. Cambridge: Cambridge University Press.

Levitt, Barbara, and James G. March (1988). "Organizational Learning," *Annual Review of Sociology*, Vol. 14, pp. 319–40.

Lieberman, Evan S. (2001). "Causal Inference in Historical Institutional Analysis: A Specification of Periodization Strategies," *Comparative Political Studies*, Vol. 34, No. 9, pp. 1011–35.

——— (2003). "Nested Analysis in Cross-National Research," *APSA-CP: Newsletter of the APSA Comparative Politics Section*, Vol. 14, No. 1, pp. 17–20.

Lieberson, Stanley (1985). *Making It Count: The Improvement of Social Research and Theory.* Berkeley: University of California Press.

——— (1997). "The Big Broad Issues in Society and Social History: Application of a Probabilistic Perspective," in Vaughn R. McKim and Stephen P. Turner, eds., *Causality in Crisis? Statistical Methods and the Search for Causal Knowledge in the Social Sciences*, pp. 359–85. Notre Dame, Ind.: University of Notre Dame Press.

Liebowitz, S. J., and Stephen E. Margolis (1990). "The Fable of the Keys," *Journal of Law and Economics*, Vol. 22, pp. 1–26.

——— (1995). "Path Dependence, Lock-In, and History," *Journal of Law, Economics, and Organization*, Vol. 11, No. 1, pp. 205–26.

Lijphart, Arend (1992). "Democratization and Constitutional Choices in Czecho-Slovakia, Hungary, and Poland, 1989–91," *Journal of Theoretical Politics*, Vol. 4, pp. 207–23.

——— (1999). *Patterns of Democracy: Government Forms and Performance in Thirty-Six Countries.* New Haven: Yale University Press.

Lindblom, Charles E. (1959). "The Science of Muddling Through," *Public Administration Review*, Vol. 19, pp. 79–88.

——— (1977). *Politics and Markets.* New York: Basic Books.

Lipset, Seymour Martin, and Stein Rokkan (1967). "Cleavage Structures, Party Systems and Voter Alignments: An Introduction," in Lipset and Rokkan, eds., *Party Systems and Voter Alignments*, pp. 1–64. New York: Free Press.

Luebbert, Gregory M. (1991). *Liberalism, Fascism, or Social Democracy: Social Classes and the Political Origins of Regimes in Interwar Europe.* New York: Oxford University Press.

Lukes, Steven (1974). *Power: A Radical View.* London: Macmillan.

Macy, Michael W. (1990). "Learning Theory and the Logic of Critical Mass," *American Sociological Review*, Vol. 55, pp. 809–26.

Mahoney, James (1999). "Nominal, Ordinal, and Narrative Appraisal in Macro-Causal Analysis," *American Journal of Sociology*, Vol. 104, pp. 1154–96.

——— (2000). "Path Dependence in Historical Sociology," *Theory and Society*, Vol. 29, pp. 507–48.

——— (2001). *The Legacies of Liberalism: Path Dependence and Political Regimes in Central America*. Baltimore: Johns Hopkins University Press.

——— (2003). "Knowledge Accumulation in Comparative Historical Research: The Case of Democracy and Authoritarianism," in James Mahoney and Dietrich Rueschemeyer, eds., *Comparative Historical Analysis in the Social Sciences*, pp. 131–74. Cambridge: Cambridge University Press.

Mahoney, James, and Dietrich Rueschemeyer (2003). *Comparative Historical Analysis in the Social Sciences*. Princeton: Princeton University Press.

Mahoney, James, and Richard Snyder (1999). "Rethinking Agency and Structure in the Study of Regime Change," *Studies in Comparative International Development*, Vol. 34, pp. 3–32.

Mannheim, Karl (1952). "The Problem of Generations," in Paul Kecskemeti, ed., *Essays on the Sociology of Knowledge*, pp. 276–320. London: Routledge and Kegan Paul.

March, James, and Johan Olson (1989). *Rediscovering Institutions: The Organizational Basis of Politics*. New York: Free Press.

Markovits, Andrei S., and Steven L. Hellerman (2001). *Offside: Soccer and American Exceptionalism*. Princeton: Princeton University Press.

Marwell, Gerald, and Pamela Oliver (1993). *The Critical Mass in Collective Action: A Micro-Social Theory*. Cambridge: Cambridge University Press.

Mayhew, David R. (2002). *Electoral Realignments: A Critique of an American Genre*. New Haven: Yale University Press.

McAdam, Douglas (1982). *Political Process and the Development of Black Insurgency, 1930–1970*. Chicago: University of Chicago Press.

McCubbins, Mathew D., and Thomas Schwartz (1984). "Congressional Oversight Overlooked: Police Patrols versus Fire Alarms," *American Journal of Political Science*, Vol. 28, pp. 165–79.

McCubbins, Mathew D., Roger G. Noll, and Barry R. Weingast (1987). "Administrative Procedures as Instruments of Political Control," *Journal of Law, Economics and Organization*, Vol. 3, pp. 243–77.

McDonald, Terrance J. (1996). *The Historic Turn in the Human Sciences*. Ann Arbor: University of Michigan Press.

Melnick, R. Shep (1994). *Between the Lines*: Washington, D.C.: Brookings Institution Press.

Meyer, John W., and Brian Rowan (1977). "Institutionalized Organizations: Formal Structure as Myth and Ceremony," *American Journal of Sociology*, Vol. 83, No. 2, pp. 340–63.

Meyer, John W., John Boli, George M. Thomas, and Francisco O. Ramirez (1997). "World Society and the Nation-State." *American Journal of Sociology*, Vol. 103, No. 1, July, pp. 144–81.

Milgrom, Paul, and John Roberts (1990). "The Economics of Modern Manufacturing: Technology, Strategy, and Organization," *American Economic Review*, Vol. 80, pp. 511–28.

Milgrom, Paul, Yingi Qian, and John Roberts (1991). "Complementarities, Momentum, and the Evolution of Modern Manufacturing," *American Economic Review*, Vol. 81, No. 2, pp. 84–88.

Miller, Gary (2000). "Rational Choice and Dysfunctional Institutions," *Governance*, 13, 4, pp. 535–47.

Moe, Terry (1984). "The New Economics of Organization," *American Journal of Political Science*, Vol. 28, pp. 739–77.

——— (1990). "The Politics of Structural Choice: Toward a Theory of Public Bureaucracy," in O. E. Williamson, ed., *Organization Theory: From Chester Barnard to the Present and Beyond*, pp. 116–53. Oxford: Oxford University Press.

——— (2003). "Power and Political Institutions," paper presented at the Conference on Crafting and Operating Institutions, Yale University, New Haven.

Moore, Barrington, Jr. (1966). *Social Origins of Dictatorship and Democracy: Lord and Peasant in the Making of the Modern World*. Boston: Beacon Press.

Morrow, James (1994). *Game Theory for Political Scientists*. Princeton: Princeton University Press.

Mueller, Dennis C. (1989). *Public Choice II*. Cambridge: Cambridge University Press.

Munck, Gerardo (2001). "Game Theory and Comparative Politics: New Perspectives and Old Concerns," *World Politics*, Vol. 23, No. 2.

Myles, John, and Paul Pierson (2001). "The Comparative Political Economy of Pension Reform," in Paul Pierson, ed., *The New Politics of the Welfare State*, pp. 305–33. Oxford: Oxford University Press.

Nelson, Richard R. (1995). "Recent Evolutionary Theorizing about Economic Change," *Journal of Economic Literature*, Vol. 33, March, pp. 48–90.

Neustadt, Richard E. (1990). *Presidential Power and the Modern Presidents*. New York: Free Press.

Nordlinger, Eric A. (1968). "Political Development: Time Sequences and Rates of Change," *World Politics*, Vol. 20, No. 3, pp. 494–520.

North, Douglass C. (1990a). *Institutions, Institutional Change and Economic Performance*. Cambridge: Cambridge University Press.

——— (1990b). "A Transaction Cost Theory of Politics," *Journal of Theoretical Politics*, Vol. 2, No. 4, pp. 355–67.

——— (1993). "Institutions and Credible Commitment," *Journal of Institutional and Theoretical Economics*, Vol. 149, No. 1, pp. 11–23.

——— (1999). "In Anticipation of the Marriage of Political and Economic Theory," in James E. Alt, Margaret Levi, and Elinor Ostrom, eds., *Competition and Cooperation: Conversations with Nobelists about Economics and Political Science*, pp. 314–17. New York: Russell Sage Foundation.

North, Douglass C., and Weingast, Barry R. (1989). "Constitutions and Commitment: The Evolution of Institutions Governing Public Choice in Seventeenth- Century England." *Journal of Economic History*, 49, pp. 803–32.

O'Donnell, Guillermo, and Philippe Schmitter (1986). *Transitions from Authoritarian Rule: Tentative Conclusions about Uncertain Democracies*. Baltimore: Johns Hopkins University Press.

Olson, Mancur (1965). *The Logic of Collective Action: Public Goods and the Theory of Groups*. Cambridge, Mass.: Harvard University Press.

——— (1981). *The Rise and Decline of Nations*. New Haven: Yale University Press.

Orren, Karen (1991). *Belated Feudalism: Labor, the Law, and Liberal Development in the United States.* Cambridge: Cambridge University Press.

Orren, Karen, and Stephen Skowronek (1994). "Beyond the Iconography of Order: Notes for a 'New Institutionalism,'" in Lawrence Dodd and Calvin Jillson, eds., *The Dynamics of American Politics,* pp. 311–30. Boulder, Colo.: Westview Press.

——— (2004). *The Search for American Political Development.* New York: Cambridge University Press.

Padgett, John F., and Christopher Ansell (1993). "Robust Action and the Rise of the Medici, 1400–1434," *American Journal of Sociology,* Vol. 98, No. 6, pp. 1259–1319.

Page, Benjamin, and Robert Shapiro (1992). *The Rational Public: Fifty Years of Trends in Americans' Policy Preferences.* Chicago: University of Chicago Press.

Pempel, T. J., ed. (1990). *Uncommon Democracies: The One-Party Dominant Regimes.* Ithaca, N.Y.: Cornell University Press.

Perrow, Charles (1984). *Normal Accidents.* New York: Basic Books.

Persson, Torsten, and Guido Tabellini, eds. (1994). *Monetary and Fiscal Policy.* 2 vols. Cambridge, Mass.: MIT Press.

Pierson, Paul (1993). "When Effect Becomes Cause: Policy Feedback and Political Change," *World Politics,* Vol. 45, pp. 595–628.

——— (1994). *Dismantling the Welfare State? Reagan, Thatcher, and the Politics of Retrenchment.* Cambridge: Cambridge University Press.

——— (1996). "The Path to European Integration: A Historical Institutionalist Analysis," *Comparative Political Studies,* Vol. 29, No. 2, pp. 123–63.

——— (forthcoming). "Public Policies as Institutions," in Ian Shapiro and Stephen Skowronek, eds., *Crafting and Operating Institutions.*

———, ed. (2001). *The New Politics of the Welfare State.* Oxford: Oxford University Press.

Pierson, Paul, and Theda Skocpol (2002). "Historical Institutionalism and Contemporary Political Science," in Helen Milner and Ira Katznelson, eds., *The State of the Discipline.* New York: W. W. Norton.

Polsby, Nelson W. (1963). *Community Power and Social Theory.* New Haven: Yale University Press.

Polsky, Andrew (1989). "The Odyssey of the Juvenile Court: Policy Failure and Institutional Persistence in the Therapeutic State," *Studies in American Political Development,* Vol. 3, pp. 157–98.

Powell, Walter W., and Paul DiMaggio, eds. (1991). *The New Institutionalism in Organizational Analysis.* Chicago: University of Chicago Press.

Przeworski, Adam (1991). *Democracy and the Market: Political and Economic Reforms in Eastern Europe and Latin America.* Cambridge: Cambridge University Press.

Przeworski, Adam, and Fernando Limongi (1997). "Modernization: Theories and Facts," *World Politics,* Vol. 49, No. 2, pp. 155–83.

Przeworski, Adam et al. (2000). *Democracy and Development: Political Institutions and Well-Being in the World, 1950–1990.* Cambridge: Cambridge University Press.

Putnam, Robert (2000). *Bowling Alone.* New York: Simon and Schuster.

Ragin, Charles C. (1987). *The Comparative Method: Moving beyond Qualitative and Quantitative Strategies.* Berkeley: University of California Press.

——— (2000). *Fuzzy-Set Social Science.* Chicago: University of Chicago Press.

Riker, William H. (1955). "The Senate and American Federalism," *American Political Science Review,* Vol. 49, pp. 452–69.

———— (1980). "Implications from the Disequilibrium of Majority Rule for the Study of Institutions," *American Political Science Review*, Vol. 74, pp. 432–46.

———— (1986). *The Art of Political Manipulation.* New Haven: Yale University Press.

Rogowski, Ronald (1989). *Commerce and Coalitions: How Trade Affects Domestic Political Alignments.* Princeton: Princeton University Press.

Rokkan, Stein (1974). "Entries, Voices, Exits: Towards a Possible Generalization of the Hirschman Model," *Social Science Information*, Vol. 13, No. 1, pp. 39–53.

Romer, Paul M. (1986). "Increasing Returns and Long-run Growth," *Journal of Political Economy*, Vol. 94, pp. 1002–37.

———— (1990). "Are Nonconvexities Important for Understanding Growth?" *American Economic Review*, Vol. 80, pp. 97–103.

Rose, Richard (1991). "Inheritance before Choice in Public Policy," *Journal of Theoretical Politics*, Vol. 2, No. 3, pp. 263–91.

Rose, Richard, and Paul Davies (1994). *Inheritance in Public Policy: Change without Choice in Britain.* New Haven: Yale University Press.

Rueschemeyer, Dietrich, and John D. Stephens (1997). "Comparing Historical Sequences: A Powerful Tool for Causal Analysis," *Comparative Social Research*, Vol. 17, pp. 55–72.

Rueschemeyer, Dietrich, Evelyne Huber Stephens, and John D. Stephens (1992). *Capitalist Development and Democracy.* Chicago: University of Chicago Press.

Sartori, Giovanni (1970). "Concept Misinformation in Comparative Politics," *American Political Science Review*, Vol. 64, pp. 1033–53.

Scharpf, Fritz W. (1988). "The Joint-Decision Trap: Lessons from German Federalism and European Integration," *Public Administration*, Vol. 66, pp. 239–78.

———— (1997). *Games Real Actors Play: Actor-Centered Institutionalism in Policy Research.* Boulder, Colo.: Westview Press.

Schattschneider, E. E. 1960. *The Semi-Sovereign People.* New York: Holt, Reinhart and Winston.

Schelling, Thomas (1978). *Micromotives and Macrobehavior.* New York: W. W. Norton.

Schickler, Eric (2001). *Disjointed Pluralism: Institutional Innovation and the Development of the U.S. Congress.* Princeton: Princeton University Press.

Schmitter, Philippe C., and Gerhard Lehmbruch, eds. (1979). *Trends toward Corporatist Intermediation.* Beverly Hills, Calif.: Sage Publications.

Schneiberg, Marc, and Elisabeth Clemens (forthcoming) "The Typical Tools for the Job: Research Strategies in Institutional Analysis," in Walter W. Powell and Dan L. Jones, eds., *How Institutions Change.* Chicago: University of Chicago Press.

Schwartz, Herman (n.d.). "Down the Wrong Path: Path Dependence, Markets, and Increasing Returns," unpublished manuscript, University of Virginia, Charlottesville.

Seabrook, John (1997). "Tackling the Competition," *New Yorker*, August 18, pp. 42–51.

Sewell, William H. (1996). "Three Temporalities: Toward an Eventful Sociology," in Terrance McDonald, ed., *The Historic Turn in the Human Sciences*, pp. 245–80. Ann Arbor: University of Michigan Press.

Shalev, Michael (1999). "Limits of and Alternatives to Multiple Regression in Macro-Comparative Research," unpublished manuscript, Hebrew University, Jerusalem.

Shefter, Martin (1977). "Party and Patronage: Germany, England, and Italy," *Politics and Society*, Vol. 7, pp. 403–52.

Shepsle, Kenneth A. (1986). "Institutional Equilibrium and Equilibrium Institutions," in

Herbert F. Weisberg, ed., *Political Science: The Science of Politics*, pp. 51–81. New York: Agathon Press.

———— (1989). "Studying Institutions: Lessons from the Rational Choice Approach," *Journal of Theoretical Politics*, Vol. 1, pp. 131–47.

———— (1991). "Discretion, Institutions and the Problem of Government Commitment," in Pierre Bourdieu and James Coleman, eds., *Social Theory for a Changing Society*. Boulder, Colo.: Westview Press.

———— (2003). "Losers in Politics (and How They Sometimes Become Winners): William Riker's Heresthetic," *Perspectives in Politics*, Vol. 1, No. 2, pp. 307–15.

Shepsle, Kenneth A., and Barry Weingast (1987). "The Institutional Foundations of Committee Power," *American Political Science Review*, Vol. 81, pp. 86–108.

Simon, Herbert A. (1957). *Models of Man*. New York: Wiley.

Skocpol, Theda (1979). *States and Social Revolutions*. Cambridge, Mass.: Harvard University Press.

———— (1992). *Protecting Soldiers and Mothers: The Political Origins of Social Policy in the United States*. Cambridge, Mass.: Belknap Press of Harvard University Press.

———— (1999). "How Americans Became Civic," in Theda Skocpol and Morris P. Fiorina, eds., *Civic Engagement in American Democracy*, pp. 27–80. Washington, D.C.: Brookings Institution Press and the Russell Sage Foundation.

Skocpol, Theda, and Somers, Margaret (1980). "The Uses of Comparative History in Macrosocial Inquiry," *Comparative Studies in Society and History*, Vol. 22, pp. 174–97.

Skowronek, Stephen (1993). *The Politics Presidents Make: Leadership from John Adams to George Bush*. Cambridge, Mass.: Belknap Press of Harvard University Press.

Soskice, David (1999). "Divergent Production Regimes: Coordinated and Uncoordinated Market Economies in the 1980s and 1990s," in Herbert Kitschelt et al., *Change and Continuity in Contemporary Capitalism*, pp. 101–34. Cambridge: Cambridge University Press.

Soskice, David, Robert Bates, and David Epstein (1992). "Ambition and Constraint: The Stabilizing Role of Institutions," *Journal of Law, Economics, and Organization*, Vol. 8, No. 3, pp. 547–60.

Spruyt, Hendrik (1994). *The Sovereign State and Its Competitors*. Princeton: Princeton University Press.

Stanger, Allison (2003). "Leninist Legacies and Legacies of State Socialism in Postcommunist Central Europe's Constitutional Development," in Grzegorz Ekiert and Stephen E. Hanson, eds., *Capitalism and Democracy in Central and Eastern Europe*, pp. 182–209. Cambridge: Cambridge University Press.

Steinmo, Sven, and Jon Watts (1995). "It's the Institutions, Stupid!" *Journal of Health Politics, Policy and Law*, Vol. 20.

Steuerle, Eugene, and M. Kawai, eds. (1996). *The New World Fiscal Order*. Washington, D.C.: Urban Institute Press.

Stevens, William K. (2000) "The Oceans Absorb Much of Global Warming, Study Confirms," *New York Times*, March 24, p. A14.

Stinchcombe, Arthur (1965). "Social Structure and Organizations," in James March, ed., *Handbook of Organizations*, pp. 123–63. Chicago: Rand McNally.

———— (1968). *Constructing Social Theories*. New York: Harcourt, Brace.

———— (1974). "Merton's Theory of Social Structure," in L. Coser, ed., *The Idea of Social Structure: Papers in Honor of Robert Merton*. New York: Harcourt, Brace.

——— (1991). "The Conditions for Fruitful Theorizing about Mechanisms in Social Science," *Philosophy of the Social Sciences*, Vol. 21, No. 3, pp. 367–87.

——— (1997). "Tilly on the Past as a Sequence of Futures," in Charles Tillly, ed., *Roads from Past to Futures*, pp. 387–409. Latham, Mass.: Rowman and Littlefield.

Stone Sweet, Alec (2000). *Governing with Judges: Constitutional Politics in Europe*. Oxford: Oxford University Press.

——— (2002). "Path Dependence, Precedent, and Judicial Power," unpublished manuscript.

Stone Sweet, Alec, Neil Fligstein, and Wayne Sandholtz (2001). "The Institutionalization of European Space," in Stone Sweet, Fligstein, and Sandholtz, eds., *The Institutionalization of European Space*. Oxford: Oxford University Press.

Strom, Kaare, and Wolfgang Muller, eds. (1999). *Policy, Office or Votes? How Political Parties in Western Europe Make Hard Decisions*. Cambridge: Cambridge University Press.

Swank, Duane (2001). "Political Institutions and Welfare State Restructuring: The Impact of Institutions on Social Policy Change in Developed Democracies," in Paul Pierson, ed., *The New Politics of the Welfare State*. Oxford: Oxford University Press.

Tarrow, Sidney (1992). "Mentalities, Political Cultures, and Collective Action Frames: Constructing Meanings through Action," in Aldon D. Morris and Carol Mueller, eds., *Frontiers in Social Movement Theory*, pp. 174–202. New Haven: Yale University Press.

Teles, Stephen (1998). "The Dialectics of Trust: Ideas, Finance and Pensions Privatization in the U.S. and U.K.," paper presented to the Max Planck Institute Conference on Varieties of Welfare Capitalism, Cologne, June.

Thelen, Kathleen (1999). "Historical Institutionalism and Comparative Politics," *Annual Review of Political Science*, Vol. 2, pp. 369–404.

——— (2000). "Timing and Temporality in the Analysis of Institutional Evolution and Change," *Studies in American Political Development*, Vol. 14, p. 103.

——— (2003). "How Institutions Evolve: Insights from Comparative-Historical Analysis," in James Mahoney and Dietrich Rueschemeyer, eds., *Comparative Historical Analysis in the Social Sciences*. Cambridge: Cambridge University Press.

——— (2004). *How Institutions Evolve: The Political Economy of Skills in Germany, Britain, Japan and the United States*. New York: Cambridge University Press.

Thelen, Kathleen, and Steinmo, Sven (1992). "Historical Institutionalism in Comparative Politics," in Sven Steinmo, Kathleen Thelen, and Frank Longstreth, eds., *Structuring Politics: Historical Institutionalism in Comparative Politics*. Cambridge: Cambridge University Press.

Tilly, Charles (1975). "Reflections on the History of European Statemaking," in Charles Tilly, ed., *The Formation of National States in Western Europe*. Princeton: Princeton University Press.

——— (1984). *Big Structures, Large Processes, Huge Comparisons*. New York: Russell Sage Foundation.

Tilly, Charles (1995). "Democracy Is a Lake," in George Reid Andrews and Herrick Chapman, eds., *The Social Construction of Democracy*, pp. 365–87. New York: New York University Press.

Tsebelis, George (1990). *Nested Games: Rational Choice in Comparative Politics*. Berkeley: University of California Press.

——— (1995). "Decision Making in Political Systems: Veto Players in Presidentialism,

Parliamentarism, Multicameralism, and Multipartyism," *British Journal of Political Science*, Vol. 25, pp. 289–326.

——— (2000). "Veto Players and Institutional Analysis," *Governance*, Vol. 13, No. 4, pp. 441–74.

Tyson, Laura D'Andrea (1993). *Who's Bashing Whom? Trade Conflicts in High-Technology Industries*. Washington, D.C.: Institute for International Economics.

Van Parijs, Philip (1982). "Perverse Effects and Social Contradictions: Analytical Vindication of Dialectics?" *British Journal of Sociology*, Vol. 33, pp. 589–603.

Watts, Ronald L. (1987). "The American Constitution in Comparative Perspective: A Comparison of Canada and the United States," *Journal of American History*, Vol. 74, pp. 769–81.

Weingast, Barry R. (1998). "Notes on a Possible Integration of Historical Institutionalism and Rational Choice Theory," prepared for Russell Sage Foundation Meeting, New York, November.

——— (2002). "Rational Choice Institutionalism," in Ira Katznelson and Helen Milner, eds., *The State of the Discipline*, pp. 660–92. New York: W. W. Norton.

Weingast, Barry R., and William J. Marshall (1988). "The Industrial Organization of Congress; or, Why Legislatures, Like Firms, Are Not Organized as Markets," *Journal of Political Economy*, Vol. 96, pp. 132–63.

Weir, Margaret, and Theda Skocpol (1985). "State Structures and the Possibilities for 'Keynesian' Responses to the Great Depression in Sweden, Britain, and the United States," in Peter B. Evans, Dietrich Rueschemeyer, and Theda Skocpol, eds., *Bringing the State Back In*, pp. 107–62. Cambridge: Cambridge University Press.

Wendt, Alexander (1999). *Social Theory of International Relations*. Cambridge: Cambridge University Press.

——— (2001). "Driving with the Rearview Mirror: On the Rational Science of Institutional Design," *International Organization*, Vol. 55, pp. 1019–50.

Williamson, Oliver E. (1975). *Markets and Hierarchies: Analysis and Antitrust Implications*. Chicago: Free Press.

——— (1993). "Transaction Cost, Economics, and Organization Theory," *Industrial and Corporate Change*, Vol. 2, pp. 107–56.

Winter, Sidney G. 1986. "Comments on Arrow and on Lucas," Robin M. Hogarth and Melvin W. Reder, eds., in *Rational Choice: The Contrast Between Economics and Psychology*. Chicago: University of Chicago Press.

Wolfinger, Raymond A. (1971). "Nondecisions and the Study of Local Politics," *American Political Science Review*, Vol. 65, pp. 1063–80.

Wood, Stewart (1997). "Capitalist Constitutions: Supply-Side Reform in Britain and West Germany, 1960–1990," Ph.D. diss. Department of Government, Harvard University.

Wuthnow, Robert (1989). *Communities of Discourse: Ideology and Social Structure in the Reformation, the Enlightenment, and European Socialism*. Cambridge, Mass.: Harvard University Press.

Young, H. Peyton (1998). *Individual Strategy and Social Structure: An Evolutionary Theory of Institutions*. Princeton: Princeton University Press.

Zolberg, Aristide R. (1986). "How Many Exceptionalisms?" in Ira Katznelson and Aristide R. Zolberg, eds., *Working Class Formation: Nineteenth-Century Patterns in Western Europe and the United States*, pp. 397–455. Princeton: Princeton University Press.

INDEX

Abbott, Andrew, 161–62, 168–69
adaptation, 150, 152–53; of expectations 24, 33
Alexander, Gerard, 143, 146, 146n
asset specificity, 147–53. *See also* institutional resilience.
Aminzade, Roy, 55–56
Arrow, Kenneth, 59–60, 68–69
Arthur, Brian, 17–18, 22–24, 27

Bates, Robert, 59, 63
Boix, Carles, 124–25
boundary conditions, 169–72

Carmines, Edward, 83, 96, 101
Carpenter, Daniel, 2–3, 101
causal chains, 68, 87–90
Clemens, Elisabeth, 135, 138, 139n, 154
collective action, 31–34, 84–85
Collier, David, 69–70
Collier, Ruth, 69–70
Colomer, Josep, 152, 153, 157n, 161
competition, 40–41, 126–29; over political space, 71–74
complementarities. *See* institutional complementarities
complexity, 37–40; in politics, 37–40. *See also* learning
conjunctures, 55–58
context, 167–72
Cook, James, 135, 139n
coordination, 24, 31–34, 143–44
cumulative causes, 82–83

David, Paul, 23–24
decontextual revolution, 167–69
democracy, disenfranchisement in, 36–37; transitions to, 62n, 67–68, 100–101, 102
Diamond, Jared, 71

electoral realignment, 85–86
Elias, Norbert, 115
Elster, Jon, 6–7, 99, 176
entrepreneurs, 136–37, 139–42
Ertman, Thomas, 3–4, 67
event chains. *See* causal chains

federalism, 163–64
Freeman, John, 126, 129, 156
functionalism, 46–48; actor-based, 104–22, 143–44, 152–53; societal, 105–6, 126–29

game theory. *See* rational choice theory
Gerschenkron, Alexander, 75–76
Goldstone, Jack, 57, 83, 169
Goodin, Robert, 119
Gourevitch, Peter, 148
Greif, Avner, 147n

Hacker, Jacob, 51–52, 76–77, 155–56
Hannan, Michael, 126, 129, 156
historical causation, 45–46, 95
historical institutionalism, 8–9, 134–42
history: in the social sciences, 4–5
Horowitz, Donald, 111, 112, 117
Huber, Evelyn, 85

ideology, 39–40
institutional change, 52–53, 133–66; barriers to, 42–44; through conversion, 138, 155–56; through diffusion, 138–39, 155–56; entrepreneurs and, 136–37, 139–42, 155; in historical institutionalism 134–42; through layering, 137, 155–56; long-term processes of, 164–65; "losers" as instigators of, 135–36, 139, 154; menus of, 160–62; in sociological institutionalism, 134–42
institutional complementarities, 149–50, 162
institutional resilience, 142–53, 157–60; asset specificity and, 147–53; coordination problems and, 143–44; positive feedback and, 147–53; veto points and, 144–46
institutions, 14–15, 34–36, 47–48; and credible commitments, 43, 144–45; deep equilibria in, 157–60; development of, 14–15, 122–29, 133–66; functional explanations of, 14–15, 46–48, 104–22; path dependence and, 26–27, 29–30, 34–35, 147–53; resilience of, 142–53; unintended consequences and, 115–19. *See also* functionalism; institutional change
isomorphism. *See* diffusion

Jepperson, Ronald, 8, 9–10
judiciary, power of, 158–59, 163–64

Karl, Terry, 65
Keohane, Robert, 121
Keyssar, Alexander, 36–37
Knapp, Peter, 57
Krugman, Paul, 25, 26n
Kurth, James, 75–76

Laitin, David, 147n
learning, 38–39, 40–41, 124–26
Leibowitz, Stan, 28–30, 42
Lijphart, Arend, 152, 164n
long-term processes, 13–14, 79–102, 164–65.
    See also causal chains; cumulative causes;
    replacement; outcomes, slow-moving;
    structural causes; thresholds
Luebbert, Gregory, 69

Mahoney, James, 68, 174
March, James, 150
Margolis, Stephen, 28–30, 42
Mayhew, David, 85–86
McAdam, Douglas, 84–85, 86, 165
mechanisms, 6–7, 175–76
Melnick, R. Shep, 136
methods, 5, 168–69, 170–75
Miller, Gary, 145
Moe, Terry, 145

North, Douglass, 26–27, 38–39, 52, 95–96,
    126, 150, 165

Olsen, Johan, 150
Olson, Mancur, 32, 33n
Orren, Karen, 56, 58n, 77, 136
outcomes, slow-moving, 90–92

path dependence, 10–11, 17–53, 95–96;
    characteristics of, 18; collective action and,
    31–34; cognition and, 38–40; critiques of,
    28–30, 48–53; in economics, 22–30; and
    functionalism, 46–48; implications of,
    44–48; institutions and, 26–27, 29–30,
    34–35, 147–53; in politics, 30–48; positive
    feedback and, 20–22; and power relations,
    36–37; sequencing and, 44–45, 63–77;
    sources of, 24–25, 31–40
policies, development of, 150–51, 165–66
political space, 71–74

power, 36–37, 47–48
proportional representation, 157–58
Putnam, Robert, 82

rational choice theory, 177; and decontextual
    revolution, 168; history in, 4, 8–10; institu-
    tional enhancement in 122–29; institutional
    selection in, 105–22, 131–32; path depen-
    dence arguments in, 22–30; sequencing
    arguments in, 13, 58–63, 74; short-term bias
    of, 99–100
replacement, 90–92
Riker, William, 116, 123–24, 135, 135n, 153
Rueschemeyer, Dietrich, 174

Scharpf, Fritz, 7, 57, 60n, 60–61, 62, 63
Schickler, Eric, 109–10, 136, 137, 139–40,
    154–55
Schneiberg, Marc, 138, 154
separatism, 158
sequencing, 11–13, 44–45, 54–78. See also
    conjunctures; path dependence
Shefter, Martin, 66–67, 95
Shepsle, Kenneth, 112–13
Skocpòl, Theda, 34, 56n
Skowronek, Stephen, 56, 58n, 77, 136
social capacities, development of, 74–77
sociological institutionalism, 110–12, 135–37,
    138, 177–78
Stanger, Allison, 122
state building, 3–4, 65, 66–67, 170–71
Stephens, John, 85
Stimson, James, 83, 96, 101
Stinchcombe, Arthur, 11, 45–46, 75n, 95, 177–78
structural causes, 93–95
Swank, Duane, 87–88

Teles, Steven, 137
Thelen, Kathleen, 49, 50, 72–73, 134–35,
    137–38, 139
thresholds, 83–86
time horizons: of causes and outcomes, 79–82;
    of social actors, 29, 41–42, 112–15
timing. See sequencing

unintended consequences, 15, 115–19

welfare state, development of, 76–77, 85,
    87–88, 92, 120, 160–61
Williamson, Oliver, 28, 107, 123, 125, 126
Wuthnow, Robert, 39